Pension Provision:
Government Failure around the World

Pension Provision: Government Failure around the World

EDITED BY PHILIP BOOTH,
OSKARI JUURIKKALA AND NICK SILVER

The Institute of Economic Affairs

First published in Great Britain in 2008 by
The Institute of Economic Affairs
2 Lord North Street
Westminster
London SW1P 3LB
in association with Profile Books Ltd

The mission of the Institute of Economic Affairs is to improve public understanding of the fundamental institutions of a free society, by analysing and expounding the role of markets in solving economic and social problems.

A CIP catalogue record for this book is available from the British Library.

ISBN 978 0 255 36602 1

Many IEA publications are translated into languages other than English or are reprinted. Permission to translate or to reprint should be sought from the Director General at the address above.

Typeset in Stone by MacGuru Ltd
info@macguru.org.uk

Printed and bound in Great Britain by Hobbs the Printers

CONTENTS

THE AUTHORS

Laveesh Bhandari

Laveesh Bhandari heads Indicus Analytics, an economics research firm in New Delhi that conducts studies on socio-economic development, finance, policy and governance issues. After completing his doctoral studies from Boston University, he worked with the National Council of Applied Economic Research, Delhi, as Senior Economist, and the Indian Institute of Technology, Delhi. He has conducted a wide range of studies on Indian economic geography and socio-economics and has published extensively. He writes frequently in newspapers and magazines such as *Indian Express, India Today*, etc.

Philip Booth

Philip Booth is Editorial and Programme Director at the Institute of Economic Affairs and Professor of Insurance and Risk Management at Cass Business School, City University. He has an undergraduate degree in economics from the University of Durham and a PhD in finance. He is a Fellow of the Institute of Actuaries and of the Royal Statistical Society. Previously, Philip Booth worked at the Bank of England on financial stability issues. He has written widely on social insurance, insurance regulation and on the relationship between Catholic social teaching and economics. He is editor of *Economic Affairs* and Associate Editor of the *British Actuarial Journal* and the *Annals of Actuarial Science*.

Deborah Cooper

Deborah Cooper is an actuary at Mercer Limited, where she leads its Retirement Resource Group. She holds a PhD in Mathematics from the University of Wales. Before working at Mercer she was a lecturer in the Department of Actuarial Science and Statistics at City University. Deborah qualified as an actuary in 1990. She is a member of the UK Actuarial Profession's Council and chairs the Research Committee of its Pensions Executive Committee. She is also a member of the profession's Pensions Executive Committee and its Public Affairs Advisory Committee.

David Gladstone

Having recently taken early retirement from the University of Bristol, David Gladstone is currently Honorary Visiting Fellow in its School for Policy Studies. A historian by training, he has also worked in the Scottish Office and at the University of Exeter. He is especially interested in aspects of – and the interrelationship between – British social policy past and present. He has authored and edited several books and book series.

Oskari Juurikkala

Oskari Juurikkala is Research Fellow with the Institute of Economic Affairs, and CEO at Larsson & Fellows. He holds a first-class honours degree in Law from the London School of Economics and an MSc in Economics from the Helsinki School of Economics.

Sumita Kale

Sumita Kale is Chief Economist at Indicus Analytics, New Delhi. She has also been a visiting member of faculty at Gokhale Institute of Politics and Economics, Department of Economics, University of Pune, and the National Insurance Academy. After her master's at the University of Cambridge, she completed her doctorate in financial economics at the University of Pune. She has a number of awards and publications and writes regularly for financial news-papers in India.

Meng Li

Meng Li is currently an economics undergraduate at the University of Cambridge. Since coming to the UK from China at the age of eight she has had a keen interest in the development of China. Her life, and ideologies, are still works in progress.

Eugen Mihaita

Dr Eugen Mihaita is a lecturer in Business Policy and Economics at the University of Derby. He studied economics at the Academia de Studii Economice, Bucharest, Romania, and received his PhD from Nottingham Trent University, Nottingham. His research is centred on the area of social security reform, with emphasis on the experience of the central and eastern European transitional economies. His research on public pension reform simulations and empirical estimates of private pension fund investment performance in Romania has been disseminated at conferences, seminars, and as working papers.

Krzysztof Ostaszewski

Krzysztof Ostaszewski received a master's degree in Mathematics from the University of Lodz and a PhD in mathematics from the University of Washington. He is a Chartered Financial Analyst, a member of the American Academy of Actuaries, and a Fellow of the Society of Actuaries. He was a Fulbright Senior Specialist. He is now a professor of mathematics and the Actuarial Program Director at Illinois State University. He has authored or co-authored research monographs on mathematics published by the American Mathematical Society, and research books on actuarial science, as well as several other books, including five volumes of poetry. He has worked in asset-liability management and modelling, as well as investment management, at Hartford Life, Providian Capital Management, and his own consulting practice. He is an Associate Editor of the *Journal of Insurance Issues*. He served on the Society of Actuaries' Education and Research Council, the Social Security Committee of the Society of Actuaries, the Social Insurance Committee of the American Academy of Actuaries, and the Joint Committee for Career Encouragement of the Casualty Actuarial Society and the Society of Actuaries. He is a member of the Advisory Board of the Cato Institute Social Security Choice project. He has also written extensively on political issues. He is an expert for the Adam Smith Research Centre, a free market think tank in Warsaw, Poland.

Alan Pickering

Alan Pickering joined Watson Wyatt in June 1992, having spent the previous twenty years with the Electrical and Plumbing Trade Union. He has chaired the UK's National Association of Pension Funds and the European Federation for Retirement Provision (EFRP). He is a non-executive director of the Pensions Regulator, chairman of both the Plumbing Industry Pension Scheme and the financial literacy charity Life Academy. In 2001, he led a review for the Secretary of State for Work and Pensions into the possible simplification of the rules governing the operation of all forms of private pension provision. His report 'A simpler way to better pensions' was published on 11 July 2002.

Nick Silver

Nick Silver is chief actuary at Parhelion Capital Limited and director of Silver Actuarial Services. He is a Fellow of the Institute of Actuaries and the IEA, Senior Honorary Visiting Fellow at Cass Business School, and chairman of the actuarial profession's Environmental Research Group. He holds an MSc in Public Financial Policy from the London School of Economics.

FOREWORD

It is easy to make the assumption that the state has a major role to play in retirement income provision. In many countries we have become used to established state pension systems and significant state regulation of private pension provision. It can be difficult to imagine things being any other way. But the authors of this book mount an important challenge to the assumption of an automatic role for the state in providing for our old age. They outline the scope for failures and unintended consequences arising from the state's involvement. Private provision of retirement income may face problems, but the potential for market failures in private provision needs to be set against potential ineffectiveness and inefficiency in the actions of governments in attempting to correct them.

The authors of this volume develop some interesting arguments in terms of the possible detriment from state involvement. In the absence of state provision of retirement income, extended family networks have typically played a major role in supporting the elderly. State involvement has tended to crowd out this valuable mechanism. Another important point is the ability of formal pension systems to create incentives for early retirement, as the working of the pension system means the financial rewards of work become low, or even negative, when the effect on pension income is considered. The authors also discuss how public choice theory provides important insights into the continued existence of pay-as-you-go state pension arrangements, where current generations of voters can vote themselves benefits to be paid for by future generations as yet unable to vote.

As evidence grows that many existing forms of retirement income provision are unsustainable in the face of current demographic trends, we need to consider the prospects for reform. There are various options for improving the situation, not all of which imply more state provision and state control. The solution to growing imbalances and problems in pay-as-you-go pension systems isn't necessarily state compulsion of private savings. As one of the authors points out, the best solution to unhealthy eating habits isn't necessarily to force everyone to eat the set menu at a government-run canteen.

This book has been written by an experienced and knowledgeable team of authors from a variety of backgrounds. It provides important lessons from the experience of both developed and developing countries, and makes provocative suggestions for reform of the mechanisms for retirement income provision. You may not agree with all of the analysis and suggestions made in the book, but hopefully, like me, you will welcome it as an important contribution to a debate that is of concern to us all.

ALISTAIR BYRNE

University of Edinburgh and the Pensions Institute at Cass Business School

August 2008

ACKNOWLEDGEMENTS

The Institute of Economic Affairs would like to thank the Templeton Foundation for the financial support it provided for the IEA Empowerment Through Savings project, but stresses that the views expressed in this publication are, as in all IEA publications, those of the authors and not those of the Templeton Foundation or of the Institute of Economic Affairs (which has no corporate view), its managing trustees, Academic Advisory Council or senior staff.

SUMMARY

- The combination of ageing populations and state-backed unfunded pay-as-you-go (PAYGO) pension systems means that many high-income democracies will face severe fiscal problems in years to come.
- Reform of PAYGO systems, as currently designed, will be practically impossible as they create large vested-interest groups that benefit from the system. Older people in retirement or approaching retirement form a large voting block that can capture the political process, making political parties unwilling and unable to effect meaningful reform.
- State systems crowd out private savings systems. The private sector, while not perfect, achieves far better outcomes than state PAYGO systems, but is often hampered by myopic legislation, which makes pensions savings in many countries incomprehensible and needlessly expensive.
- PAYGO systems often lead to misappropriation of funds. In many countries that do not benefit from properly functioning legal systems, this comes in the form of corrupt officials. In high-income democracies, however, opaque legislation often results in savings funds being used to pay current pensions or fund general government spending.
- A combination of PAYGO systems and inappropriate legislation provides incentives for older people to cease work

and to have fewer children, thus reducing the workforce and tax base and hence the ability of the systems to sustain themselves. This is often to the detriment of the older people themselves, who would be healthier, wealthier and more fulfilled if they were to stay in work.

- Many middle-income countries have similar demographic structures to those of richer countries. Many are also hampered by unsuitable PAYGO systems inherited from former socialist regimes. While some countries, for example Chile, have undertaken promising reforms and have effectively privatised the system, other countries' attempted reforms have been half-hearted or undermined by excessive government interference and legislation. Success of reform is usually inversely proportional to government involvement.

- The large emerging economies of India and China are in particularly poor shape. China faces a demographic time bomb more severe than any developed country, caused by its one-child policy. India has a much younger population, so its demographic problems are deferred. The pension landscape in India is, however, characterised by state interference and harmful legislation.

- In the absence of state pension systems, people display a great deal of innovation. Examples abound in less-developed countries, where formal savings vehicles often do not exist. In Hong Kong, which until recently had no state pension system, retirement incomes were far higher than in other countries with state systems. In the USA, individual initiatives provide innovative solutions despite the interference of the government.

- The influential World Bank reform approach assumes that

the government should be at the centre of old-age security, even if some of the tasks are undertaken by the private sector. This is an essentially socialistic view of society which should be reversed. The individual and family should be at the core of the provision of old-age security with governments providing the legal and institutional framework, and occasionally more substantive assistance, to help individuals meet their aspirations.

- Governments should focus on ensuring that the legal and financial infrastructure exists to allow people to make proper provision for their retirement. PAYGO systems should be cut back, and people given the freedom to save for themselves as only they can decide the most appropriate vehicle for their own circumstances. So-called 'market failure' will always ensure that the result is imperfect. But, by comparison, government failure around the world has had catastrophic effects.

TABLES AND FIGURES

EDITORS' PREFACE

There are so many difficulties with state pension schemes throughout the world that one should be surprised that there is not more favourable discussion of the concept of private provision for income replacement in old age. Nearly all serious discussion regarding pension reform takes the current state-oriented model as a framework of reference. This has been clear in the UK with the Turner Commission and the various reactions to it (see, for example, their second report: Pensions Commission, 2005). It is even clearer in continental Europe, where substantial pay-as-you-go (PAYGO) systems seem impervious to reform. Even the reforming countries, such as some in central and eastern Europe, have retained substantial state pension provision and regulation of private provision. Indeed, the so-called privatisation of pensions in these countries normally involves the government requiring workers to pay a high percentage of salary into heavily regulated, though privately managed, savings vehicles. There is little by way of genuine free choice. The investments are, however, at least privately owned, though they will often be in government-issued securities.

These state-oriented pension arrangements are grossly unsatisfactory. In some countries they have left the old in dire poverty as benefits that are fixed in domestic currency terms have been eroded by inflation. Corruption, stealing and the misuse of the revenue streams generated by social security taxes are also not uncommon. Though we think of these problems as being confined to less developed countries, in developed countries the misappropriation of funds is masked by complex legislation. For example, the government in the UK has decided to use social security tax rebates – designed to be invested to provide the future (private) pensions of those who opt out of the state pension system – to pay higher state pensions to the current generation of pensioners instead. In other words, today's young are being plundered to provide benefits to the electorally more significant older generation. Unfunded or partially funded state pension schemes also leave unjustifiable and opaque burdens on younger generations; they override the principle of private property and the security that comes from private property; they are self-destructive in the face of changing demographics; and they are inimical to the capital accumulation that should be at the heart of long-term saving.

So why does state pension provision persist? One of the answers is discussed at length in this monograph. The vested interests that support state provision are overwhelming and entrenched. The potential beneficiaries of reform do not represent a coherent democratic interest group and, in many cases, are either too young to vote or not yet born. A second reason is because at the heart of much economic thinking on pensions lies the failed paradigm of market failure.[1] Politicians, and their advisers, often speak as if they have swallowed an inadequate A-level economics textbook when they discuss the potential failings of private markets in pensions. They talk about the unsuitability of financial

---

1   Often so-called 'market failure' in this field is caused by government interference through myopic legislation in the savings system. See, for example, Silver (2006).

markets for transferring resources across long periods of time – as if governments are especially effective at performing that function. Politicians wax lyrical about information asymmetries, myopia and cost inefficiencies in private markets. Of course, private pensions, with all their arrangements for investing funds, might appear more expensive to run than state pension schemes that do not have any investments. But then a pension scheme without investments is like a car without an engine: a car without an engine is, of course, cheaper than one with an engine, although it is not fit for purpose.

The other arguments against private schemes fall into the usual trap of assuming that, because markets are not perfect, then the outcome must be better if markets are either controlled (in the case of compulsory, heavily regulated, private schemes) or under-mined completely (in the case of government-provided pensions). But we see that the outcome of government pension provision is not perfection but, often, poverty, unjust inter-generational transfers and bankruptcy. Whereas private, funded pensions have self-correcting mechanisms governed by the price system and competition that help to move markets closer to a welfare-maximising position, the failures of government pension provision are self-reinforcing.

This point can be illustrated very clearly. When the population ages, there will tend to be a rise in returns to labour (due to labour shortages). When pensions are privately provided, this effect will attract prospective pensioners back into the labour market, thus leading retirement to be deferred. When a pension scheme is a government-run PAYGO scheme, an ageing population will reduce the very tax revenues that are necessary to pay the pensions. Because a PAYGO government pension institutionalises inter-generational redistribution, it will also increase the incentives for the growing number of older people in the electorate to exercise their influence on policy, thus making it harder for governments to reform those schemes. The resulting rise in tax rates, as the tax base falls relative to the number of pensioners, will also have the effect of further choking off the labour supply, reducing tax revenues further – thus a vicious circle ensues.

Indeed, many of the problems with private pensions are caused by their interaction with government regulation, taxation codes and social security pensions. The problems these cause for private pensions are too numerous to discuss in this preface and are not the main focus of this monograph but are analysed, with respect to the UK, in Booth and Cooper (2005).

Perhaps the main blind spot that politicians have is their narrow conception of private pension provision. They see what is out there at the moment, dictated by state regulation and the overwhelming influence of state pension provision, and point to the difficulties. It is rather like the government saying, in 1970s Britain, that the state should own the car industry because nobody can build a Morris Oxford quite as efficiently as a nationalised company. Of course, this very proposition is arguable, but the point is that the British public did not want the motor cars that their political masters envisaged for them. It is also so in the provision of income for old age. There is a diverse range of mechanisms that individuals can use for old-age income provision when they are free to choose. These mechanisms are dependent on culture, employment prospects, the number of children in a family, and a whole range of other factors. Individuals and families do not need a long-term savings vehicle to be designed for them.

An overview of the monograph

We begin with an introductory discussion of the main themes of
the monograph and a challenge to the prescriptive World Bank
model of pension provision. After the introduction, Part One of
the monograph looks at pensions policy in high-income countries.
The first chapter in Part One examines the disincentives inherent
in state pension schemes: as noted above, they encourage the very
type of behaviour that undermines their foundations. The second
chapter is a public choice analysis of the difficulty of reforming
state pension systems once populations start to age. There is
then an analysis of retirement income provision in the USA. The
conclusions of the US chapter are interesting, because they are so
similar to the conclusions of those authors looking at the poorest
parts of the world in Part Three: individual initiative manages to
overcome the obstacles that our political masters put in our way so
that, despite the efforts of politicians, we can be optimistic about
the future. Part One then moves on to examine the problems in the
UK created by an extraordinarily complex social security system
that provides strong incentives not to save. In the last chapter in
this part, Alan Pickering, in a style different from that of the other
authors, examines the 'problem' of longevity. He shows how, even
if we start with the view that the state should play a substantial
role in providing a basic income in retirement, detailed central
planning and regulatory frameworks have turned what would
have been a relatively benign intervention into one that has had
seriously adverse consequences. Pickering argues that the government should provide a framework within which individuals and
their employers can plan: governments should not try to dictate
outcomes.

In Part Two, middle-income and emerging economies are

examined. The authors find no evidence that systems involving a greater level of state intervention have achieved their goals effectively. The first chapter in this part examines 'Chilean-style' reforms that have been pursued in many countries – especially in South America and in central and eastern Europe. Over-regulation is identified as a key problem limiting the effectiveness of such reforms. The experience of the paternalistic approach to pensions in Singapore is then compared with the more liberal Hong Kong. The former approach has led to very low rates of return in state-run funds: the author does not recommend it as a model. This chapter is included in Part Two, rather than in Part One, because the pension systems in Hong Kong and Singapore were developed when these countries were low-to-middle-income countries. Of course, the UK was once a low-income and, until relatively recently, a middle-income country by today's standards. It is important to study not just current developments but also how we got to where we are today. David Gladstone's chapter charts the development of the UK state pension system, which 'celebrates' its centenary this year. Part Two finishes with an analysis of the problems facing China. China is in a poor demographic position, which makes PAYGO pension arrangements unstable. Chinese people also work in a wide variety of cultures and economic circumstances. The authors therefore suggest that the most important reforms are those to liberalise and strengthen property rights in financial markets so that long-term savings can evolve organically rather than being forced by government.

The monograph finishes by looking, in Part Three, at low-income countries. Can such countries avoid the mistakes of the emerging economies and developed democracies? The first chapter in this part shows once again how resourceful individuals and families can be in the most difficult of circumstances. Where inflation is endemic, corruption is common and property rights are not protected, there is little point in the government institutionalising and favouring long-term pensions savings vehicles – whether they are based on taxation or private saving. Families find their own ways of making inter-generational transfers in these circumstances. Meanwhile, the government first needs to perform its proper functions properly. If governments do that, more formal long-term savings vehicles will emerge.

The position in India is perhaps a little different from that in African countries, which are the main focus of the work of the first chapter in Part Three. In the chapter looking at India, more formal vehicles are proposed, but it is also recognised that, as in China, the government must ensure that the legal infrastructure to support the development of free financial markets is also in place.

Overall, most of the authors find that when the state fails in this area of pension provision, individuals – even those who are very poor and who have little education – are incredibly resourceful in finding appropriate methods of income replacement for old age. There is no question that the state, represented by politicians, underestimates the capacity of its citizens and overestimates its own capacity. The objective of the authors is to be holistic. The monograph does not look narrowly at the situation we see in developed countries today to see how incremental reforms could improve the situation. Rather, taken as a whole, it examines the experience of both developed and underdeveloped countries and emerging economies. It is only through doing this that important common threads and lessons are identified. Perhaps the most important common theme that the editors have found is that the state often displaces rather than assists personal and family initiative. The signals that governments send when they provide or mandate retirement income provision lead to a reduction in saving, work and family support. State pension systems and compulsory private provision also provide a disincentive to have children. Ironically, this causes the very demographic scenario that makes state pay-as-you-go pension schemes so difficult to reform.

The chapters in this monograph complement the articles in the March 2008 edition of *Economic Affairs* on 'New perspectives on the economics and politics of ageing'. Some of the authors of chapters in this monograph would conclude less emphatically than others, and it should not be assumed that the authors would agree with the sentiments expressed in the Editors' Preface. Most of the authors would certainly agree, however, that state pension systems are very badly designed and will not cope with the process of population ageing that has already hit most OECD countries and which will hit many other countries within a generation. Most would also argue that state systems are incorrigible, that developed countries should move towards private sector systems of income replacement in retirement, and that less-developed countries should learn from the mistakes of the richer countries.

References

Booth, P. M. and D. R. Cooper (2005), *The Way out of the Pensions Quagmire*, Research Monograph 60, London: Institute of Economic Affairs.

Pensions Commission (2005), *A New Pension Settlement for the Twenty-first Century: The Second Report of the*

Pensions Commission, London, available online at www.
    pensionscommission.org.uk/.
Silver, N. (2006), 'The trouble with final salary pension schemes',
    Economic Affairs, 26(4): 53–60.

**Pension Provision:
Government Failure around the World**

1 INTRODUCTION: OLD AGE IN A FREE SOCIETY – A PROPOSAL FOR PENSIONS REFORM

Oskari Juurikkala and Philip Booth

Introduction

In the coming decades, many public pension systems around the world[1] will face a major crisis because of the absence of pre-funding, declining older-worker labour force participation rates, falling fertility and rising life expectancy. In the developing world old-age security is also an important issue, as decisions are made on the best way ahead. Many countries are adopting pension institutions similar to those in the developed world, despite clear lessons that this may be imprudent. Similarly, current attempts to tinker with rules in developed countries will not deliver the long-term, sustainable approach to old-age security that is needed.

In this introductory chapter we propose a radical solution that could be adopted widely. In a sense it summarises much of the analysis that is presented later in the monograph, although not all the authors of this monograph would agree with the proposed reforms. The essence of this solution is to remove state involvement in old-age security matters altogether. This means abolishing the current pay-as-you-go (PAYGO) schemes, which have been the main source of confusion, harmful incentives and short-term political opportunism. It also means rejecting compulsory

---

[1] Most notably western Europe, the USA, Japan, China and the former Soviet bloc countries.

savings schemes, because they favour powerful interest groups at the expense of efficient resource allocation and the interests of the general population. We do accept, however, that, in a liberal regulatory environment with strong protection of property rights, compulsory private savings schemes could be a workable 'second best' solution for some countries, if designed and implemented correctly.

State involvement: common problems
Fallacious assumptions

The implicit starting point of most policy discussion regarding pensions and retirement is that, first, there is a problem of old-age income security to be solved, and second, the state can solve the problem in a satisfactory manner. Neither of these beliefs bears careful scrutiny.

First of all, there is no evidence that there ever was a problem with old-age security before the advent of compulsory, state-managed pension systems. There were numerous institutions that provided old-age security: such as the extended family, mutual help societies and savings institutions. Of course, they were not as extensive as we might expect to see in high-income countries today. When incomes are very low, however, it may not be possible to save from one's income to have a period of full-time leisure at the end of one's life. Low-income people often have relatively low life expectancy; it would therefore not be rational for them to save for retirement. Presently, in less-developed countries (LDCs), there are well-established informal institutions that provide social insurance for old age, illness and unemployment.

Even assuming deficiencies in old-age security before states got involved, there is reason to believe that the state has not done a satisfactory job. There are at least four reasons to be sceptical of government attempts to solve societal problems: lack of information, the law of unintended consequences, public choice dilemmas, and the principle of subsidiarity.

Lack of information

The first problem faced by governments with social issues is that they lack necessary information. Of course, governments may be good at gathering official, statistical information. But it is harder to acquire relevant and useful information for solving the real needs of real human beings; commonly neither these needs nor the efficient solutions to them can be captured in statistical data (Hayek, 1945). Market economies communicate information through the price system, which reflects the simultaneous and independent decisions of thousands and millions of individuals. Socialist governments, in contrast, cannot access this information, and they are left blind as to what people really value and how their needs can be satisfied efficaciously.

Lack of relevant information has been a major source of trouble in public pension systems. First, they have failed to address the real desires of individuals. Instead of allowing people to pursue different options as they grow older, these systems have imposed an institutionalised period of leisurely non-activity. This might sound attractive, but in reality several studies attest that full-time retirement contributes to deteriorating mental and physical well-being, especially when the person feels that retirement was not a free choice (Dave et al., 2006; Bender, 2004). A 'one size fits all' approach has neglected differences in personality, work habits, life situation and preferences. Second, estimating the long-range forecast information required to manage a state pensions system, such as long-range mortality projections, is inherently difficult. Mortality, for example, has been consistently underestimated.

Third, governments have not managed their pension schemes satisfactorily. Contribution rates have been on the rise throughout the history of those schemes, but no solution has been found to reverse the trend; this resembles the inability of socialism to innovate. Many governments have also neglected or dismissed negative information, owing mainly to public choice problems discussed below.

Unintended consequences

Another problem of state involvement in old-age security is that government intervention tends to have unintended consequences, especially for inter-temporal issues such as pensions (Hayek, 1978; Merton, 1979). Private solutions too may bear unintended consequences, but they respond and adapt themselves more effectively. In contrast, when government programmes are amended, they often become increasingly complex and difficult to handle.

This is particularly true of public pension systems. A major problem is that they have created harmful incentives, such as opportunities for 'free-riding' and 'moral hazard' (Holmström, 1978). This makes the systems more expensive and undermines their sustainability. Some examples of such incentives, discussed in more detail later, are the following: implicit penalties for working longer, penalties for having more children, and incentives to abuse disability retirement rules. The unintended consequence of public pension systems is that people retire earlier than ever before, and fertility rates are below replacement levels in many countries: thus these systems contribute to their own insolvency.

Public choice and private interests

The third problem with state solutions is embedded in the nature of democratic decision-making processes. These are analysed in what is known as 'public choice theory' (Buchanan and Tullock, 1962; Tullock, 2006). The key idea is that politics is not just about the benevolent pursuit of general welfare; political decisions are often dictated by individuals and groups seeking their own private interests. The general public has weak incentives to monitor government, and well-organised special-interest groups can therefore force through their own agendas. Politicians, too, are human beings, and may pursue policies in line with their personal interests. But even when politicians act benevolently, there will be a tendency to engage in 'log rolling', i.e. buying support from different social segments by providing tangible benefits to them.

Public choice problems are hugely important for understanding the existing public pension systems, and more on this will be said later. It is also a reason for scepticism about the ability of governments to solve the current situation satisfactorily (see the chapter by Booth).

The principle of subsidiarity

Local decision-making often yields better solutions and outcomes and can help ease public choice problems. Needs are best understood and satisfied by people who are closest to them and who act as neighbours to those in need – and this includes the very personal needs of the elderly. Arguably the most important deficiency of public pension systems – one that has been almost completely ignored in the public arena – is that they undermine all the local institutions, family, voluntary associations, etc. Unlike governments, these can give something more than cold cash. Meeting need in old age is not just about monetary income, and policies that replace intermediary institutions in old-age security will eventually contribute to the demise of those institutions.

Pensions problems: the state is the cause, not the remedy

It is worth delving more deeply into government pension policies to see why the state is not the solution but actually is the origin of problems with old-age security and care. Although state retirement policies come in all sorts of sizes and shapes, most of them can be reduced to two general alternatives: public PAYGO pension systems and compulsory savings systems.

Public pay-as-you-go pension systems

The most common general form of governmental pension scheme is the PAYGO type. This means that the government makes inter-generational transfers from the working population to those in retirement. In practice, these systems vary in many ways. At one end there is the 'Bismarckian' model where private pension provision is virtually non-existent; at the other end there is the more liberal 'Beveridge' model adopted in the UK and the USA, where occupational and other private schemes play a major role.[2] In some countries, such as France, public pension schemes are strictly speaking non-governmental, but they are compulsory and sanctioned by law, so that the difference is administrative only. Also, some governments partially fund their pension scheme, which means that there is a savings aspect, but in practice these do not differ much from pure PAYGO schemes.

The following sections present a brief critique of public PAYGO pension systems. The main points of criticism are that they induce early retirement and cause low fertility rates. They have also been a disaster in less-developed countries and should be avoided by their governments. PAYGO schemes tend to be popular, however, because democratic politics favours their expansion.

Problems of PAYGO pension systems
Induced early retirement

One common problem with the existing public PAYGO systems is that they induce early retirement. It is well established that labour force participation rates among older workers have been declining ever since the creation of public pensions (Gruber and Wise, 1998, 1999). Between the 1960s and 1990s, the proportion of men at work aged between 60 and 64 reduced from over 80 per cent to around 50 per cent in many countries. People are retiring earlier than ever before.

The explanation is simple; public pension schemes not only

---

2   In the USA, public pensions are called 'social security', but we avoid using this term, because in Europe it refers to other kinds of welfare benefits, excluding public pensions.

allow people to retire early, but they positively encourage it: 'What has not been widely appreciated is that the provisions of [public pension] programs themselves often provide strong incentives to leave the labor force. By penalizing work, social security systems magnify the increased financial burden caused by aging populations and thus contribute to their own insolvency' (Gruber and Wise, 2005).

The disincentives to continue working differ from country to country. In the USA, Butrica et al. (2004) estimate that at age 67 most people will earn the same by retiring as by continuing to work, and after that age one is financially punished for working. In many European countries, incentives for early retirement tend to be ever greater, though some countries have made minor reforms in recent years.

Induced early retirement is a classic case of how government solutions can go awry. Artificial incentives have created free-riding, making the systems ever more expensive – an example of unintended consequences. It displays public choice problems, because earlier retirement ages did not come accidentally, but were consistently pushed for by labour unions. Indeed, Sefton et al. (2005) argue that there is an inherent bias in democratic systems towards more generous pension benefits, even at the cost of future generations. Finally, there is lack of innovation and subsidiarity. Disability benefit rules are rigid and bureaucratic, and they have failed to adapt to their exploitation.

Declining fertility rates

Another reason for the looming bankruptcy of public pension systems is population ageing and low fertility rates. In many

European countries, fertility rates are now far below replacement levels.[3] An increasing number of sociologists and economists are blaming this on public pension schemes (Ehrlich and Kim, 2007; Boldrin et al., 2005; Cigno and Rosati, 1996).

The reason why public pensions affect fertility is twofold. First, in the absence of formal pension schemes, the main vehicle for old-age security is the extended family. This gives rise to the so-called *old age security motive for fertility*, which is strong in less-developed countries (Nugent, 1985). The establishment of public pensions removes this incentive to have children. But, what is more, public PAYGO pensions positively penalise childbearing (Ehrlich and Kim, 2007). This is because a compulsory pension scheme imposes the costs of retirement on all workers, regardless of how many children they have had (if any), so that families that raise more children carry a larger burden of the cost of PAYGO pensions.

The empirical evidence linking fertility decline to the growth of public pensions is striking and undeniable. Only some of it can be cited here.[4] Ehrlich and Kim (2007) show, using data from 57 countries between 1960 and 1992, that higher pensions taxes have a negative and significant effect on total fertility rates in all plausible regression specifications. Puhakka and Viren (2006) report similar findings with data going farther back, and Cigno and Rosati (1996) reach the same conclusion with a different time-series regression method. Overall, the effect seems very strong indeed: simulations estimate that the growth of public PAYGO pensions can explain as much as 50 per cent of the decline in

---

3   The EU average is just 1.5, and the Mediterranean countries are as low as 1.3. See en.wikipedia.org/wiki/List_of_countries_and_territories_by_fertility_rate.

4   See Juurikkala (2007) for a detailed discussion.

fertility rates in Europe and the USA between 1950 and 2000 (Boldrin et al., 2005).

Expansive dynamics

If public PAYGO schemes really are so bad, one wonders why they were ever created. Public choice theory provides a simple answer: it paid off for the first generation of voters. A public PAYGO system transfers money from workers to retirees. Hence those who design the system, the first generation to retire, get a windfall. They reap the benefits of generous retirement income without having to contribute much or anything at all. This was how the system was publicised in Britain (Bartholomew, 2006).

Public choice theory also demonstrates an inherent expansive dynamic in public PAYGO systems (see the chapter by Booth and also Mulligan and Sala-i-Martin, 1999, 2003). Elderly voters have a strong focus on their retirement benefits when taking voting decisions, whereas workers have a more diffuse set of interests. There is an inbuilt tendency for PAYGO pension systems to over-expand. Many of the losers from expansion cannot yet vote or have not even been born. This explains why it is so difficult for countries to change their flawed policies.

Problems of compulsory savings schemes

Instead of public PAYGO schemes, some governments have pursued compulsory savings schemes to provide retirement security (see the chapter by Mihaita). The most famous example is Chile, where, in the early 1980s, the bankrupt PAYGO scheme was replaced by individual retirement accounts into which workers had to contribute a predetermined proportion of their salary. In the USA, the second Bush administration strongly advocated a similar reform.

There is a lot to be said for compulsory savings schemes (Piñera, 1996). They provide better returns to contributions, and they create fewer harmful incentives. In Chile, pensions have been much more generous under the new scheme, and the political manipulation and favouritism of the previous system have largely disappeared. More private savings have also stimulated the economy as a whole, and employment incentives are better, because one owns every penny saved for retirement. Comparing Chile with other Latin American countries, pensions are fairer, more generous and more widely spread.

There are, however, reasons to oppose this as a general solution. At the outset, one wonders what the benefits of compulsion are over the free decisions of individuals and families. At best, state direction *may* be helpful in developing capital markets where they are lacking, but even that is doubtful. Indeed, the Chilean model has fared poorly precisely in those countries where financial markets were not sufficiently advanced. Moreover, in Chile a unique set of political circumstances meant that strong vested-interest groups were ignored during the transition period, facilitating a well-designed system. Other countries that have attempted 'Chilean-style' reforms have not been as successful.

Making retirement savings compulsory may actually do more harm than good. First, they create inefficiencies through over-regulation. In Chile, despite a generally flexible framework in which specialised companies manage the funds, there are various onerous limits on investments; investments in foreign assets have been particularly restricted. This is not a minor matter, because international diversification is one of the key methods for protecting the investments against national shocks and bad government policy, such as monetary inflation. In Chile, investment returns have been remarkably good, but this is more likely to be due to a period of rapid economic liberalisation and development, not to the merits of the compulsory savings scheme.

Second, compulsory savings causes a prima facie resource misallocation (Booth and Cooper, 2005). Instead of allowing people to allocate their earnings to their most highly valued ends, the government forces them to place an arbitrarily defined amount in an inflexible savings vehicle, which they cannot access until old age. This prevents people from making their own judgements about how to use scarce economic resources. There is, moreover, an implicit assumption behind compulsory savings, namely that financial markets are the best medium for providing old-age security, but this is doubtful. Indeed, for reasons explained later, there is reason to believe that personal savings should play a subsidiary, not a primary, role in many situations. This is especially the case in less-developed countries, where other risks such as illness or unemployment are far more important issues. Compulsory retirement savings force poor people to use scarce resources on saving for retirement, which may be wholly inappropriate if their life expectancy is less than their expected retirement age.

Third, there is the risk of corruption and mismanagement. Wherever there is a significant accumulation of capital concentrated within organisations ultimately accountable to government there is the potential for problems. In many African countries, savings schemes known as Provident Funds have been subject to large-scale corruption (Tostensen, 2004; Barbone and Sanchez,

1999). In Chile, the experience has been better owing to the implementation of a well-designed scheme with good institutional checks and balances.

An argument commonly used for compulsory savings is that people are too short-sighted to save otherwise; this is discussed in detail later. But note also that public choice theory may explain the recent push for compulsory savings: there are many institutions that benefit from it. For politicians too, a compulsory savings system can be an instrument of political manipulation. It is important to note, however, that in Chile and many other countries the compulsory savings systems have been an improvement on the systems they replaced. Wholesale repeal of state pension systems was probably not a realistic option. Compulsory savings systems, up to a degree, can also be justified if other social security systems provide means-tested benefits to the elderly, though it could be argued that this problem should be tackled at its root.

Old-age security and care: alternatives to the state

It is easy to find reasons to criticise government attempts to provide meaningful, efficient and long-term old-age security. The harder question is whether there could be adequate security and care without government intervention, and what that might look like. If the state were to withdraw from pension provision, the argument goes, many people in old age would rely on means-tested social security benefits. Surely, it is further argued, one cannot simply withdraw such benefits and watch old people starve to death.

If the state were to withdraw, the elderly might actually receive better security and care than through the state. Markets are not the only alternative to state provision. There are at least three sources of old-age security that are alternatives to the state: the extended family, capital markets, and other civil society institutions such as charities and mutual help societies.

Extended family: a private pay-as-you-go system

Governments did not invent PAYGO pensions. There is a much older, and arguably more efficient, PAYGO mechanism. It is called the family. In the absence of public social security systems, families function as a type of private, informal PAYGO insurance mechanism, in which parents look after their children, and children care for their parents in sickness and old age in return. This is the most common form of savings in much of the developing world today – just as it was in the West a hundred years ago.

Some individuals cannot have children of their own, or their children may fall ill and die. The natural solution to these risks is to *pool* them in the informal social insurance market – hence the norm in traditional societies is not the nuclear family but the *extended family* (Ehrlich and Lui, 1991). Indeed, this form of support can be found operative even in highly developed societies. For example, Rendall and Bahchieva (1998) show that co-residence and functional support by the extended family are a major source of poverty alleviation among elderly Americans: around 11 per cent of all unmarried elderly, and almost one third of disabled elderly, stay above the poverty line by living with family members.

Implicit 'insurance' within the extended family has several advantages. For one, it is actually more effective than formal systems in solving informational and monitoring problems, because all members know and have constant dealings with each

other. Emotional ties also give strong internal incentives to participate for the common good. This results in less moral hazard,
adverse selection and free-riding – problems that are common
in formal insurance markets and pension schemes. For example,
elderly people in informal systems do not retire early and they
continue working, perhaps part time, even if they have some
disability (Nugent, 1985).

Family-based old-age security also better aligns private interests with public interests. Fertility is a case in point: childbearing
is actually economically sound in the absence of public PAYGO
pensions, which is one reason why people used to have large
families – and continue to do so in LDCs. Higher fertility in turn
contributes to more human capital and economic growth (Ehrlich
and Lui, 1991; Simon, 1994, 1996).

Capital markets, savings and insurance

The capital markets are not the sole source of old-age security, but
in developed economies they would undoubtedly play a major
role. Indeed, private retirement savings and insurance already
constitute an important part of retirement incomes in countries
such as the USA and the UK.

Private saving has many advantages over government pension
schemes: it leads to lower taxes, better incentives to work, higher
productivity due to capital accumulation and more efficient
resource allocation. It seems that a given contribution will yield
a much larger pension than in public PAYGO systems, as the
Chilean experience testifies (Corbo and Schmidt-Hebbel, 2003).
Also, apart from purely economic benefits, emphasis on saving
promotes cultural benefits, such as cultivation of prudence, a

long-term perspective on life, wider capital ownership and greater personal responsibility.

A further benefit of relying on the voluntary choices of individuals and families is that they can choose how much, through what vehicles and when in their life cycle to save. How can the state know whether it is better for somebody to pay off their mortgage or increase saving at a particular time? How can the state know the balance between spending on children's education and pension provision that is appropriate? How can the state know whether people would want to save more and retire early or save less and continue to work part time after formal retirement age? Of course, these questions highlight the problem of compulsory private pension schemes just as much as state pension provision. It might even happen that the very concept of 'retirement' should be allowed to erode; to a large degree it is a creation of the state. The idea of working until one drops for 35 years and then spending a period of complete leisure is in many respects bizarre. Arguably, the abolition of pure retirement would reduce depression and other health deterioration associated with social isolation and physical inactivity (Dave et al., 2006). It would also reduce the social marginalisation of the elderly.

Civil society: charities and mutual help

Provision of old-age security in a free society is not limited to families and financial markets. An equally important provider is 'civil society': especially charities and mutual help organisations. In developed countries, private charities have played an increasingly important role in solving needs not looked after by formal markets or states.

In addition to traditional charities, there would be mutual help societies, which are a kind of middle way between the extended family and formal insurance. Popular especially in the eighteenth and nineteenth centuries, mutual help societies came in various sizes and shapes, such as trade unions, friendly societies, credit unions, self-help groups and fraternal organisations. They were often based on some common religious or ideological convictions that help to establish loyalty and commitment (Beito, 1992, 2000).

Such organisations have numerous advantages over the state, such as the use of voluntary action, local knowledge, local action, commitment and ability to innovate. Put to the test, they can improve on the performance of governmental welfare organisations. This is supported by both past and present experience (Olasky, 1992; Beito, 2002).

Before the advent of the welfare state, mutual help societies impressed by both the extent of their work and their efficiency (Beito, 1992, 2000). Fraternal societies, for example, provided practically every kind of welfare service imaginable, including orphanages, hospitals, job exchanges, homes for the elderly and scholarship programmes. They also supplied health insurance at much lower rates than the present-day formal schemes subsidised by tax incentives. Moreover, mutual help organisations were anything but elite groups, as they were mainly manned by working-class men and women, who wanted to look after each other and knew how to go about it.

Mutual help societies lost their role for a simple reason: public welfare programmes, backed up by taxpayers' money, crowded them out. Beito (1992, 2000) argues that something very important was lost in the transition. The greatest virtue of mutual help societies was their commitment to helping individuals where they needed it most, not paralysing those who asked for assistance, but fostering self-reliance, thrift and self-control. They also provided valuable services such as business training and leadership skills. Now, instead of approaching a voluntary organisation marked by reciprocity and fraternal spirit, the poor and unfortunate must go to unfriendly bureaucracies dominated by legalism and collective frustration. If mutual help societies sought to put people back on their feet, government welfare programmes make passive the poor and positively penalise effort: not surprisingly, the welfare state has not put an end to poverty.

Predicting the unpredictable

It is not possible to predict exactly what old age would look like without government intervention. We do know that individuals, families and other institutions will develop new solutions, combining past and present wisdom, if state systems are wound down. This much can be known, without knowing what a private system of care and income provision would look like in detail. One of the principles of free market economics is that the market – and the civil society just as much – is a discovery procedure (Hayek, 1945; Kirzner, 1992). It is driven by human creativity, which can never be fully anticipated.

There is a tendency to assume that various services financed through compulsory tax payments would not be provided if governments did not provide them. The market provides food, houses, cars and education where it is allowed to do so, however, as well as other basic necessities. Once artificial barriers to human creativity are removed, one sees all sorts of solutions cropping up, which no one would have thought of before.

There are sometimes barriers to human creativity even when the government is not making income provision in old age. For example, lack of property rights, contractual uncertainty, etc. This explains why, in less-developed countries, prosperity is so thinly spread. Arguably, in many less-developed countries, the government is the direct or indirect cause of those very barriers. Some other challenges are 'natural' – for example, informational asymmetries. When people are left free to solve their problems, however, they are surprisingly responsible and creative. In contrast, when they are being 'looked after' by public programmes, people develop cultures of dependency that have an economic cause but which harm not just economically but also emotionally and spiritually.

Possible problems rebutted

Now, one might be tempted to think that, if the state did not provide old-age security, old-age provision would just revert back to the level before the welfare state or to the level of provision in less-developed countries (LDCs). This is obviously incorrect. For example, it is true that an extended-family solution to income risks in present-day LDCs is clearly more risky than a public welfare system in developed countries. It does not mean, however, that public systems are better than private ones, but simply that developed countries are in all respects better off than LDCs, which is rather self-evident. If one wishes to compare public with private systems, one should, for example, compare governmental systems in LDCs with private solutions in similar countries. In Africa, state pension schemes have been a disaster; they have not just failed to deliver what they promised, but they have also eroded the existing private solutions and left many people without either public or private security (Barbone and Sanchez, 1999; Silver et al., 2007). In contrast, private market and family systems seem to function relatively well there, taking into account very low incomes, high inflation and insecure property rights.

There are, however, also more genuine concerns about old-age security in the absence of state involvement. First, there are real risks in the market provision of income security, and some individuals may lack the skills to make prudent choices in managing their wealth. Second, assuming markets can handle that challenge, some individuals may fail to look after themselves if they are not compelled to do so. Finally, there are concerns about the employability of older workers, which will be important to individuals that do not have sufficient savings. The following sections respond to each of these challenges.

Limits and risks of private provision

There are two common worries people have about the market provision of old-age security. One is that companies are less stable than governments and, if they go bankrupt, some individuals will lose all their savings. Another concern is that purchasing savings and insurance instruments calls for a solid understanding of financial affairs, which many people do not have, and this could result in poor service and ruthless exploitation of innocent people.

Regarding the issue of security, the market itself, together with the legal system, produces solutions to this problem. Indeed, markets have produced solutions to this problem from the earliest days of their development. In the UK and the USA (and common-law jurisdictions in general) pension fund assets are held in trust funds. A trust fund is a legally separate entity, which neither the sponsoring company nor its creditors can access. Hence, even if the company goes bust, savers still have interests in the fund. Of course, problems can arise, as in the Maxwell scandal in the mid-1990s. It is worth noting, however, that this was not a failure of regulation but involved a systematic theft of funds. No system can completely protect people from theft in this way – but such events are very rare.

The UK government is having to deal with criticism at the current time about the inadequacy of pension funds where the sponsoring employer has gone bankrupt. These are genuine problems. We are not arguing that free markets are perfect markets – merely that they are better than the alternatives. It is, nevertheless, worth noting that the problems for particular groups of workers in insolvent pension funds in the UK have been exacerbated by government regulation that imposed a greater share of any losses on specific groups of members within the schemes. Also, savings institutions can protect their assets most effectively in a free market, which allows them to pool risks by investing internationally and using suitable investment vehicles to control risks.

Moreover, it is uncertain that government pensions are less risky. Government pensions in LDCs have historically been anything but safe, and even in developed countries public pension benefits can be changed at will by any government in power. Workers are given nothing but political promises, which generally have no value when tested in courts of law. Although political promises have mostly been fulfilled, it is very likely that more dire times are ahead owing to the looming bankruptcy of public PAYGO pension systems – the risk of loss to a PAYGO 'saver' might be lower than in a private system, but the now non-zero probability of a PAYGO system going bankrupt would be disastrous.

Ignorance

The second problem concerns the ability of individuals to buy the right products, given their limited know-how. While deciding the 'optimal' amount to save and the 'optimal' vehicle through which to save may be difficult technical decisions, real life does not require the determination of such technically optimal solutions. Evidence suggests that, given the right set of incentives, individuals will make provision for their future. Furthermore, in the absence of state intervention, individuals have incentives to either avoid complex products or pay for appropriate advice. Indeed, close-to-optimal solutions tend to require little technical knowledge in a world of reasonably competitive markets. Competition leads to an improvement in product quality in general so that, if a product is chosen at random, it will normally suffice, even if it is not optimal. The market for technical white goods such as refrigerators illustrates the point. Finding the 'best' refrigerator for a particular family is a difficult technical decision. Finding a reasonably good product requires much less information. But, even if a product is chosen more or less at random, that product would almost certainly be better than the product that would be supplied in a centrally planned market with a state producer. It should be added that regulation and government tax policies significantly add to the complexity, variety and opacity of financial products. The market is moreover not limited to pure savings, but there is scope for different kinds of old-age insurance, and markets will adapt to new needs and demands. Moreover, even if people were to buy products that give a poor return, their retirement income would still be much larger than under public PAYGO schemes, in which the return to contributions is often negative.[5]

There is in fact no reason to take it as a given that many people understand little about financial markets. It is generally not necessary for individuals to understand the basic principles of finance, given that about half of the population (for example in the UK) have very little saving because of state involvement in pension provision. If people could benefit from becoming more educated, there is no reason to believe they would not do so.

A related issue is the complex but fundamental problem of inflationary monetary policies. In many countries, saving for retirement is difficult because the real value of savings is lost in depreciating currencies. Indeed, even in developed countries, confidence in long-term nominal investment instruments and contracts was eroded in the 1970s. Factoring in expected inflation, comparing actual with expected inflation and monitoring the uneven effects of inflation on different parts of the economy add to the opacity of private sector pension provision through capital markets. Even modern financial instruments with returns linked to retail prices may not offer such good net outcomes: there is a growing debate on whether official government reporting of inflation figures is honest and truthful, and real returns to investments

---

5   In PAYGO schemes, the theoretical rate of return on contributions is equal to the growth rate of the population (in the absence of any funding and ignoring changes in other factors such as employment rates). In countries with below-replacement fertility rates, this translates into a negative rate of return. As tax rates have to rise to allow pension promises to be fulfilled, economic inactivity increases, thus raising the cost per taxpayer still further.

may be smaller than is usually thought.[6] In any event, inflationary monetary policies are a key factor that makes individuals economically vulnerable and dependent on the state: monetary reform is a central part of reforming old-age security.

Access to the market

It could of course be that, in some cases, there is no access to market provision for old-age security. For example, in many LDCs there are effectively no financial markets in which to invest. This is not, however, a problem that can be solved by state intervention in pension provision; often the state is the real cause of those very problems, as it fails to maintain reliable legal institutions and monetary stability. Imposing forced PAYGO schemes on top of this has only exacerbated the harm when governments should be using their limited capacity to provide the institutional framework within which people can save. Surprisingly, people in these settings do manage to save through informal markets reliably and relatively efficiently. A good example of this is the widespread custom of 'Roscas' (Rotating savings and credit associations), which are a type of informal lending and savings institution (Anderson and Baland, 2002; Besley et al., 1993). The problem is neither the unavailability of formal savings schemes, nor the lack of government intervention; the problem is bad governance by corrupt governments that have failed to create a legal and political environment conducive to thrift and economic enterprise.

---

6   According to calculations by Walter J. Williams, US inflation figures may be underestimated by as much as 4–7 percentage points (Williams, 2006; Welling, 2006). If this is true, real returns on low-risk investments may have been negative in 2008.

Old-age security in free societies would most likely not depend just on formal savings schemes, thus access to the market is not necessarily the key issue – though it is a very important issue. As has been mentioned, in many circumstances, the family, or the extended family, is possibly the most efficient mechanism for providing basic income security and care. In LDCs, extended family 'insurance' has the additional benefit of providing for income replacement risks other than old age, especially unemployment, illness and physical disability (Cain, 1982, 1983). This is prima facie a more efficient allocation of scarce resources, because limited wealth does not become tied into inflexible savings instruments that one cannot access before old age – something that is a feature of even free-market-oriented reforms such as those in Chile.

Short-termism and 'under-saving'

Another big concern about the free decisions of individuals and families is that people might be tempted to make short-term decisions and consequently save too little for retirement. This concern is one motivation for compulsory savings schemes, and the report of the UK Turner Commission expressed such fears (Pensions Commission, 2005). It is supported by research in behavioural economics, which shows that people do not always behave fully 'rationally' over time.[7] For example, people may fall prey to various behavioural 'anomalies', such as over confidence, weakness of will and various biases in judgement (Kahneman et al., 1982; Earl, 1990). Making optimal decisions may be especially

---

7   See Mitchell and Utkus (2004) for an excellent overview of the issue and relevant literature.

hard when they involve events far in the future, as is the case with retirement (Wärneryd, 1989; Thaler, 1990).

The crucial question is what conclusions one should draw from this. The mere fact of uncertainty does not mean people will save too little – the presence of uncertainty regarding the future could well mean that people have a tendency to over-save rather than under-save. Empirically, it does seem that some people under-save, but this may be a consequence of the current institutional incentives, such as compulsory pension contributions and high taxes.[8] In fact, there is evidence that, by and large, those not affected by social safety nets tend to 'over-save'; most retirees are generally wealthier and better off than those of working age (HSBC, 2006). This implies that many people save more than they actually need in order to sustain their lifetime consumption levels in retirement.

Assuming the concern is valid for some groups of people, the question remains whether the state should intervene, and how. To use an analogy, many people have unhealthy eating habits (owing to problems of self-control and lack of information), but this does not mean we should all be forced to eat bureaucratically designed diets in government canteens. Government pension schemes may not be more effective than even imperfect private systems, as has been demonstrated. More subtle ways of influencing behaviour

---

8   Thaler (1994) claims that lack of self-control may lead people to save too little. His argument for this is that 'many households undoubtedly think they should be saving more but find saving is a luxury they cannot afford' (p. 187). But perhaps that is precisely what further saving is: a luxury. This is not evidence of lack of self-control, but of rational allocation of scarce resources to their most highly valued ends. Of course, part of the reason why most people cannot afford to save is that they are forced to pay vast proportions (around 50 per cent in most EU countries) of their nominal earnings in taxes, public pensions contributions, etc.

may be wiser: education, information, tax incentives, default rules, opting-out, etc.

Of course, there are individuals who suffer poverty in retirement. They tend, however, to be people who suffered poverty and unemployment during their lifetime too. Therefore, this is not evidence of under-saving, because these individuals had more pressing needs than a comfortable retirement. Moreover, elderly poverty tends to be marked in countries with substantial means-tested retirement benefits, such as the UK, the USA and Australia. The problem here is that means-tested benefits penalise savings, especially in the years just before retirement (Neumark and Powers, 1998, 2000). It is because of this that means testing exacerbates income inequalities in retirement (Sefton et al., 1998). It is therefore unfair to assume that the less well off are merely short-sighted and unable to make long-term decisions. The provision of means-tested benefits can make saving irrational, so that failing to save has become economically optimal for those with smaller incomes (Hubbard et al., 1995). The tangible evidence from LDCs shows that people can and do save for 'rainy days', when they benefit from it, even if they have to sacrifice a lot to do it.[9]

Employment of older workers

Another cause of concern is the possibly limited employment

---

9   A good example again is the widespread use of 'Roscas'. Bouman (1995) estimates that between 50 and 95 per cent of the adult population in Africa participate in Roscas. This is a highly significant number given the low incomes that most people live off. Quantitative savings data is of course scant owing to the underdevelopment of formal savings institutions, but the main reason for this is bad government and legal institutions that undermine formal contracts and investments (De Soto, 2000).

prospects of older workers. If there is no state-provided or compulsory pension scheme, some individuals may need to work longer. The question is whether they will find suitable employment later on, as companies may wish to make older workers redundant and they may be less productive in alternative occupations.

In general, there is no reason to assume this is the case. Before the establishment of public pension schemes, the majority of people worked beyond age 65. Indeed, the concept of retirement was foreign to most people, who at least did some part-time work even as they grew older. Moreover, the fertility decline of recent decades should encourage working longer, because a diminishing population will make labour relatively scarcer and increase its price (Miles, 1999).

It could of course be that times have changed and companies no longer wish to retain older employees. One would expect this to vary, however, between industry and type of job. On the one hand, certain cognitive and technical abilities deteriorate with age, so that crude productivity goes down. On the other hand, older workers are more experienced, reliable and loyal to the company, which are highly valued attributes in some jobs, and explains why older workers are generally much better paid (Skirbekk, 2003).

In line with this, the evidence of employer attitudes to older workers tends to be mixed. Munnell et al. (2006) report that age is particularly valued in white-collar jobs, because older managers and professionals are overwhelmingly seen as more productive than younger ones; also nearly one half of respondents saw older blue-collar workers as more productive. Age tends to increase the cost of employment, however, owing partly to higher health-care costs (in the USA) as well as larger salaries on average. This may explain why older workers find it more difficult to obtain a new job than younger workers do (Chan and Stevens, 1999). Another reason seems to be that companies expect workers to retire at specific ages, which reduces the value of investing in their training.

Assuming that the concern is justified, there are at least two responses to it. One is to reduce the cost of employing older workers by abolishing laws that require employers to bear the burden of employee healthcare costs – after all, if the individuals are inactive, their healthcare costs would not be borne by employers.[10] Moreover, if it is true in some jobs that older workers are less productive, one could simply allow companies to pay lower wages to them. The usual trend is that wages go up with age, but there is no reason why this should always be the case. Finally, if elderly employment became a real issue, various policies could be employed to alleviate it. For example, there could be tax incentives to employ older people (though, in practice, one should, however, avoid creating special taxation categories, because they add to the complexity of the tax system). Alternatively, there could be a modest basic pension, given to workers above, say, 75 with no early retirement provision.

Conclusion and an analysis of the World Bank approach

The majority of pension reform proposals focus on fine-tuning the existing systems. Such incremental reform may be valuable, but it is insufficient. The World Bank has proposed a broader policy approach that has become very influential (World Bank, 1994, 2001). After discussing the various challenges posed by old-age

---

10 This is not applicable in the UK, of course, where general taxation bears most healthcare costs.

security in different cultural, social and economic environments, the World Bank research group concluded that governments should develop a three-pillar pension system. The pillars are: (1) a public scheme (either universal or means-tested), which has the goal of reducing poverty; (2) a mandatory savings scheme, managed by the private sector; and (3) voluntary private savings. The details of each pillar should depend on the conditions in each country, but the goal is to combine the three pillars instead of relying on just one type of income protection.

This approach has its merits: it really seeks to provide a global, long-term approach, which builds on experiences in different countries. There are problems too, however. A World Bank report by Holzmann and Hinz (2005) noted that there were important omissions, especially when one considers less-developed countries. So they added two more pillars: (4) a basic defined benefit pension and, more importantly, (5) informal support, i.e. family and other informal sources of old-age security. Later, an independent evaluation group of the World Bank (World Bank, 2006) criticised the implementation of the approach on several grounds. They claimed that there had often been a failure to understand local economic and institutional environments. Consequently fully funded systems fared badly when local financial markets were ill prepared to sustain and support them, resulting in poor diversification and limited coverage. There was also lack of analytical depth regarding assumptions on the living conditions of the aged, investigation of the limits of formal pension coverage, etc. Finally, there was inconsistency in how the pillar combination was adopted in different countries.

These criticisms are not fundamental, but there are deeper problems with the World Bank approach. For one thing, the

World Bank is suggesting that all pillars should be employed. Adding the fourth and fifth pillars makes the picture more complete, but the research group fails to take a real stand on what works and what does not – the implication is that they are all fundamentally good. Of course, all solutions to old-age security have some weaknesses, and the World Bank seems to hope that, by combining all the pillars, a country can get 'the best of both worlds'. The five-pillar approach overlooks the fact that the state pillars erode the non-state sectors, resulting in all the problems of government regulation while dulling the self-correcting and evolutionary mechanisms of the private sector.

This chapter has shown that there are real problems with public PAYGO schemes, and indeed a basic state pension may simply be unnecessary. There is also no obvious need for mandatory savings, certainly in the absence of means-tested social security systems where payments are linked solely to old age. Finally, family support and private savings are inextricably linked to the provision of compulsory pension schemes, because compulsion will tend to crowd out voluntary solutions, including civil societies, associations and charities.

The fundamental flaw of the World Bank approach, then, lies in its basic assumption that the government should be at the centre of old-age security, even if some of the tasks are undertaken by the private sector. It further assumes that it is the task of the government to ensure that everything is in place. This is an essentially authoritarian view of society, one that fails to understand the limits and deficiencies associated with any governmental interference with the lives of individuals and communities. Instead, we argue, this outlook should be reversed. The individual and family should be at the core of the provision of old-age security, with governments providing the legal and institutional framework, and occasionally more substantive assistance, to help individuals meet their aspirations.

References

Anderson, S. and J. M. Baland (2002), 'The economics of ROSCAS and intra-household resource allocation', *Quarterly Journal of Economics*, 117(3): 963–95.

Barbone, L. and L.-A. Sanchez (1999), 'Pensions and social security in sub-Saharan Africa: issues and options', Africa Region Working Paper Series no. 4, World Bank, available online at www.worldbank.org/afr/wps/wp4.htm.

Bartholomew, J. (2006), *The Welfare State We're In*, 2nd revised edn, London: Politico's.

Beito, D. T. (1992), *From Mutual Aid to Welfare State: Fraternal Societies and Social Services*, Cambridge: University of North Carolina Press.

Beito, D. T. (2000), *From Mutual Aid to Welfare State: How Fraternal Societies Fought Poverty and Taught Character*, Heritage Foundation Backgrounder no. 677, available online at www.heritage.org/Research/PoliticalPhilosophy/h1677.cfm.

Beito, D. T. (ed.) (2002), *The Voluntary City: Choice, Community, and Civil Society*, Ann Arbor: University of Michigan Press.

Bender, K. A. (2004), *The Well-being of Retirees: Evidence Using Subjective Data*, Working Paper 24–2004, Center for Retirement Research at Boston College, available online at www.bc.edu/centers/crr/papers/wp_2004–24.pdf.

Besley, T., S. Coate and G. Loury (1993), 'The economics of Rotating Savings and Credit Associations', *American Economic Review*, 83(4): 792–810.

Boldrin, M., M. de Nardi and L. E. Jones (2005), 'Fertility and social security', NBER Working Paper no. 11146, available online at www.nber.org/papers/w11146.

Booth, P. and D. Cooper (2005), *The Way out of the Pensions Quagmire*, London: Institute of Economic Affairs.

Bouman, F. (1995), 'Rotating and Accumulating Savings and Credit Associations: a development perspective', *World Development*, 23(3): 371–84.

Buchanan, J. M. and G. Tullock (1962), *The Calculus of Consent*, Ann Arbor: University of Michigan Press, Ann Arbor, available online at www.econlib.org/library/Buchanan/buchCv3Contents.html.

Butrica, B. A., R. W. Johnson, K. E. Smith and E. Steuerle (2004), *Does Work Pay at Older Ages?*, Working Paper, Center for Retirement Research at Boston College, available online at www.bc.edu/centers/crr/wp_2004–30.shtml.

Cain, M. (1982), 'Perspectives on family and fertility in developing countries', *Population Studies*, 36(2): 159–75.

Cain, M. (1983), 'Fertility as an adjustment to risk', *Population and Development Review*, 9(4): 688–702.

Chan, S. and A. H. Stevens (1999), 'Employment and retirement following a late-career job loss', *American Economic Review*, 89: 211–16.

Cigno, A. and F. C. Rosati (1996), 'Jointly determined saving and fertility behavior: theory and estimates for Germany, Italy, UK, and USA', *European Economic Review*, 40: 1561–89.

Corbo, V. and K. Schmidt-Hebbel (2003), *Efectos macroeconómicos de la reforma de pensiones en Chile*, available online at www.josepinera.com/text/corbo-schmidt.pdf.

Dave, D., I. Rashad and J. Spasojevic (2006), 'The effects of retirement on physical and mental health outcomes', NBER Working Paper no. 12123, available online at www.nber.org/papers/w12123.

De Soto, H. (2000), *The Mystery of Capital*, New York: Basic Books.

Earl, P. E. (1990), 'Economics and psychology: a survey', *Economic Journal*, 100.

Ehrlich, I. and J. Kim (2007), 'Social security and demographic trends: theory and evidence from the international experience', *Review of Economic Dynamics*, 10(1): 55–77.

Ehrlich, I. and F. Lui (1991), 'Intergenerational trade, longevity, intrafamily transfers and economic growth', *Journal of Political Economy*, 99(5): 1029–59.

Gruber, J. and D. A. Wise (1998), 'Social security and retirement: an international comparison', *American Economic Review*, 88(2): 158–63.

Gruber, J. and D. A. Wise (eds) (1999), *Social Security and Retirement around the World*, Chicago, IL: University of Chicago Press.

Gruber, J. and D. A. Wise (2005), 'Social security program and retirement around the world: fiscal implications. Introduction and summary', NBER Working Paper no. 11290.

Hayek, F. A. (1945), 'The use of knowledge in society', *American Economic Review*, 35(4): 519–30, available online at www.econlib.org/library/Essays/hykKnw1.html.

Hayek, F. A. (1978), *New Studies in Philosophy, Politics, Economics and the History of Ideas*, Chicago, IL: University of Chicago Press.

Holmström, B. (1978), 'Moral hazard and observability', *Bell Journal of Economics*, 10: 74–91.

Holzmann, R. and R. Hinz (2005), *Old-Age Income Support in the 21st Century: An International Perspective on Pension Systems and Reform*, Washington, DC: World Bank.

HSBC (2006), *The Future of Retirement: What the world wants*, London, available online at www.thefutureofretirement. com/.

Hubbard, R. G., J. Skinner and S. P. Zeldez (1995), 'Precautionary saving and social insurance', *Journal of Political Economy*, 103(2): 360–99.

Juurikkala, O. (2007), 'Pensions, fertility and families', *Economic Affairs*, 27(4): 52–7.

Kahneman, D., P. Slovic and A. Tversky (eds) (1982), *Judgment under Uncertainty: Heuristics and Biases*, Cambridge: Cambridge University Press.

Kirzner, I. (1992), *The Meaning of Market Process: Essays in the Development of Modern Austrian Economics*, Routledge.

Merton, R. K. (1979), *Sociological Ambivalence and Other Essays*, New York: Free Press.

Miles, D. (1999), 'Modelling demographic change upon the economy', *Economic Journal*, 109: 1–36.

Mitchell, O. S. and S. P. Utkus (2004), 'Lessons from behavioral finance for retirement plan design', in Mitchell and Utkus, *Pension Design and Structure: New Lessons from Behavioral Finance*, Oxford: Oxford University Press, pp. 3–41.

Mulligan, C. B. and X. Sala-i-Martin (1999), 'Gerontocracy, retirement, and social security', NBER Working Paper no. 7117, available online at www.nber.org/papers/w7117.

Mulligan, C. B. and X. Sala-i-Martin (2003), 'Social security, retirement, and the single-mindedness of the electorate', NBER Working Paper no. 9691, available online at www.nber.org/papers/w9691.

Munnell, A. H., S. A. Sass and M. Soto (2006), *Employer Attitudes towards Older Workers: Survey Results*, Issues in Brief, Center for Retirement Research at Boston College, available online at www.bc.edu/centers/crr/wob_3.shtml.

Neumark, D. and E. Powers (1998), 'The effect of means-tested income support for the elderly on pre-retirement saving: evidence from the SSI program in the US', *Journal of Public Economics*, 68(2): 181–206.

Neumark, D. and E. Powers (2000), 'Welfare for the elderly: the effects of SSI on pre-retirement labor supply', *Journal of Public Economics*, 78(1/2): 51–80.

Nugent, J. B. (1985), 'The old age security motive for fertility', *Population and Development Review*, 11: 75–98.

Olasky, M. (1992), *The Tragedy of American Compassion*, Washington, DC: Regnery.

Pensions Commission (2005), *A New Pension Settlement for the Twenty-first Century: The Second Report of the Pensions Commission*, London, available online at www.pensionscommission.org.uk/.

Piñera, J. (1996), 'Empowering workers: the privatization of social security in Chile', *Cato Journal*, 15(2/3), available online at www.josepinera.com/pag/pag_tex_empowering.htm/.

Puhakka, M. and M. Viren (2006), 'The effects of the size of the public sector on fertility', Discussion Paper no. 8, Aboa Centre for Economics, Turku School of Economics, Finland, available online at www.tse.fi/ace/dp008.pdf.

Rendall, M. S. and R. Bahchieva (1998), 'And old-age security motives for fertility in the US?', *Population and Development Review*, 24: 293–307.

Sefton, J., J. Dutta and M. Weale (1998), 'Pension finance in a calibrated model of a saving and income distribution for the UK', *National Institute Economic Review*, 166: 97–107.

Sefton, J., J. van de Ven and M. Weale (2005), 'Means testing and retirement choices in Europe: a comparison of the British and Danish systems', *Fiscal Studies*, 26(1): 83–118.

Silver, N. (2007), 'The trouble with final salary schemes', *Economic Affairs* 27(1): 71–75.

Silver, N., E. Acquaah and O. Juurikkala (2007), 'Savings in the absence of functioning property rights', *Economic Affairs*, forthcoming.

Simon, J. L. (1994), 'More people, greater wealth, more resources, healthier environments', *Economic Affairs*, 14(3), available online at www.juliansimon.com/writings/Articles/POPENVI2.txt.

Simon, J. L. (1996), *The Ultimate Resource II: People, Materials, and Environment*, 2nd edn, Princeton, NJ: Princeton University Press, available online at www.juliansimon.com/writings/Ultimate_Resource/.

Skirbekk, V. (2003), *Age and Individual Productivity: A Literature Survey*, Max Planck Institute for Demographic Research, available online at www.demogr.mpg.de/papers/working/wp-2003–028.pdf.

Thaler, R. H. (1990), 'Saving, fungibility and mental accounts', *Journal of Economic Perspectives*, 4(1): 193–205.

Thaler, R. H. (1994), 'Psychology and savings policies', *American Economic Review*, 84(2): 186–92.

Tostensen, A. (2004), 'Towards feasible social security systems in sub-Saharan Africa', Chr. Michelsen Institute, CMI Working Paper WP 2004:5, available online at www.cmi.no/publications/publication.cfm?pubid=1816.

Tullock, G. (2006), *The Vote Motive*, Hobart Paperback 33, London: Institute of Economic Affairs, available online at www.iea.org.uk/record.jsp?type=book&ID=397.

Wärneryd, K.-E. (1989), 'On the psychology of saving', *Journal of Economic Psychology*, 10: 515–41.

Welling, K. M. (2006), 'Shadowing reality: economist keeps tabs on government's "creative" statistical reports', *Welling@Weeden*, 8(4), 21 February, available online at www.weedenco.com/welling/Downloads/2006/0804welling022106.pdf.

Williams, W. J. (2006), 'The Consumer Price Index', Part 4 of *Government Economics Reports: What You've Suspected but Were Afraid to Ask*, 1 October (update), available online at www.shadowstats.com/article/56.

World Bank (1994), *Averting the Old Age Crisis: Policies to Protect the Old and Promote Growth*, Washington, DC.

World Bank (2001), *Social Protection Sector Strategy: From Safety Net to Springboard*, Washington, DC.

World Bank (2006), *Pension Reforms and the Development of Pension Systems: An Evaluation of World Bank Assistance*, Washington, DC, available online at www.worldbank.org/ieg/pensions/.

PART ONE – PENSIONS AND PUBLIC POLICY IN HIGH-INCOME DEMOCRACIES

2 RETIRE EARLY, SAVE LITTLE: THE IRONIC DISINCENTIVES OF PUBLIC PENSION SYSTEMS
Oskari Juurikkala

Introduction

> What has not been widely appreciated is that the provisions
> of social security programs themselves often provide strong
> incentives to leave the labor force. By penalizing work, social
> security systems magnify the increased financial burden
> caused by aging populations and thus contribute to their
> own insolvency. (Gruber and Wise, 2005: 1)

Public pension systems around the world are facing a funding crisis. The principal causes include rapid population ageing and low fertility rates, but there are also less well-known reasons. One is the trend towards earlier retirement, and the other is low private saving rates. In other words, people rely increasingly on the state to look after them in old age.

This chapter surveys the evidence on the incentive effects embedded in public (state) pension systems in different countries. It shows that public pension schemes penalise those who work longer, thus inducing earlier retirement. It also cites evidence that unfunded pay-as-you-go (PAYGO) pensions depress private savings. Simple reforms such as higher retirement ages and actuarially calculated benefit accrual can result in substantial cost reductions, but a true long-term reform should also aim to deinstitutionalise retirement patterns.

Induced early retirement
Declining labour force participation

Over the last century, the developed world has witnessed a strong trend towards lower labour force participation rates among older workers (Gruber and Wise, 1998, 1999). For example the proportion of men at work aged between 60 and 64 has reduced dramatically between the 1960s and the 1990s. It has fallen from over 80 per cent to around 50 per cent in many countries; in France, Belgium and Holland, fewer than 20 per cent of those aged 60–64 were still working in the mid-1990s (see Table 1). People retire earlier than before.[1]

Table 1 **Labour force participation among men aged 60–64 in sample countries (per cent)**

	1960	*1965*	*1970*	*1975*	*1980*	*1985*	*1990*	*1995*
Sweden		82	80	74	69	65	63	56
US	81	78	75	65	61	54	55	53
UK			83		65	53		50
Germany	73		75		44		35	
Belgium	71		64		35	27	19	18

Note: Data missing for some years
Source: Gruber and Wise, 2005

---

1 The decline has been even more dramatic among older workers. For example, in the USA the proportion of married males over 65 still at work declined from 55 per cent in 1947 to below 20 per cent in 1985, while for those aged between 55 and 64 it fell from 90 per cent in 1957 to below 65 per cent in 1985 (Anderson et al., 1999). Samwick (1998) points out that the declining participation rates of older workers started around the 1930s and have continued ever since (see Lumsdaine and Wise, 1990, for more details).

In itself this is neither good nor bad: one could expect economic development to lead to more leisure and earlier retirement. The evidence suggests, however, that the trend has also been caused by artificial economic disincentives to work in old age. These disincentives, in turn, make pay-as-you-go (PAYGO) pension systems less sustainable. It also means wasting productive capacity, causing a greater tax burden for the working population, especially in countries where pensions are mainly paid out of tax revenue.[2] And besides economic harm, early retirement can damage the elderly both materially and psychologically, as many would prefer to continue working longer if that choice were not penalised. Robust empirical research shows that early retirement tends to contribute to marginalisation and depression (Dave et al., 2006).

Evidence of disincentives to work

Although pension systems differ across countries, they create similar disincentives to retire early. Two problems are particularly common (Gruber and Wise, 1998, 2005). First, most pension schemes offer generous early retirement benefits: these have made early retirement so common in some countries that few people work up until the 'normal' retirement age. Second, the pattern of benefit accrual often creates high implicit taxes on working in older ages, so that it becomes economically irrational to work after a certain age. These are bold assertions, but they are substantiated by the following evidence taken just from the USA and the UK.

---

2   Gruber and Wise (1998) estimate that the proportion of unused productive capacity among those aged 55–65 ranges from 38 per cent in the USA to over 60 per cent in France and Belgium. In macroeconomic terms this is a devastating waste, especially in times when populations are ageing rapidly.

United States

The most extensive research on this issue has been done in the USA. In the USA retirement rates peak at ages 62 and 65 (Diamond and Gruber, 1997; Coile and Gruber, 2000). These correspond exactly with the two main age thresholds in the governmental pension scheme (called social security): 62 is the earliest possible benefit entitlement age, and 65 is the normal retirement age.[3]

The system is embedded with hidden disincentives to work, as has been thoroughly demonstrated by Butrica et al. (2004). These authors measure two key aspects of the incentive structure of the public pension scheme: the implicit tax rate on work[4] and the replacement rate.[5] The authors show that both measures rise rapidly at older ages. For many individuals the replacement rate jumps to over 50 per cent at age 62 and goes beyond 80 per cent at age 65, giving strong financial incentives to retire at these ages (see Table 2). The disincentives get worse as years go by: at age 67 most people will earn the same by retiring as by continuing to work, and after that one is virtually punished for working, as one could simply earn more by retiring.[6]

---

3   Recent reforms will gradually raise the retirement age to 67.

4   Implicit tax on work is measured as the total of: traditional income tax + changes in future state pension (social security) benefits + loss on employer-provided pension benefits (in the defined contribution schemes) + changes in health benefits (specific to the healthcare system). Implicit taxes on work will tend to be much higher in Europe, where both traditional income tax and state pension benefits are higher.

5   Measured as the ratio of retirement income to work income.

6   The disincentives depend, of course, on many factors. For example, the replacement rate rises even faster for women than for men. People with more savings also face higher implicit taxes and replacement rates (e.g. the latter go to 97 per cent at age 64 and 158 per cent at age 69!). Both rates also rise very steeply for members of private defined-contribution pension schemes once they can start claiming benefits.

Table 2 **Replacement rates in the USA for a representative single male worker in good health with a defined-benefit pension scheme and no retiree health insurance**

Retirement age	Replacement rate (US, per cent)
60	5
61	5
62	53
63	59
64	62
65	82
66	90
67	98
68	110
69	119
70	73

Source: Butrica et al., 2004

These disincentives are present even though early retirement in the USA is 'penalised' (working until the normal retirement age of 65 will result in a larger pension – 6 per cent higher per extra year in employment). But the state pension still encourages early retirement in at least two ways. First, pension benefits do not grow if one continues working beyond age 65, so that paying more pension contributions will not be reflected in the benefits (this anomaly has been noticed recently, and later retirement will receive compensation in the future). Second, the system of means-tested retirement benefits encourages early retirement for many individuals. The early retirement option is mainly used by the least well off, and Neumark and Powers (2000) demonstrate that the means-tested supplement may be causing this. The reason is that, although most people permanently lose part of their pension if they claim early retirement benefits, this may not be so for the less wealthy. The means-tested supplement, which they can claim from age 65 onwards (the level of which is determined according to income and assets), may offset the early retirement penalty. Although there will not usually be a one-to-one offset, early retirement may be attractive to many individuals when the net financial penalty is not significant.

United Kingdom

The UK pension system includes a large proportion of private pension schemes, and thanks to this the state-run scheme is among the more sustainable ones in Europe (Daykin, 2002). Nevertheless, the state scheme is not free from worries. The Turner Commission showed that the existing system will deliver increasingly inadequate pensions (Pensions Commission, 2005). There is also evidence that the implicit debt of public sector employee pensions is substantially larger than official government figures suggest (Record, 2006).

The UK retirement system is rather complicated, both in its state and private aspects. Although around half of retirement income comes from private sources, the state system matters to most people. The Basic State Pension, an unfunded flat-rate pension, is normally available from age 65 for men and 60 for women. There is also an earnings-related unfunded scheme (SERPS or the State Second Pension), which is only compulsory for employees and from which people can contract out – though contracting out is increasingly allowed only on poor terms and is to be formally restricted in the near future.

Most people also participate in occupational and other private schemes.

Again, part of the problem is low labour force participation rates among older men. In 2005 average formal retirement ages were around 64 for men and 62 for women (Pensions Commission, 2005). But the proportion of full-time workers falls steadily from ages in the mid-fifties onwards, dropping sharply to 40 per cent at age 60, going farther down to 30 per cent at age 64, and then tumbling below 10 per cent at age 66 (Blundell and Johnson, 1998). The pattern is broadly similar for women. Blundell and Johnson (ibid.) argue that this pattern reflects the financial disincentives of the existing schemes and easy access to ill-health benefits. Early retirement is particularly attractive to lower earners, which fits the observation that lower-skilled workers have the lowest labour force participation rates at older ages. Ill-health retirement is particularly common in the public sector, and it is estimated that undue ill-health retirement costs the government £1 billion each year (Silver, 2006).[7]

It is worth mentioning that the problem in other EU countries is much worse. Astonishingly, the starting point in the EU is so low that its target for employment of older workers (55–64) is just 50 per cent by 2010. The level of employment among that age group in Germany was just 41 per cent in 2004. This is an increase

7   The proportion of ill-health retirement at all retirements ranges from more than 20 per cent among civil servants, teachers and NHS workers, and almost 40 per cent in local government, to staggering rates of 49 per cent in the police and 68 per cent in the fire authorities. Among policemen and firemen the reason seems to be that, in these professions, it has become an established practice that when people cannot fully perform their physically demanding jobs, they are granted ill-health retirement and the bill is forwarded to the unknowing taxpayer. Such an arrangement is unreasonable, because these people could easily find further employment in other, physically less exerting jobs.

on earlier levels of labour market participation but, nevertheless, the average age of retirement is rising less quickly than life expectation. Only three member states have seen significant rises in the proportion of older people in work in recent years and, significantly, all three (Finland, Hungary and Latvia) were not EU members over the period when the increase took place.

Depressed private saving

Another problematic trend in countries around the world is the fall in private saving rates. According to the World Bank research project 'Saving in the world', the world's average saving rate has been in long-term decline for the last two decades (Loayza et al., 2000). This trend may not have been apparent throughout the world in more recent years (witness the very high levels of saving in China, for example) but it is certainly in evidence in particular economies, such as those of the USA and the UK. A reduction in saving has several problematic consequences: it will diminish long-term economic growth; it will make it even more difficult for governments to cope with their ageing populations and the consequent reforms of pension systems; moreover, there is a greater need for private savings in order for individuals to adjust to future reductions in unfunded PAYGO pensions.

Life-cycle consumption behaviour

Private savings are influenced by numerous factors, one of them being the disincentives created by public pension systems. The irony of this is that – just as with retirement behaviour – public pension schemes create incentives that undermine the systems themselves. As governments begin to promise extensive retirement benefits and to tax people at rising rates, the consequence is inevitable: self-reliance, thrift and private saving go down, and people become more dependent on government provision and more vulnerable to systemic breakdown.

In economic theory, the common way of approaching the issue of savings is the so-called life-cycle consumption hypothesis, which views savings as a means to smooth consumption during times of low income, such as education or retirement (Ando and Modigliani, 1963). In other words, people will tend to consume beyond their income during years at university; then get a job, pay the student loans and accumulate pension wealth; and finally consume some of the accumulated wealth in retirement.[8]

The life-cycle hypothesis suggests that unfunded government pension provision will reduce private saving, because people have weak incentives to save to smooth future consumption into old age. The disposable income of the young is also reduced by social security taxes, thereby making it more difficult to accumulate wealth. Alarmingly, an additional implication of the life-cycle hypothesis is that overall population ageing should lead to lower total savings rates, as there is more wealth consumption than wealth accumulation; this means that the retirement of the baby-

---

8   Recent literature on behavioural economics reveals, however, that one should not draw too strong conclusions from the life-cycle consumption hypothesis (see Mitchell and Utkus, 2004). The hypothesis does a reasonably good job of tracking real-life behaviour, but it does so only in broad terms, not with mathematical precision. Real people are not computers which calculate their 'optimal' saving and consumption rates based on some probabilistic models of futures earnings and expenses – that would be virtually impossible. Besides, it would be irrational to waste energy on such calculations, because they would hardly make a real difference to our wellbeing and happiness. What matters is our ability to get by reasonably well in all circumstances of life: youth, professional life and old age.

boomers is likely to cause a further drop in aggregate saving rates (Feldstein, 1980).

Empirical evidence on public pensions and savings

In practice it is difficult to show the exact effect of state-run pension schemes on saving rates, because there are numerous factors at play. The seminal contribution was by Feldstein (1974), who showed with US data that public pensions are a substitute for private saving. In that paper he estimated that the government pension scheme (social security) depresses personal saving by 30–50 per cent. Feldstein (1996) came to even larger estimates with more recent data: the current US pension system appears to depress private saving by as much as 60 per cent.

Studies in other countries present a similar picture. Attanasio and Brugiavini (2003) look at Italian data, which also captures the effect of the Italian pension reform in 1992. The authors report that there is a significant substitution effect – in the range of 30–70 per cent – between pension wealth and private saving. Yamada (1990) also finds support for the substitution effect in Japan: looking at the recent development of public pensions, he finds strong evidence that the growth of public pensions encourages earlier retirement and substantially depresses private savings. One should emphasise for clarity that 'public pension wealth' is not real wealth at all, but it represents political promises about future pension benefits that may – or may not – be available when one retires.

In line with these findings are studies that compare aggregate data across several countries. Feldstein (1980) uses data from twelve major industrial countries and finds that public pensions significantly reduce private saving. He concludes that people do not ignore public pensions when they make saving decisions, and they certainly do not save more because of public pensions, so that the net effect on private savings is unambiguously negative. This is supported by much later work by Samwick (2000), who conducts an extensive cross-country study of savings using a World Bank database with observations from 121 countries. He finds that unfunded PAYGO systems are associated with lower national savings than funded systems, and moving towards more fully funded pensions will tend to go hand in hand with higher saving.[9]

Alternative arguments

Some authors have denied the negative savings effect of public pensions. For example, Leimer and Lesnoy (1982) estimate, using US data, that the effect of public pensions on private saving is not significant. Barro (1978) even argues that public pensions do not necessarily affect aggregate private saving at all, because people may also save so as to give more to their children, compensating them for their larger pension taxes in the future. In other words, parents, recognising the burden they are leaving their children, will alter their bequests appropriately.

Cigno and Rosati (1996) try to show that public pension schemes may actually encourage private savings. Their theory puts saving decisions in the context of childbearing choices, which

---

9   Strictly speaking, net national saving and private saving are different things. Public saving cannot be equated with private saving, because their economic consequences differ significantly.

they show to be negatively affected by public pensions.[10] Lower fertility rates in turn make it easier for individuals to save, and this indirect effect, they argue, is not captured by previous studies. Cigno and Rosati claim that their theory is supported by time-series data from the USA, the UK, Germany and Italy.

These are important challenges to the standard model of public pensions and savings, but their significance is doubtful. First, one should not be surprised to find ambiguities at the empirical level. Attanasio and Brugiavini (2003) point out that there are inherent difficulties in measuring public pension wealth, and cross-sectional differences in private saving rates can be caused by a variety of observable and unobservable factors, which render it difficult to say anything certain about causalities. Second, as far as theory is concerned, Barro's hypothesis of offsetting private transfers may realise itself in some hypothetical circumstances, but there seems to be no tangible evidence for this: indeed, Feldstein (1996) shows that the depressive effect of public pensions on saving is very real even when one builds Barro's theoretical hypothesis into the model. Finally, the argument of Cigno and Rosati sheds lights on more complex consequences of public pensions, but it really implies that savings may be increased only indirectly owing to the reduced fertility effect of public pensions, whereas the direct effect on savings is nevertheless negative. If this is actually correct, it may explain why the net effect is not clear cut in all empirical data. Lower fertility rates are themselves, however, causing other and probably much more significant challenges to the unfunded pension systems of the affluent world.

---

10   This has been argued by several other authors too, including Ehrlich and Kim (2007), and Boldrin et al. (2005).

Reversing the trend
Quick fixes: higher retirement ages and actuarially fair benefits

There are some simple reforms that would improve public pension systems in the short term. Minimum retirement ages can be raised, and benefit accrual can compensate those who work longer. Many European countries, such as Germany and Italy, have already taken steps towards these directions, yet much remains to be done. The Turner Commission in the UK has also recommended higher retirement ages (Pensions Commission, 2005).

Higher retirement ages and actuarially fair benefits accrual can reduce the costs of public pension schemes, as Gruber and Wise (2005) have shown. They rely on extensive country-based studies, which have been used to create simulations of the behavioural consequences of reforms. Thus the authors distinguish between two effects: one is the mechanical effect of changing the rules; the other is the effect of adapted behaviour, such as working longer. They also take into account the fact that working longer implies higher tax revenue for governments.

One reform option they consider is the raising of all benefit eligibility ages – early retirement, normal retirement and disability benefits – by three years. In the twelve countries studied, this would, on average, save 27 per cent of current programme costs, or nearly 1 per cent of GDP. In some countries the effect would be even larger: in the UK, over 40 per cent of programme costs could be saved (ibid.).

Another important reform is to adjust early retirement benefits so that they are actuarially equivalent at all ages. In developed countries, increases in benefits for working during the mid-sixties should be roughly 6 per cent for each year retirement is postponed (ibid.). Early retirement should reduce the pension by a similar figure. This creates stronger incentives to retire later.

Actuarially fair benefit accrual is likely to have a significant behavioural effect in countries in which benefit accrual is currently not properly adjusted. Gruber and Wise (ibid.) show that this would on average save 26 per cent of current programme costs. The most striking result is obtained for Germany, where savings are estimated at 43 per cent.

A word of caution should be noted regarding these simulation estimates. Some authors argue that there are people with a strong subjective preference to retire early and who are insensitive to economic incentives (Chan and Stevens, 2004): these could include people in ill health who do not expect to live long in retirement. Moreover, it has been shown that older workers tend to underestimate future benefit flows and how much longer they will live (Kahn, 1988; Gustman and Steinmeier, 2005a). Some individuals may also have a high time preference (or subjective discount rate), which means that they perceive late retirement augmentations to pensions as poor value even if they are actuarially fair to the average person at market interest rates (Gustman and Steinmeier, 2005b). If this is the case, it may be more effective to raise minimum retirement ages than to use financial penalties within public pension systems. But it is also necessary to consider the pension system in conjunction with other aspects of the tax and benefit system.

Long-term reform: deinstitutionalising retirement patterns

Long-term reform could go farther. First, the reforms discussed above tackle only the problem of early retirement ages, but they do nothing about declining savings rates. Second, they leave pension systems vulnerable to population ageing and other changes in the support ratio. Third, forcing people to work longer undermines the personal freedom of individuals because, in theory, there is no reason why people should not retire early as long as they bear the costs themselves. The root of all these problems lies in the very nature of public PAYGO pension schemes, which institutionalise retirement patterns.

Broader reform could involve the deinstitutionalisation of retirement patterns. This means that people should be free to retire whenever and however they think is suitable for them, as long as they do not impose the economic burden on others. Essentially, the ordinary pension should be a flexible savings vehicle, so that one can use it early or late, fully or partially, as a lump-sum payment or as an annuity. People should also remain free to raise larger families and receive support from children in an informal manner. Individual circumstances differ just as subjective preferences do.

Some of the reforms already discussed would contribute to this goal. Ideally, however, there should be no limit to early retirement. Some people might prefer to work hard when young, buy a modest annuity at the age of 50 and continue working part time. Others might choose to raise a large family and look after their grandchildren in exchange for old-age support. There is an endless array of plausible retirement possibilities which are ignored by most people because public pension schemes impose one option on everyone.

But the effective deinstitutionalisation of retirement ages would require other changes too (see Booth and Cooper, 2005). For example, tax qualification rules often restrict how pension funds are used in retirement. Similarly, occupational pension schemes tend to limit partial retirement (although UK rules have just been relaxed in this respect). In practice, defined-benefit pension schemes can also limit flexible retirement though defined-contribution schemes are more flexible.

Even labour market regulation may contribute to inflexible retirement patterns. Although most employers tend to view older workers in a positive light (Munnell et al., 2006), elderly workers experience greater difficulties in finding a new job (Chan and Stevens, 2001). Many factors may contribute to this: for example, employers may expect older workers to retire and therefore invest less in the training of older employees. If this, itself, results in earlier retirement, the expectation is reinforced. Older workers may have to accept lower wages in order to find employment, although this need not be so in all employment sectors (see Oshio and Yashiro, 1997, for a study of Japan). Thus it might be appropriate to remove restrictions on age-based wage discrimination in order to give older people more opportunity to re-enter the workforce.

Conclusion

Public pay-as-you-go pension systems encourage earlier retirement and depress private savings. Thus they contribute to their own insolvency while also making people more vulnerable to systemic collapse. Empirical studies show that the decline in labour force participation rates among older workers may be largely the result of financial penalties on working longer. The evidence also suggests that public pensions are a significant substitute for private saving for old age.

Simple reforms will include higher retirement eligibility ages as well as actuarially fair adjustments for early and late retirement. But a truly long-term retirement policy should deinstitutionalise retirement patterns and favour greater flexibility based on individuals bearing the costs of the retirement decisions they make.

References

Anderson, P., A. Gustman and T. Steinmeier (1999), 'Trends in male labor force participation and retirement: some evidence on the role of pensions and social security in the 1970s and 1980s', *Journal of Labor Economics*, 17(4): 757–83.

Ando, A. and F. Modigliani (1963), 'The life cycle hypothesis of saving: aggregate implications and tests', *American Economic Review*, 53(1): 55–84.

Attanasio, O. P. and A. Brugiavini (2003), 'Social security and households' saving', *Quarterly Journal of Economics*, 118(3): 1075–1119.

Barro, R. J. (1978), *The Impact of Social Security on Private Saving*, Washington, DC: American Enterprise Institute.

Blundell, R. and P. Johnson (1998), 'Pensions and labor-market participation in the United Kingdom', *American Economic Review*, 88(2): 168–72.

Boldrin, M., M. de Nardi and L. E. Jones (2005), 'Fertility and social security', NBER Working Paper no. 11146.

Booth, P. and D. Cooper (2005), *The Way out of the Pensions Quagmire*, London: Institute of Economic Affairs.

Butrica, B. A., R. W. Johnson, K. E. Smith and E. Steuerle (2004), *Does Work Pay at Older Ages?*, Working Paper, Center for

Retirement Research at Boston College, available online at www.bc.edu/centers/crr/wp_2004-30.shtml.

Chan, S. and A. H. Stevens (2001), 'Job loss and employment patterns of older workers', *Journal of Labor Economics*, 19: 484–521.

Chan, S. and A. H. Stevens (2004), 'Do changes in pension incentives affect retirement? A longitudinal study of subjective retirement expectations', *Journal of Public Economics*, 88(7/8): 1307–33.

Cigno, A. and F. C. Rosati (1996), 'Jointly determined saving and fertility behaviour: theory and estimates for Germany, Italy, UK and USA', *European Economic Review*, 40(8): 1561–89.

Coile, C. and J. Gruber (2000), 'Social security and retirement', NBER Working Paper no. 7830.

Dave, D., I. Rashad and J. Spasojevic (2006), 'The effects of retirement on physical and mental health outcomes', NBER Working Paper no. 12123.

Daykin, C. D. (2002), *Pensions Systems: The EU and Accession Countries – Lessons for the UK*, London: Politeia.

Diamond, P. and J. Gruber (1997), 'Social security and retirement in the US', NBER Working Paper no. 6097.

Ehrlich, I. and J. Kim (2007), 'Social security and demographic trends: theory and evidence from the international experience', *Review of Economic Dynamics*, 10(1): 55–77.

Feldstein, M. (1974), 'Social security, induced retirement, and aggregate capital accumulation', *Journal of Political Economy*, 82(5): 357–74.

Feldstein, M. (1980), 'International differences in social security and saving', *Journal of Public Economics*, 14(2): 225.

Feldstein, M. (1996), 'Social security and saving: new time series evidence', *National Tax Journal*, 49(2): 151–64.

Gruber, J. and D. A. Wise (1998), 'Social security and retirement: an international comparison', *American Economic Review*, 88(2): 158–63.

Gruber, J. and D. A. Wise (eds) (1999), *Social Security and Retirement around the World*, Chicago, IL: University of Chicago Press.

Gruber, J. and D. A. Wise (2005), 'Social security program and retirement around the world: fiscal implications. Introduction and summary', NBER Working Paper no. 11290.

Gustman, A. L. and T. L. Steinmeier (2005a), 'Imperfect knowledge of social security and pensions', *Industrial Relations*, 44(2): 373–97.

Gustman, A. L. and T. L. Steinmeier (2005b), 'The social security early entitlement age in a structural model of retirement and wealth', *Journal of Public Economics*, 89(2/3): 441–63.

Kahn, J. A. (1988), 'Social security, liquidity, and early retirement', *Journal of Public Economics*, 35(1): 97–117.

Leimer, D. and S. Lesnoy (1982), 'Social security and private saving: new time series evidence', *Journal of Political Economy*, 90(3): 606–29.

Loayza, N., K. Schmidt-Hebbel and L. Servén (2000), 'What drives private saving across the world?', *Review of Economics and Statistics*, 82(2): 165–81.

Lumsdaine, R. L. and D. A. Wise (1990), 'Aging and labor force participation: a review of trends and explanations', NBER Working Paper no. 3420.

Mitchell, O. S. and S. P. Utkus (2004), 'Lessons from behavioral finance for retirement plan design', in Mitchell and Utkus,

Pension Design and Structure: New Lessons from Behavioral Finance, Oxford University Press, pp. 3–41.

Munnell, A. H., S. A. Sass and M. Soto (2006), 'Employer attitudes towards older workers: survey results', *Issues in Brief*, Center for Retirement Research at Boston College, available online at www.bc.edu/centers/crr/wob_3.shtml.

Neumark, D. and E. Powers (2000), 'Welfare for the elderly: the effects of SSI on pre-retirement labor supply', *Journal of Public Economics*, 78(1/2): 51–80.

Oshio, T. and N. Yashiro (1997), 'Social security and retirement in Japan', NBER Working Paper no. W6156.

Pensions Commission (2005), *A New Pension Settlement for the Twenty-first Century: The Second Report of the Pensions Commission*, London, available online at www.pensionscommission.org.uk/.

Record, N. (2006), *Sir Humphrey's Legacy: Facing Up to the Cost of Public Sector Pensions*, London: Institute of Economic Affairs.

Samwick, A. (1998), 'New evidence on pensions, social security, and the timing of retirement', *Journal of Public Economics*, 70(2): 207–36.

Samwick, A. (2000), 'Is pension reform conducive to higher saving?', *Review of Economics and Statistics*, 82(2): 264–72.

Silver, N. (2006), 'Commentary: the unnecessary burden of public sector pension schemes', in Record (2006).

Yamada, T. (1990), 'The effects of Japanese social security retirement benefits on personal saving and elderly labor force behavior', *Japan and the World Economy*, 2: 327–63.

3 THE IMPOSSIBILITY OF PROGRESS – A PUBLIC CHOICE ANALYSIS OF STATE PENSION PROVISION

Philip Booth

Introduction

In a paper published in *Economic Affairs* (Booth, 2008) I examine and quantify the incentives that exist within the UK state pension system for voters to increase pension provision through the state system. Those who do not pay the full cost of higher pensions have strong incentives to vote for higher pensions while imposing the costs on others. In response to these incentives, we have seen all major political parties in the UK promise higher incomes to pensioners either through increases to the level of pensions, through extending the scope of the state pension system, through increased social security benefits or through special tax concessions for pensioners. This behaviour of political parties is perfectly understandable in the context of our understanding of public choice economics (see, for example, Tullock, 2006, and Galasso, 2006, who focuses entirely on pensions policy). Table 3 below shows the main proposals from the three main parties at the 2005 election that were specifically designed to assist old people.

Table 3 **Special benefits promised to pensioners in the 2005 general election***

Labour[†]	• Increase in means-tested benefits in line with earnings, not prices.
	• Provision of free off-peak local bus travel.
	• £200 reduction in council tax bill.
	• Elimination of 'fuel poverty'.
	• Abolition of hospital fees.
	• Greater assistance with long-term care costs.
Conservative	• Linking of the Basic State Pension to earnings.
	• Use of unclaimed bank assets to bail out insolvent pension funds.[‡]
	• 50% reduction in council tax bills up to a maximum of £500.
	• Increased entitlement of carers to a Basic State Pension.
	• Meeting of all long-term care costs after three years.
Liberal Democrats	• Removal of requirement to contribute to a Basic State Pension through the National Insurance system for those over 75[¶] (citizens' pension).
	• Increase the citizens' pension in line with wages.
	• Provision of free off-peak local bus travel.
	• Meeting of all long-term care costs.

*The sources were the election manifestos and official statements made during the campaign.

†Labour also withdrew plans to reduce benefits within public sector pension schemes just before the election.

‡This is especially interesting in a public choice framework. The people who own the unclaimed bank assets do not, of course, know that they own them and thus the policy would not affect how they vote. The people who have suffered from pension fund insolvency are a group with very homogeneous preferences whose voting intentions could be changed by specific proposals to benefit them.

¶And gradually extend this to all ages.

These promises are interesting because in many cases they proposed straightforward exemptions for older people from otherwise perfectly standard aspects of the tax system (such as council tax) or the provision of benefits in kind (such as free bus travel) for which there is no clear economic case. The proposals were clearly designed to harvest the votes of older voters who were targeted in a way no other voter group was targeted.

Since 2005 there have been a number of changes to pensions policy in the UK, such as the decision to index the Basic State Pension to wages starting from between 2012 and 2015. In general, younger voters have paid for these changes. For example, contracting out of the Second State Pension is going to be limited considerably from 2012 (at the latest). Because many individuals will then no longer be able to contract out of a major part of the state scheme, pension liabilities to future generations of taxpayers will increase and the government will spend the money saved from not paying contracting-out rebates to young people on *current* pensions for older people. Future benefits in the Second State Pension are also going to be reduced, and this change is being phased in so that it affects only younger and not older voters.

Pension policy is part of a more general shift in policy that is moving resources away from the younger generation to the older generation. Such resource transfers can manifest themselves in increased health spending and spending on long-term care for the elderly; in reduction in government finance in areas such as higher education; or in changes to the tax system that increase taxes on families with children and reduce them for older people. The influence of a 'greying' electorate is a phenomenon that is being understood and studied more widely, including by pressure groups.[1] In the last 100 years the extended franchise of unlimited democracies

---

1   See, for example, the very interesting study by Davidson (n.d.) which was undertaken for the pressure group Age Concern.

has given organised voter groups considerable potential power to take the property of others through the tax and social security system. Older people are beginning to realise that potential.

In this chapter we focus specifically on pensions policy and examine the problems for public pensions systems that are predicted by public choice economics. We then show how electorates in a number of countries, not just in the UK, are ageing dramatically and relate that ageing process to public choice economics and the prospects for pension reform. Finally, we discuss various mechanisms for delivering pension provision that can overcome the problems predicted by public choice economics.

Policy platforms and voter behaviour

It is worth noting that there are two different ways in which voter preferences can reveal themselves in the policy positions of political parties. Different parties can stand on different platforms and voters can then vote for the platform they prefer. Alternatively, particularly in a two-party model, parties wishing to attain power may shift their policy positions to maximise the probability of being elected. The platforms of the parties will then become increasingly similar.[2]

As we have seen above, this is what seems to have happened in the UK on pensions issues. Indeed, Budge et al. (2001) state that the three main parties in the UK were closer together in the 2001 election than at any other time since 1945, and this drift seems to have continued. If parties shift their policies to be as

---

2   See Mueller (2003) for a full discussion of the theory.

close as possible to the median voter then parties will be judged on their ability to *deliver* as their programmes will be similar. This is known as the 'valence' model (see Mueller, 2003). Whitely et al. (2005) show that the valence model strongly influenced voting for the Labour and Conservative parties in 2001. Thus it is clear that political parties and voter groups can respond in various ways to help promote the self-interest of their supporters. How does this apply to pensions policy?

The relevance of public choice economics

If a state pension scheme is established, it cannot be assumed that the scheme will be one that can achieve theoretical ideals of equity, security and cost efficiency which some authors ascribe to state pension schemes. State pension schemes are not designed by benevolent and omniscient public servants. Rather, they arise as a result of a complex combination of decisions taken by voters, politicians and civil servants – with interest groups such as trade bodies also being influential.

As a population ages, it is possible for a country to reach a situation where a majority of voters are in receipt of a pension or close to state pension age. At this point, the shape of the political marketplace is such that beneficial reform of pension schemes may be impossible. Imperfections in schemes, once established, may be impossible to rectify.

It may be felt that there is little point debating these issues – they have a fatalistic aspect to them. If it is in the interests of a majority of the population not to reduce the size of state pension schemes, why would it help if we had private schemes instead? That same majority could just vote for the winding up of private schemes and establish systems to transfer money from a minority of taxpayers to itself. There is, however, an institutional aspect to this problem too. While voters may well try to pursue their own interests through the ballot box, it is possible to put in place institutional impediments that make change more difficult. It is easier to muster a majority in favour of extending accepted principles than it is to develop schemes based on a whole new set of principles. Substantive changes in policy have much more complex ramifications on voter groups than a mere increase in the size of an existing pension system. Such a substantive change may also affect current vested interests; as such, it requires a broader consensus for implementation than a simple majority (see Galasso, 2006).

We also learn from public choice economics that interest groups have an incentive to promote a particular policy if the benefits are concentrated and the costs are relatively dispersed. Also, the more aligned are the interests of a given group, the easier it will be for that group to get its policy proposals accepted. In a straightforward state pension system that transfers money between generations on a pay-as-you-go (PAYGO) basis, the interests of all those over pension age are very clearly aligned. Younger voters, who may wish to oppose expansion of the state pension system, will have much more diffuse preferences because their economic interests lie with a much broader range of issues. Indeed, many of those who will bear the main costs of an expansion of the state pension system will not be of voting age – or may not even be born.

The Browning model

The theoretical model was developed by Browning (1975),

who demonstrated that, in a pure democracy, there are strong incentives to increase the size of social security systems beyond their optimal level. When PAYGO pension systems are expanded, the only group that pays the full cost of the expansion is that just beginning its working life. That group will pay a working lifetime of contributions to obtain a pension from retirement age. Anybody older than this will receive some form of subsidy from later entrants to the workforce, as older workers will pay the higher contributions needed to finance higher benefits for only a portion of their working life, yet receive a higher pension throughout their retirement. Thus, even where the economics of state pensions systems become inferior to those of private systems, the refusal to use the market mechanism allows one generation to impose huge externalities on another generation. If this were to occur in a market system, politicians would be rushing to interfere to 'correct the externality'.

The basic Browning model assumes an even distribution of people across the age range. The worst problems arise, however, when there is population shrinkage in conjunction with increased longevity, because this increases the proportion of voters who are in the retired population dramatically: the number of employed falls while the number of retired people rises.

There are some inconsistencies in the Browning model. Most notably, in theory, policy could be changed continually, yet we assume that at any given election the electorate votes for a policy change that it believes to be permanent. These inconsistencies do not, however, invalidate the main messages of the model. There is inertia built into the system; voting is infrequent; and though it may be possible to change pension levels in a particular system, getting agreement on general reform may be harder. These factors make it reasonable to follow the implicit assumption of Browning that electors will vote for a system that, at a given point in time, will give them the largest lifetime utility if there are no further changes.

The importance of nuances in pension systems

So far we have focused on inter-generational redistribution and have ignored the issue of redistribution between poorer and richer individuals – something that is also a feature of state pensions systems. Casamatta et al. (2000) distinguish between Bismarckian systems that are not redistributive within generations (for example, those that provide earnings-related pensions in return for earnings-related contributions) and Beveridgean systems that imply redistribution between people on different levels of income. As a historical point, it is worth noting that the original Beveridge system did not involve significant income redistribution because fixed contributions were required, at first, for fixed benefits (see Booth, 2002). Also, the earnings-related part of the UK system (State Earnings Related Pension – SERPS) did, from its origins, involve earnings-related contributions and earnings-related benefits. It was only when that system was overhauled in 2002, with the introduction of State Second Pension (S2P), that subtle and highly complex redistributive elements were introduced (see Booth and Cooper, 2005).

Any system in which contributions or taxes are linked to earnings while benefits are flat rate will redistribute income. The young poor will then have a stronger incentive to vote for bigger pensions, though well-off older people have a weaker incentive. There are also other ways of redistributing money between generations that, in a fully comprehensive public choice analysis, should be taken into account. These can include other government spending programmes (health, education, etc.), off-balance-sheet financing of capital projects and the accumulation of government debt.

It is also worth noting that, if pensions are financed from taxes levied on all voters, including pensioners (for example, using a sales tax rather than an income tax), older voters will bear some costs of their decisions.[3] This will lessen the incentives for expansion of the system.

In a fully funded scheme – even one administered by the state – there are no incentives for inter-generational redistribution because voting behaviour cannot affect pension rights already accrued. Also, an unfunded state pension scheme based on an accruals system where, in effect, contractual rights are given to those who accrue benefits have similar characteristics, from a public choice perspective, to a fully funded scheme. Indeed, we could say that a state scheme based on the accruals principle is implicitly funded by government debt (see Minford, 1998).

Casamatta et al. (2000)[4] conclude that a social security system will be bigger if it is an unfunded system, because of the behaviour of retired voters. It will also be smaller if taxes cause greater distortions because there will be a welfare loss from increased taxes that impact on most groups of voters, including the retired. Of course, if tax rates reach the top of the Laffer curve, even retired individuals in a PAYGO system would have no incentive to vote for increased taxes to finance increased pensions. A social

3   Though, as has been noted, pensioners in the UK campaign to be exempt from taxes levied on the general population.

4   See also Cremer and Pestieau (2000).

security system might grow bigger if it is Bismarckian, rather than Beveridgean, for two reasons. First, the taxes used to finance it are not as distortionary (because the increased taxes are reflected in increased future pension benefits accruing to the same individual – workers get something directly in return for their taxes, which reduces the disincentive effects of higher taxes). Also, in a Bismarckian system, higher income groups are more likely to accept a bigger social security system.

Importantly, Cremer and Pestieau (2000) suggest that a contributory system can set up 'entrenched interests' against reductions in the size of the system that are harder to overcome using the sheer weight of voters. Individuals who have accrued entitlements hold a political weight stronger than their numbers suggest. This would make general reforms of the system easier as long as they did not affect current entitlements, but changes to accrued entitlements would be harder. We will come back to this point below. It is certainly the case in the UK that most reforms to the earnings-related part of the state pension system have left existing accrued benefits unchanged, but that changes to future accrual have been relatively easy to implement. In continental Europe, there has been strong resistance to any reform that reduces accrued benefits, whether explicitly or implicitly, throughout state pension systems.

Some evidence for the public choice model from voting behaviour

Breyer and Craig (1997) tested public choice models for twenty OECD countries over four decades. The size of public sector pension programmes grew dramatically over the period, although some programmes did reduce in size as a proportion of GNP. The timing of growth in different countries' schemes was also different and there was a substantial difference between the sizes of programmes (for example, in 1985, pension spending ranged from 2.1 per cent of GNP in Portugal to 14.5 per cent of GNP in Austria).

The authors found that the fraction of pension programmes financed by taxes on employers did not affect programme size. This is interesting as it suggests that there is no fiscal illusion: voters behave as if they are aware that the burden of taxes levied on employers falls ultimately on employees. Breyer and Craig found a very strong relationship between median voter age and pension programme size. An increase in median voter age of one year added 0.5 per cent to the share of GNP taken by the pensions programme. The authors also found that, for a given age of median voter, the ratio of the retired to working population affected pension programme size.

It is also worth noting that Breyer and Craig discovered that there is a secular component of public sector pension programme growth that appears to be independent of demographic effects. The authors are unable to explain this. One possibility is that voters make decisions on issues of principle as well as on the basis of self-interest. It is possible that there was a general drift among the electorate towards more socialist principles in the post-war period. This suggests that it may be possible to resist the influence of the median voter by establishing a consensus behind the principles of a particular approach to policy, though that consensus would have to rely on the acceptance of certain political principles and not on self-interest. Even if this were possible, however, trying to restrain government pension programmes while the population was ageing would be like pushing a heavy barrel uphill.

Overall, according to this research at least, the public choice model is depressingly resilient.

Trends in the age of the median voter

Using population projection models based on generally accepted assumptions,[5] it is possible to determine the likely trends in the age of the median voter over the coming generations. The age of the median voter is defined as a particular age that marks the point at which 50 per cent of voters are older and 50 per cent younger than this age. We have used the population model to examine the age profile of voters in various countries over the coming generation. Our analysis is more detailed in the UK than for other countries, as, for the UK, we have allowed for variables such as migration and the tendency of people of different ages to exhibit differential turnout at elections.

Table 4 below shows the projected age of the median voter at specimen dates over the next 50 years. It also shows the median age if reasonable assumptions are made about differential turnout and about immigration. With regard to turnout, we have used information drawn from current voting patterns.

It can be seen that the age of the median voter, already high if we allow for differential turnout of people of different ages, will rise dramatically. To change this sharp upward trend in the age of the median voter will require a considerable rise in the birth rate very soon. Ignoring migration, the shape of the electorate until

5   See Booth (2008) for a discussion of the construction of the model and the data sources.

Table 4 **Age of the median voter**

Date	Projected age of median voter: no immigration	Projected age of median voter: no immigration but allowing for turnout	Projected age of median voter: with immigration
2005	46	50	46
2015	49	52	48
2025	52	56	49
2035	53	58	50
2045	54	59	52
2055	55	60	52

Figure 1   **Proportion of UK voting population over 55**

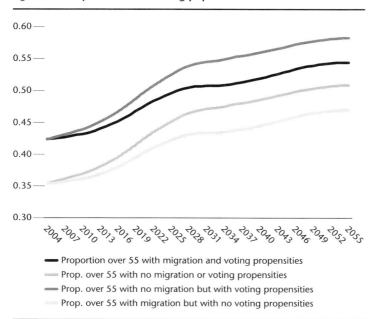

Proportion over 55 with migration and voting propensities
Prop. over 55 with no migration or voting propensities
Prop. over 55 with no migration but with voting propensities
Prop. over 55 with migration but with no voting propensities

2034 is more or less already settled today. Reasonable assumptions about immigration do prevent the age of the median voter from rising as quickly (see column four) but, nevertheless, the age of the median voter would still rise substantially (by six years) over the next 50 years even if we allow for migration.

The ageing of the electorate can also be shown by looking at the proportion of voters aged 55 or over (that is, within ten years of UK state pension age). This is shown in Figure 1 (p. 107).

The proportion of the population over 55 is projected to rise to over 50 per cent by 2050 from just 35 per cent today. Making allowance for reasonable assumptions about future migration keeps the proportion a little lower. If, however, we adjust the population projections for differential age-related turnout at general elections the expected proportion of active voters over 55 will be nearly 60 per cent by 2055 and will reach 50 per cent by 2010.

'Rates of return' from voting for increased pensions

Booth (2008) computed the rates of return that the median voter could obtain by successfully voting to increase pensions. The cost to the median voter would be the increase in social security taxes (National Insurance contributions) in the short period before retirement. The benefit would be the increased pension after retirement. The net benefit can be expressed in the form of a rate of return that equates the present value of the additional contributions that the median voter has to make when pensions are increased to the present value of the additional pension he will

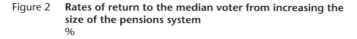

Figure 2   Rates of return to the median voter from increasing the
size of the pensions system
%

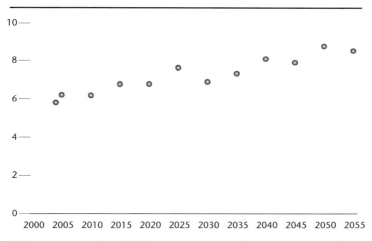

receive.[6] Not surprisingly, these rates of return were found to be
very high and are set to increase because of the rising age of the
median voter. They are shown in Figure 2. These rates of return
did not assume differential voter turnout so, in fact, the rates of
return are lower than is perhaps realistic.

At the current time, the rate of return to the median voter from
expanding the pension system is 5.8 per cent. The rate of return
will rise quickly to 7.6 per cent by 2025 and then rise more slowly
to 8.8 per cent by 2050. This suggests very strong, and increasing,

---

6   In Booth (2008) the technical formulae are developed. Allowance is made for
mortality. There is also a discussion of whether the rates of return are real or
nominal or relative to salaries. The rates of return can reasonably be regarded as
real rates of return.

incentives for the median voter to vote to increase the size of state pensions. One would expect politicians to respond to those incentives by offering financial packages that benefit the median voter and raise the level of government help for pensioners. In turn, reducing benefits to pensioners will be very difficult. These figures can be compared with the risk-free real rate of return that the median voter can obtain from saving for pensions in financial markets – currently about 1.6 per cent per annum.[7]

Once the median voter is above state pension age there is a strong incentive for voters to expand the state pension system to its maximum possible size, which would occur when tax rates are at the top of the Laffer curve. Reform of pensions systems to reduce their size, at this point, would become very difficult.

Differential turnout

In column three of Table 4, the age of the median voter was recalculated to allow for differential voter turnout at different ages. Given that somebody has decided to vote, it is reasonable to use public choice theory to analyse the results of voting. The decision to vote cannot, however, be made along wholly economic lines. The probability of influencing an election is so small that, on economic grounds alone, it is difficult to justify voting at all – yet we know that people do vote. Given this, it is difficult to know precisely how age-determined differences in turnout at general elections will develop in the future. If it is assumed that today's older generation feel a public duty to vote, perhaps because of

---

7   There are some qualifications to this comparison discussed in Booth (2008) and in Galasso (2006). In particular, the rates of return that might be received from an increase in government pensions are subject to political risk.

their experience of world war and the threat of totalitarianism (as well as having distant memories of their parents being aware of a time when the franchise was not fully extended), then turnout will become more uniform with age over the coming generations (though it will fall on average). On the other hand, it is possible that young people will become more and more disaffected with the democratic system (or will simply decide to take the economically rational decision not to vote) and thus differential turnout between the age groups will widen still further.[8] More generally the old have a stronger incentive to vote because they have a lower opportunity cost of time than younger people and potentially less diffuse economic interests. Thus the above figures, showing the considerable ageing of the median voter, after factoring in assumptions for differential turnout, are only illustrative. They are, though, alarming – the median voter will be nearly sixty years old within one generation.

We have not adjusted the age of median voter figures for other countries to allow for differential turnout (see below). But a similar pattern of voting propensities prevails outside the UK (see Galasso, 2006: 33). In the USA, for example, older voters are twice as likely to vote as younger voters; in France, turnout is almost 50 per cent higher among older voters than among younger voters.

---

8   It was suggested by a referee that, if young people see actions being taken that are clearly against their interests, then they may be motivated to vote in greater numbers. This is possible, though the pure economic incentives will still be weak. One cannot rule out, though, that emotional factors, based on indignation, may motivate young people – though, equally, disillusionment may increase and young people be further turned off voting.

Other countries

The situation in other countries is similar to that in the UK – though the magnitude of the problem varies. In this section, we will examine the trends in the age of the median voter and the proportion of voters over 55 in four other countries: Italy and Germany (examples of EU countries with looming demographic problems); New Zealand (a small open economy); and Bosnia–Herzegovina (a relatively poor country with significant emigration of those of working age). The projected age of the median voter at various times over the 50 years from 2005 is shown in Table 5 below. Reasonable assumptions about migration have been used.

Table 5 **Projected age of the median voter, four selected countries and the UK**

Date	Germany	Italy	New Zealand	Bosnia–Herzegovina	UK
2005	47	47	44	42	46
2015	50	49	47	43	48
2025	53	52	48	45	49
2035	54	55	49	49	50
2045	56	56	50	54	52
2055	57	57	50	59	52

It can be seen that the median voter is ageing faster in both Italy and Germany than in the UK, though less quickly in New Zealand. In both Italy and Germany, within a generation or so, the majority of the electorate will be very close to state pension age. In both countries, the majority of the electorate will be over 55 within 30 years (see Figure 3). The ageing tendency is rather less extreme in New Zealand. In Bosnia–Herzegovina, the median voter starts at a lower age but ages much faster than in the other countries. It

Figure 3   **Proportion of voters over 55**

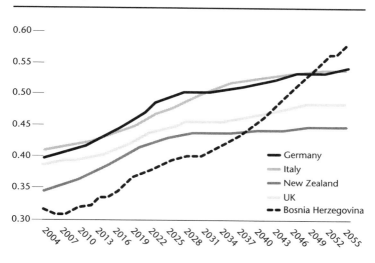

is not surprising that considerable reform of state pension systems has proven impossible in most EU countries: there would seem to be little prospect of meaningful reform happening in the future unless ways are found to deal with public choice interest groups.

The population models used to project the figures above assumed that migration was an exogenous variable. In fact, it is likely to be endogenous. As taxes to provide for extensive state pension systems increase, we might expect working people to migrate from high-tax countries with a substantial pension burden to lower-tax countries. This will make the demographic situation worse in the countries where young working people are in shortest supply.

Reform in the face of public choice pressures

Pension reform in the developed world has not proved impossible, though it has rarely been radical. For example, pension reform has recently been undertaken in Sweden. This is perhaps surprising given the demographic background there. The state pension system was established at the beginning of the twentieth century. Since that time, the age of the median voter has increased by eight years to 47.5; young people, defined as those between ages 20 and 25, have fallen by half as a proportion of the electorate; and the replacement ratio has risen dramatically.

A new Swedish pension system was introduced in 2000 based on notional defined contributions. The notional contributions receive 'interest' based on the increase in population of working age and on productivity. An annuity is then paid at retirement by taking the accumulated account and dividing by life expectancy. Thus the new scheme reduces the risk that costs for the working population will increase by reducing the level of pension as labour supply decreases and as life expectancy increases. Older people (aged over 57) were not affected by the change as they had their rights under the former system protected. They therefore had no incentive to vote against the proposals. In a sense this is a similar effect to creating an accruals-based system (see below). Very young people had an incentive to vote for the reform as they were promised a more sustainable system with lower contributions. The voting behaviour of middle-aged groups would depend on their specific income characteristics but, overall, votes in favour of the reform were expected to outnumber votes against the reform using a public choice analysis. Kruse's (2005) analysis of the Swedish reforms concludes that it was a 'smart use of the transition rules' (p. 14) which made reform possible.

In the reformed scheme, the accruals mechanism has now been formalised using a defined contribution system, with the provision of certain guarantees but with devices for risk-sharing between the working and retired populations. This experience suggests that the principle of accrual can be important in dealing with the public choice dilemma in state pension systems. Older people were not given the option, at the time of the reform, to increase their benefits, and now that option is removed unless the whole principle of the system is overturned – and that is an issue on which it would be hard to attain a consensus.

Meeting the costs of transition

The Swedish example shows one way in which reform was possible in a very specific situation. More generally, if radical pension reform involves a move to funded pension provision, then there is a 'transition cost'. As has been noted, the pensions of people who accrued rights under the old PAYGO systems still have to be met by young taxpayers while the same young taxpayers also have to fund their own pensions. Such radical reforms have generally been achieved by removing the costs of reform from the older generation of the population entirely. For example, where Chilean-type reforms, based on compulsory personal accounts, have been implemented, older people have often been excluded from the new arrangements altogether and have their benefits under the existing scheme preserved (see Stroinski, 1998, for discussion of reform in Poland, for example). From a public choice point of view, this may have been necessary to facilitate any reform at all. It does mean, however, that the younger generation pay for the liabilities accrued by the older generation (which they would have had to do in any case), but, interestingly, the younger generation seem willing to forsake having their own pensions paid for by the generation that follows them and younger people seem to support reform.[9, 10]

In practice, pension reform might be easier to achieve if the burden of transition is spread over a number of future generations. It is difficult to make a moral case for this approach because it would mean that current voters imposed the costs of meeting past accumulated commitments on people too young to vote. The whole public choice framework involves voter interest groups using the electoral system to impose costs on other groups of people, however, so this is merely an extension of that practice – as indeed is government borrowing more generally. This approach can be used to formally recognise and freeze past commitments and move to a new system. Tradable (or non-tradable) government bonds could be issued to those who had accumulated rights in a PAYGO system equal to the present value of their pension promises. The bonds would then be serviced, as with all government debt, over a given period. This would explicitly recognise implicit state pension commitments and also provide better information to the electorate regarding the true size of the government debt. This is broadly the approach followed in Chile.

Reform can also be financed by the privatisation of state assets (see also Booth, 1998). State assets should theoretically provide taxpayers with revenue streams from the returns on the assets. These assets can include nationalised industries but

---

9   Of course, in recognition of this, they could reduce bequests to their children.
10   Galasso (2006) mentions that limited reform was also achieved in France, Italy and Germany after more fundamental reform had failed to gain a political consensus. Those more limited reforms mainly affected young workers.

also roads, schools, airport slots, mobile phone networks and so on. The proceeds from the sale of state assets can then be used to reduce explicit government debt, and pension debt can then be recognised by giving those who have accrued pension rights government bonds, in the way explained above. The two transactions – the privatisation of state assets and the privatisation of state pension liabilities – will at least partially offset each other. In addition to easing the burden of transition to pension reform, such a move should create value from at least three sources: we would expect assets to have a higher value in the private than in the public sector; pension promises would be crystallised and no longer subject to political risk; finally, those who have pension promises would have them backed by tradable securities and they could make portfolio adjustments to suit their risk preferences.

Reform by raising state pension age

At various times, the UK government has successfully reduced the cost of future state pensions by raising state pension age. Governments in other parts of the world have sometimes done so too.[11] Legislation was passed to increase the female state pension age from 60 to 65 in 1995 – though implementation will be gradual from 2010 to 2020. It is also currently proposed that the state pension age is raised for all people from 65 to 68 over the period 2024 to 2044 (with full implementation being 38 years after the initial announcement!).

This type of reform also 'buys off' the median voter by imposing the costs of reform entirely on younger people. In the

---

11   The German government is raising the minimum age for the standard statutory pension from 65 to 67, phased in over seventeen years to 2029.

case of the two occasions when the UK state pension age has been raised, only a small percentage of the existing electorate was affected. Interestingly, in fact, this type of reform becomes easier as the voting population ages. Assuming that the aim of a political party is to capture the median voter then, as the age of the median voter rises, the implementation lag necessary before a rise in the state pension age affects the median voter falls as the population ages. When the state pension age is below the age of the median voter, for example, a political party could promote the raising of the state pension age with immediate effect and still capture the median voter.[12] Thus, raising pension ages is one of the few meaningful reforms that seem possible in a public choice model.

Raising the state pension age also has beneficial public choice effects (Galasso, 2006). The move clearly lowers the age of the median voter relative to pension age. It should be noted, however, that, as with any other reforms that seem possible in a public choice model, the distributional cost of raising state pension ages falls entirely on the younger generations.

System design and public choice

Our analysis above suggests that reform of public sector pension schemes may become impossible at the very time when reform is most urgent, although it has been seen that reform may be easier when the accrued rights of older voters are maintained. This leads us to ask whether, in a pure democracy, there are design features of state pension schemes that can make them

---

12   Indeed, the median voter may gain from any dynamic effects arising from lower tax rates.

more impervious to rent-seeking by voter groups. We will then examine these desirable design features in the context of the UK.

The contributory principle and accruals system

Most importantly, state pension schemes can be designed on an accruals basis. This would mean that for every year of contributions[13] a given pension entitlement is accrued. For example, if the maximum pension required 35 years of contributions, every year of contributions would entitle the individual to 1/35th of a full pension. This is broadly the same as the methods used in theory in both the Basic State Pension and State Second Pension systems in the UK. There are, however, important practical differences between the two systems. With the Basic State Pension, the contribution record determines the proportion of the full Basic State Pension that an individual receives. The level of that Basic State Pension is then determined by Parliament. At various times since its inception decisions have been taken to vary the level of the pension and the basis of indexation. Most recently, it has been proposed that the pension will be indexed to earnings when in payment from between 2012 and 2015. The State Second Pension system is based on a much more secure accruals principle. The amount of pension accrued from each year of contributions is set out in legislation and the index to which the accrued amount is linked both before and after retirement is also predetermined. Major adjustments to pension rights that have already

---

13   A contribution record can still be assigned to an individual who is too poor to make contributions or who is not in paid work, as happens in both the UK Basic State Pension and State Second Pension systems, without any loss of the advantages of this system.

been accrued have not been made in the State Second Pension system (or in its predecessor, the State Earnings Related Pensions system), though changes to rules for future accrual have been made. Regrettably reforms to the system have taken the system farther from the accruals principle by making the link between benefits and contributions more opaque.

A further important feature of the State Second Pension system is that individuals are allowed to contract out of the system and an age-related rebate is given to those who do so. In recent times, those rebates have not properly reflected the value of the pension lost by contracting out. Contracting out provides a further guard, however, against the manipulation of the state pension system by voter interest groups. The existence of contracting out further institutionalises this part of the state pension as a service – a year of pension accrual – that is provided by the state upon receipt of a price (the price being the contracted-out rebate forgone).

Under an explicit accruals system if, for example, a 60-year-old voter successfully votes for higher pensions to be financed by higher social security taxes, he will receive an increase only on a small proportion of his total pension – that to which he gains entitlement from his next five years of higher taxes, assuming a retirement age of 65.[14] There are no external costs of increasing the pension that any generation can deflect on to another generation. The accruals principle, buttressed by contracting out, can therefore provide a guard against rent-seeking.

---

14   This will be discussed farther below.

A citizens' pension: a public choice nightmare

Many proponents of pensions reform in the UK have proposed a 'citizens' pension'.[15] This is the most undesirable model from a public choice point of view. With a citizens' pension, all individuals would receive a state pension regardless of their contribution record. The pension would be set by the government of the day (or by a body set up by the government) and any increase in pension would be received by all people, regardless of their contribution record. This system is highly manipulable by the median voter. Older voters can vote for the pension to increase, without bearing any significant costs themselves.

A better approach

It would be better to move the whole UK pensions system in the direction of the former State Earnings Related Pension Scheme. For every year of contributions (or of attributed contributions) an individual could accrue an entitlement to (for example) 1/35th or 1/40th of a full state pension, linked to an index until retirement (for example, an index of earnings or an index of prices). If the amount of the full pension were increased (and National Insurance contributions were increased commensurately) it would only be future years of contributions which would bring an entitlement to a higher pension. An individual with one fifth of his full working life left at the time of an increase in the base level of the pension would pay higher National Insurance contributions for those remaining years and receive a higher level of pension only in respect of one

---

15 For example, see reference to the Liberal Democrat 2001 election manifesto above. The National Association of Pension Funds has supported this proposal, and see also O'Connell (2004) on behalf of the Pensions Policy Institute.

fifth of his entitlement. The median voter would pay the full cost of voting to increase pensions – the same as young voters: the problem identified by the Browning model is thus resolved. Indeed, the government could go farther and turn pension accruals into a contractual entitlement. This could be further reinforced if accrued rights within state pension schemes were funded (even if only with government debt), explicitly appeared on government balance sheets and were contractual. Contracting out of all state pensions, for a rebate of National Insurance contributions, should be allowed too. Government pensions could then be explicitly seen as a service being provided by a nationalised corporation, but one that allowed private competition.

It might be asked why a different state pensions system would be more impervious to public choice pressures. Could the older generation not simply vote to overturn the system and increase their incomes? This is always possible. As has already been mentioned, however, substantive changes to a system require a broader consensus than a simple majority (Galasso, 2006). Thus it is more difficult for such a system to be overturned.

Conclusion

All political parties nakedly flirt with older voters, exactly as predicted by public choice theory. At the 2005 UK general election, there was no other voter group that political parties tried to attract so explicitly. Given the information above about the ageing of the median voter, this is not surprising.

The ageing of the median voter makes it highly likely that state pension reforms will become more difficult to implement. As such, it is essential that those elements that most nearly approximate to ensuring that a given age group pays for the pension rights it promises itself remain and, preferably, are strengthened. In the UK, these include the accruals system in the State Second Pension – which should be extended to the Basic State Pension system. Also, contracting out opportunities should be expanded, not reduced. The UK government's recent reforms are entirely predictable in public choice theory, but entirely wrong. State pensions are going to be increased, with relatively little delay, with all those of median age and above benefiting from the increase. On the other hand, there is an increase in state pension age being proposed which will not fully take effect until long after the median voter has retired.

Given the rates of return the median voter can obtain from voting for a bigger state pension system, the probability of meaningful reductions in the size of the state pension system looks to be very small. Spending on the middle-aged and old in general is likely to take taxation in the UK close to the top of the Laffer curve – and keep it there.

References

Booth, P. M. (1998), 'The transition from social insecurity', *Economic Affairs*, 18(1): 2–12.

Booth, P. M. (2002), 'Pension provision: liberalism or corporatism?', in A. Deacon (ed.), *Debating Pensions: Self-Interest, Citizenship and the Common Good*, London: Civitas.

Booth, P. M. (2008), 'The young held to ransom – a public choice analysis of the UK state pension system', *Economic Affairs*, 28(3): 4–10.

Booth, P. M. and D. R. Cooper (2005), *The Way out of the Pensions Quagmire*, Research Monograph 60, London: Institute of Economic Affairs.

Breyer, F. and B. Craig (1997), 'Voting on social security: evidence from OECD countries', *Journal of Political Economy*, 13: 705–24.

Browning, E. K. (1975), 'Why the social insurance budget is too large in a democracy', *Economic Inquiry*, XIII: 373–88.

Budge et al. (2001), *Mapping Policy Preferences*, Oxford: Oxford University Press.

Casamatta, G., H. Cremer and P. Pestieau (2000), 'The political economy of social security', *Scandinavian Journal of Economics*, 102(3): 503–22.

Cremer, H. and P. Pestieau (2000), 'Reforming our pension system: is it a demographic, financial or political problem', *European Economic Review*, 44: 974–83.

Davidson, S. (n.d.), 'The growing importance of older voters: an electoral demographical model for analysis of the changing age structure of the electorate', Report prepared for Age Concern, Loughborough University, Loughborough.

Galasso, V. (2006), *The Political Future of Social Security in Aging Societies*, Cambridge, MA: MIT Press.

Kruse, A., (2005), 'Political economy and pensions in ageing societies – a note on how an "impossible" reform was implemented in Sweden', Mimeo, Department of Economics, Lund University.

Minford, P. (1998), 'The economic principles of pension provision', *Economic Affairs*, 18(1): 13–17.

Mueller, D. C. (2003), *Public Choice III*, Cambridge: Cambridge University Press.

THE IMPOSSIBILITY OF PROGRESS

O'Connell, A. (2004), *Citizen's Pension: Lessons from New Zealand*, Pensions Policy Institute Discussion Paper.

Stroinski, K. (1998), 'Poland: the reform of the pensions system', *Economic Affairs*, 18(1): 29–33.

Tullock, G. (2006), *The Vote Motive*, Hobart Paper 33, London: Institute of Economic Affairs.

Whitely, P., M. C. Stewart, D. Sanders and H. D. Clarke (2005), in P. Norris and C. Wlezien (eds), *Britain Votes 2005*, Oxford: Oxford University Press.

4 THE GREAT INVISIBLE PENSION REFORM IN THE UNITED STATES
Krzysztof Ostaszewski

Is the US bankrupt? Or to paraphrase the Oxford English Dictionary, is the United States at the end of its resources, exhausted, stripped bare, destitute, bereft, wanting in property, or wrecked in consequence of failure to pay its creditors?

LAWRENCE KOTLIKOFF

Introduction

The retirement income system in the USA combines a social insurance scheme and pension systems of federal and state governments with a multitude of private retirement systems, resulting in a structure of great complexity and diversity. The upcoming retirement of the generation of 'baby boomers' is looming. This potential major crisis of public and private finance has caused alarming prognoses, but there has been no substantial reform. How will the US economy solve this problem? This author believes that the resolution is unlikely to arrive from government, but rather will arise from the human action of individual decision-makers who have already begun the process of adjustment of their lifestyle, work and leisure behaviour in order to cope with this problem. There remain, however, many explicit and implicit interventions from government which will act as obstacles to this naturally occurring human action resolution.

The economics of social insurance

Participants in any retirement income system perceive it as either a part of the private insurance system, or as a part of a welfare system. These are dramatically different perspectives. In the context of a private insurance system, a person gives up a part of their income during their working years and purchases capital assets in order to exchange them for income in the later years of life. The individual faces great uncertainties concerning the amount of income needed in retirement and the amount of savings needed to provide it. Financial intermediaries such as insurance companies, pension plans or investment funds offer help in the process, but the uncertainties are too great even for them to fully overcome. For example, the purchasing power of retirement income is not merely a function of the amount of savings and the rate of return on them, but of the rate of inflation before and after retirement, often as far in the future as 60 years beyond the beginning of the process of retirement planning, and clearly beyond the control of private financial institutions, or individual consumers. Additionally, the later years of life are exactly the years when the consumer is most vulnerable, usually unable to work, in great need of financial stability, and facing irreversible consequences of past decisions concerning retirement planning. That vulnerability is given as the key reason for inclusion of retirement provision in welfare systems in all countries that created any form of welfare state. But the welfare state provides retirement income in a different manner from private retirement systems. The most common form of state retirement provision is so-called *social insurance.* Social insurance, as opposed to private insurance, is defined by the following features:

- the system is administered by the state, and is typically universal or nearly universal;
- benefits paid and 'premiums' (more precisely taxes, as they are collected by the state) are prescribed by law, not by a private contract, and may be changed any time the appropriate law is changed, even for current participants who have earned benefits and paid 'premiums'.

One more standard feature common to social insurance is that the system is financed on a pay-as-you-go basis, which simply means that 'premiums' collected are immediately paid out as benefits, without any accumulation of assets. This is the part of any social insurance system which is subject to most frequent criticism: that by not pre-funding the benefits the system does not allow for any real investment. In the context of this statement, 'real' refers to the real economy, i.e. factories, machinery or any new productive capacity, as opposed to investments in capital assets, such as stocks or bonds, which are financial investments. Of course, the funds collected by a pay-as-you-go system, while paid out nearly immediately, in the process are used by the government, and for those who consider that a productive use, the argument about the lack of real investment is unconvincing. There are, however, significant additional issues to be considered.

In fact, a pay-as-you-go system creates only an illusion of involving no asset accumulation. Participants in a social insurance system accumulate rights to benefits, which are, to them, capital assets.[1] One could describe social insurance as a system of mandatory savings constructed as follows:

---

1   Though, as noted above, there is risk attached to these capital assets because the government can, at any time, change the benefits to be paid.

- every working participant's taxes contributed to the system are invested in government bonds;
- government bonds earn interest at a rate set by law, or by a social insurance government administrator;
- upon retirement, benefits are paid to the participant from that participant's account. But if the amount of benefit exceeds that prescribed by law, the excess is taxed at 100 per cent. If the amount is lower than the amount prescribed by law, the government subsidises the benefit to reach the desired level.

One crucial difference between the accumulation of capital assets in a private system and that in a social insurance system is the method of pricing those capital assets. The amount of income received in a private pension scheme is established based on prices of capital assets in the market. If the stock market crashes, there will be less money for benefits. If the stock market booms, benefits can be increased. On the other hand, the amount of income received from a social insurance scheme is set by law. Thus, social insurance results in government pricing of financial assets, as opposed to market pricing. Individuals are forced to participate and the return that they will receive on their contributions through the tax system is fixed by law. This results in a distortion of market signals provided by prices. Proponents of social insurance, it appears, are willing to accept such distortions in order to meet the social need for a safety net for the elderly. A further difference between private and state social insurance is that the liabilities to meet the claims of retired people on their assets built up within a social insurance system do not arise from free exchange in a market but are imposed on the next generation of participants in the system – many of whom will be too young to vote. Furthermore, the accumulation of, and accounting for, the assets and liabilities within a social insurance system is opaque in the extreme.

Some economists, notably Martin Feldstein (1974, 1977 and 1997), have argued that social insurance systems (or, specifically, the old-age social security system in the USA[2]) lower the savings rate. This phenomenon represents itself through:

- the *saving replacement effect*: the idea that people believe that the government is saving for them through the mandatory social security programme. Therefore, private savings are subsequently decreased since the government is already saving for people;
- *induced retirement effect*: social insurance prescribes the age of retirement, and resulting inflexibility will cause people to retire, in general, too early in relation to the market value of their human capital (i.e. ability to earn income).

But one could also envisage the situation where incentives work in the opposite direction, so that:

- participants could view unrealistically high future benefit promises as simply promises of higher future tax rates, and respond with higher precautionary savings, to be able to pay those higher future taxes; and
- participants could be forced to retire at an age higher than the one desired by them, and respond by increasing their savings

---

2   Throughout this chapter, when the words 'social security' are used, they refer specifically to the US Old Age Survivors and Disability programme.

in order to be able to afford at least a partial retirement at an earlier age.

But the level of savings, while important, is not the ultimate determinant of prosperity of a nation. How those savings are put to productive use matters more. The absence of price signals in a social insurance system where capital assets are not exchanged at market value is important here. Price signals in capital markets affect the real investment decisions of businesses. For example, a firm may have a choice between building a new factory or buying another firm that already owns a similar factory. If the price of that other firm, as established by the stock market, is artificially low, investment in a new factory may be abandoned, and the gain to the firm may be a loss to the society in general, because the new productive capacity of that factory is not created. In a similar way, the absence of price signals within a social insurance system leads to inefficient resource allocation.

Prices of capital assets are also affected by the changes in the relative risks of various assets as a result of social insurance provision. Because social insurance benefits enjoy government guarantee, if they are provided at an unreasonably high level, consumers may be able to increase the riskiness of the rest of their investment portfolio without overall loss to their financial well-being. Thus a stable and generous social insurance system may appear to be beneficial to the stability of society until we consider the more speculative investments undertaken by participants in their private portfolios without proper consideration for risk.

Consumers may also respond to the social insurance incent-ives by altering the balance between work and leisure, or between education and work. For example, the benefit formula of social insurance may be gamed by participants. If benefits are granted, as in the USA, based on the best 35 years of work history, with past wages indexed based on an historical wage index, the optimal strategy is to work for exactly 35 years and use the other years of life to increase earnings in those crucial 35 years: one way to do this is to acquire professional or graduate education. Thus social insurance may be one explanation for 'qualification inflation'.

Social insurance and public choice

All of the above economic considerations are only a part of the picture, because we have still not added the public choice effects of social insurance (see, e.g., Mueller, 1989). Public choice theory studies the behaviour of voters, politicians and government officials as self-interested agents. The very existence of social insurance brings about new incentives to all participants (see also the chapter by Booth):

- Because the benefit amount is not tied to contributions paid, participants can lobby government to have the tax burden shifted to other groups, such as future generations, businesses or groups and individuals viewed as more able to carry the burden (e.g. high-income or high-net-worth individuals).
- Because benefits are granted by law, special interest groups formed by the retirees (such as AARP in the USA) can lobby the government for benefit increases, programme expansion and creation of new benefits and sub-programmes. For example, in the USA a new prescription drug benefit social insurance programme was enacted in 2005 with support from AARP.

- Special interest groups can lobby the government for benefit increases or the granting of special benefits for specific professional groups (e.g. policemen, the military or teachers). Ironically, small groups can be especially successful in such rent-seeking behaviour, especially if they are well organised, closely connected with political agents, and receive concentrated benefits paid for by costs that are widely dispersed across the general population, or borne by future generations.

- Politicians holding or seeking office can offer increases in benefits in social insurance as a method of convincing voters to choose them in the election process. This is especially effective if the mechanism of shifting the cost to future generations, or to a group of voters irrelevant to a given politician, can be exploited. The actual structure of the election process becomes crucial here, because if a decisive voting block can be convinced of receiving desired benefits at the expense of others, the elections and policy implementation following it become certain, and the only counteraction will be in the form of future economic consequences (e.g. a high level of national debt leading to reductions in future state expenditures, or even some form of insolvency of the state – for an insightful discussion of such a possibility for the USA, see Kotlikoff, 2006).

All of the lobbying activities brought about by the very nature of social insurance do not, of course, remain without response. Groups targeted for tax increases respond with their own lobbying activities (although future, yet unborn, generations have been always extremely ineffective in that activity, thus there is very little lobbying against continual increases in public debt in most modern democracies). They can also respond by legal and illegal tax avoidance, which not only reduces government revenue and redirects human action to ineffective use, but also undermines the rule of law – that rule of law which is the foundation of all social activities, including the business activities usually targeted for the taxes needed for the welfare state.

The balance of public choice effects on the retirement system depends very much on the balance of relative sizes of incentives involved. If the cost of the social insurance system is relatively low, and the public good provided (a safety net for the elderly) visible and effectively delivered, incentives for lobbying and tax avoidance may be negligible. If, on the other hand, the benefits delivered are small and marred with bureaucratic rent-seeking and intrusion into citizens' lives (for a thorough presentation of the role of bureaucracy in public choice theory, see Niskanen, 1987), while the costs of social insurance are high (which is typically a situation in the case of bureaucratic rent-seeking), productive economic decision-makers are likely to seek ways to exit the social insurance system, or arbitrage against it, further exacerbating the system's high costs.

The heavy hand of government retirement planning

One final remark on the impact of a large, dominant system of social insurance should also be added. If retirement provision is the sole, or nearly sole, domain of the central government, this clearly leads to the creation of 'national retirement policy'. Retirement is planned by the social insurance system, with a normal retirement age, early retirement age, adjustments for retiring at different ages, calculation of benefits based on employment history, often requiring participants to produce and document their own employment histories, with adjustments for family status, and spouse employment history, and many, many other numerous factors. All of these require a massive, sophisticated, centralised model that is trying to replace the price system of a free market. And that attempt to replace the market by a sophisticated scientific model designed by central government authority is exactly the idea termed by Friedrich Hayek (1988) the *fatal conceit.* Hayek argued that price signals are the only possible way to let each economic decision-maker communicate tacit knowledge or dispersed knowledge to others, in order to solve the economic calculation problem. The idea was, of course, also presented in the debate on economic calculation by Ludwig von Mises (1920), and was at the heart of the *economic calculation problem*: the issue of whether a central government authority can calculate prices in the absence of free markets.

But the central idea of Hayek's work was that people often do not like the free market system because capitalism functions as an unseen extended order, while people prefer to see immediate, visible good. The invisibility of the functioning of the free enterprise system has been the constant theme of its scholars, as illustrated, of course, by the *invisible hand* metaphor of Adam Smith (1776). Capitalism is somewhat akin to electricity or any form of energy: invisible, alien, often frightening. Yet it warms or cools our houses, cooks our food, moves us around, and enriches our lives. Hayek basically told us that it is very difficult to love capitalism, because we can't touch it.

The key claim of this chapter is that the USA has entered a *Great Invisible Pension Reform.* That reform may not be loved, but unlike centrally-planned reforms it has a chance of producing results.

The invisible and incomprehensible hand of insurance markets

The free enterprise provision of retirement income generally lies within the domain of the insurance industry. While saving and investing can be done with the help of banks, investment companies or just directly, protection against risks of timing of retirement and protection against longevity in retirement require some form of insurance (by an insurance company, or through a pension plan). This industry is among the most distrusted, obscure and unintelligible to its customers. The retirement process itself is opaque and many consumers dread dealing with it. The attitudes of those consumers are, of course, part of the problem with Adam Smith's *invisible hand*: that it is invisible! Given that, is there any hope for the insurance industry to be helpful in resolving the retirement puzzle? Or, more generally, what is the social benefit of that industry? The answer can be derived from this simple question: in the absence of automobile insurance, would people drive less or more? The answer is less, of course. The consequence of the existence of the insurance industry is that economic decision-makers can undertake more risky activities. This means that firms and individuals can undertake more projects producing necessary economic output. But it also means that firms and individuals can assume more risks than they otherwise would.

When we create any insurance system, we need to ask ourselves honestly: if we offer people risk reduction through insurance, what will those additional risky things that people will do be? Different retirement schemes bring about different new incentives and resulting human activities; we should have the honesty and courage to at least consider those. Steven Tyler (2008), in an EconTalk.org podcast, quotes a sentence he heard from Robert Solow concerning centrally designed plans of economics, which reached their peak of power in the USA in the 1960s: 'We never did damage to reality. We used adequate abstraction.' The inadequacy of abstractions lay in the lack of consideration for human action, and brought about the harvest of crises in the 1970s.

We have already talked about the public choice consequences of social insurance design. But what is the moral hazard of the retirement system? The risk that pensions, annuities and other retirement products insure against is the risk of finding oneself too old to work, and yet without income to sustain life. One is fully insured against that risk if one possesses assured adequate income for the rest of one's life. And therein lies the moral hazard of retirement: that people who are able to work, and who can make a significant, valuable contribution to the society, withdraw into a life of not merely leisure, but also separation from what generally goes on in the society. The skills and the wisdom of the elderly are needed far more than we commonly assume.

The old order of central control

Most of the basic design of social insurance and private pensions worldwide was created in the late nineteenth century and the first half of the twentieth century. This approach to retirement produced generally a design in which everyone was able to retire and do no work for a significant period of their lives. Social insurance generally prescribed a retirement age, and created incentives against retirement at any other age. In the USA, the message of counting only 35 years of employment in the benefit formula is clear and understood by all workers, even those who find insurance utterly incomprehensible. Furthermore, this problem is supplemented by taxation of wages that do not earn benefits, and even punitive taxation at a certain level of income, resulting in a perception of threat of loss of benefits if one works while officially retired. Private pension plans also commonly stop accruing benefits at a certain age, or after a certain number of years of service, again producing strong incentives to stop working. Traditional retirement systems from before the reforms of the late 1970s and 1980s generally insisted that workers retire and stop working at a particular point, reflecting the earlier private paternalistic arrangements of a corporatist age.

A person who desired an increase in retirement income under those circumstances had the choice between these two clear alternatives:

- work for more years, and accept lower wages resulting from punitive taxation and possible loss of pension benefits; or
- lobby the government for pension benefit increases in social insurance, or demand through the collective bargaining process that employers increase pension benefits.

Other choices emerged more clearly in the 1980s and 1990s worldwide:

- lobby the government for lower taxes and the ability to accumulate retirement assets in an individual account, where

benefit is given not by law, but determined by the account balance; or
- lobby the government to remove disincentives to work created by pension systems.

These two additional choices seem natural and offer a socially desirable solution because they result in:

- an increase in labour supply;
- better incentives to work;
- a possible increase in national savings;
- market pricing of retirement income, and more efficient allocation of capital to real investment.

But these solutions do bring with them one problem: they require the same economic agents who want to work, and most likely work long hours already, to simultaneously lobby the government and be involved in the political process. Only a deep crisis, such as the one of the late 1970s, could bring about enough will to encourage such people, who have a high marginal utility of time, to involve themselves with the political process.

The USA never created a dominant national pension system. The American retirement system currently in existence is extremely complex, because it consists of many 'moving parts' that interact with each other (that is, various forms of retirement income provision, public and private, affect each other). In the first half of the twentieth century, pension system design was mostly centralised. In 1935 the federal government created the social security system, a universal social insurance retirement system, which, by welfare state standards, is relatively small, aiming to replace, on average, approximately a quarter of pre-retirement income. Employment-based pension plans, while in existence before World War II, became a significant factor in the national economy during that war, as labour unions lobbied employers and government for benefit increases in lieu of wage increases, while regular wages and prices were subjected to government controls. Pensions granted by social security and employers were of a defined-benefit type, and their design included strong incentives to retire upon reaching normal retirement age. But, in addition to those command economy aspects, the US economy also contained a large and established insurance industry offering retirement annuities, as well as an active private investment industry, and a private real estate market, with relatively easy access to long-term mortgage loans at fixed interest rates. There were also some defined-contribution pension plans. All of these offered either opportunities for private wealth accumulation or insurance against retirement risk. Additionally, workers in large parts of the US economy were not covered by social insurance or employment-based pensions. Nearly half of workers were initially not covered by social security, including self-employed individuals, as well as employees of states and cities – though state and city employees were generally covered by pension plans created by their employers.

Proposals to promote the 'invisible hand'

Dramatic changes to the old system started in the 1970s. In 1974 the Employee Retirement Income Security Act was implemented. The law created strict funding requirements for private defined-benefit pension plans, and created Individual Retirement

Accounts. In 1978, Congress amended the Internal Revenue Code, in Section 401(k), allowing employees not to be taxed on income they choose to receive as deferred compensation rather than direct compensation. This started 401(k) accounts, the most popular type of employment-based defined-contribution pensions. In the early 1980s, the financial projections of the Social Security Administration indicated near-term revenue from payroll taxes would not be sufficient to fully fund near-term benefits. The US government appointed the Greenspan Commission, headed by Alan Greenspan (before he became chairman of the Federal Reserve), to investigate what changes to federal law were necessary to shore up the social security programme. The adjustment to the structure of social security recommended by the Commission involved the following elements: some tax increases; substantial benefit cuts; an increase in the normal retirement age; expansion of coverage of workers to near universal; and the creation of a trust fund. This was the last major reform of US social security.

Since then, there has been political stalemate about the system's status. When the second term of President Reagan ended, social security was in a short-term and long-term surplus. This changed following the 1991 recession, and the system has remained in long-term actuarial deficit since. In 1994 the situation was judged to be so grave that an Advisory Council was appointed to address the issue. The Report of the 1994–1996 Advisory Council on Social Security outlined three options for social security reform:

- The first option sought to maintain the then current system's basic benefit structure by increasing revenues and reducing outlays. Specifically, the plan sought to increase programme revenues by extending coverage to state and local government employees hired after 1997, extending and increasing the taxation of benefits to all recipients, and increasing the payroll tax by a combined 1.6 per cent. The plan also called for an extension of the benefit computation period from 35 to 38 years by 1999, thereby reducing benefits by an average of 3 per cent. Since these revenue and expenditure measures did not completely solve the long-term solvency problem, the proposal recommended investing up to 40 per cent of the trust fund in the stock market.

- The second option sought to restore programme solvency mainly through reductions in outlays. Such reductions were to be achieved by accelerating the increase in the retirement age to 67 by 2011 and to 70 by 2083, reducing the growth of basic benefits, and extending the benefit computation period. This option would also establish a system of mandatory individual accounts to be funded by employee contributions. Specifically, workers would be required to contribute an additional 1.6 per cent of covered earnings into a personal savings account. Individuals would have limited choices on how these accounts would be invested.

- The third option was to replace the current social security system with a new two-tiered system. The first tier would provide a flat-rate benefit based on a worker's length of service. Workers with 35 or more years of covered employment would receive a monthly benefit equal to 65 per cent of the current poverty level. The second tier would supplement this basic benefit by creating a system of Personal Saving Accounts funded by 5 percentage points of the 6.2 per cent payroll tax on employees. These accounts would be individually owned and managed. Workers would be able to invest in a wide range of investment options.

These proposals were produced by different groups of the Council, and represented mutually incompatible options. Generally, the first option was supported by the Democrats, and the third by Republicans, although this party association was not universal. The resulting stalemate has lasted since the 1997 publication of the proposals, even though President Bush's election platform included a proposal similar to the third one. The long-term solvency of social security remains a problem. This, in combination with future costs of healthcare provided by the US government (through Medicare social insurance and Medicaid social assistance) and public debt, is the reason why Kotlikoff (2006) raised the possibility of US bankruptcy.

The invisible hand needs no help from government

But while the social insurance status has been deteriorating, the other parts of the US pension system have been performing rather well. The amount of assets held to meet retirement needs, as given by EBRI (2007), increased from $2.4 billion in 1985 to $14.4 billion in 2005. The growth has been particularly dramatic among plans that have a more individualist nature – specifically defined-contribution arrangements and Individual Retirement Accounts. Within this period, both the federal government and other types of government (state and local) have added and expanded defined-contribution plans. While the social security reform of creating individual accounts stalled, individual accounts prevailed in the marketplace. Notably, Individual Retirement Accounts (IRAs), non-existent in 1973, and funded sometimes with funds that do not qualify for tax relief, now constitute nearly a quarter of all retirement assets in the USA.

The mid-1990s were an ideal time for a resolution of the baby boomers' retirement puzzle. That generation was still at least ten years from retirement, so there was time for them to act and prepare. The failure of the federal government to reform social security was accompanied by failure to stop dangerous long-term trends in Medicare and Medicaid, and rising healthcare expenditures in general. But that was also the time when the trend towards individual accounts accelerated. Furthermore, that was the time when labour participation rates for older Americans started climbing. The percentage of civilian non-institutionalised Americans aged 55 or older who were in the labour force declined from 34.6 per cent in 1975 to 29.4 per cent in 1993. Since 1993, however, the labour-force participation rate has steadily increased, reaching 38.0 per cent in 2006 – the highest level over the 1975–2006 period.

We should also note that, at that time, the following two additional phenomena occurred (see Hutchens, 2007):

- phased retirement: the situation in which workers gradually decrease the number of hours worked, while beginning to receive their pension benefits, and possibly accruing defined-contribution plan balances; and
- accommodation of such phased retirement by state and city governments, which had previously used traditional incentives for early retirement, by creating systems of *re-employment of retired employees*, who do not accrue new defined-benefit pensions by working, but can accumulate defined-contribution plan balances.

At the same time Muldoon and Kopcke (2008) point out that a very large percentage of workers in the USA claim their social security benefits at the earliest possible age: 62. This means that workers seek minimum income protection from the federal government, but are not very eager to postpone receiving that minimum in return for social insurance benefit increases. The political stalemate in the reform process resulted in workers taking what they can get from social insurance and then working longer and accumulating money in defined-contribution plans in order to fully resolve the retirement puzzle.

We can see that all of the moving parts of the US retirement systems affect each other. One more example of that is the work of Friedberg and Webb (2005). Analysing data from the longitudinal Health and Retirement Study, they concluded that defined-contribution plans lead to an increase in the retirement age of nearly two years, on average, compared with defined-benefit plans. Moreover, the authors suggest that their findings may explain the recent increase in employment rates among people in their sixties, following decades of decline. They expect this trend to continue, as more workers with defined-contribution plans reach retirement age and defined-benefit plans become largely a thing of the past.

Political stalemate and human action

There are common threads in the Invisible Pension Reform in the USA:

- The federal government has instituted changes in social insurance. Normal retirement age in social insurance was increased, but Medicare eligibility age remained unchanged, and Medicare coverage was expanded. Medicare benefits can be received even while a person still works. Some reductions in benefits for working while receiving social insurance were removed. All of these spell out the message that workers should claim all social insurance benefits they can as early as possible, but continue working, full time or part time, if they can.

- Since social insurance benefits are not fully indexed to inflation, and decline in purchasing power in relation to the cost of healthcare, a major service needed by retirees, this also pushes retirees to work to supplement their income.
- State and city employees' pension plans have become very accommodating about employees receiving pensions but returning to work.
- A significant move from defined-benefit (DB) plans to defined-contribution (DC) plans, or individual accounts in general, resulted in significant incentives for working longer, as both disincentives for work in DB plans are removed, and incentives to work in DC plans are introduced.
- The trends towards working longer and towards individual accounts reinforce each other.
- While the health insurance market in the USA remains very inflexible, with health insurance tied to employment, the social health insurance for retirees, Medicare, increased its flexibility, by expanding benefits and allowing options to purchase private coverage, either replacing regular social insurance or supplementing it. The labour market in the USA is relatively flexible, but the health insurance tie-in to employment is its major inflexibility. This is not the case for retirees, as social insurance health coverage is available for them.

Thus, it can be argued that the retirement crisis in the USA is solved, albeit without major fanfares and political action. Instead, human action reform is implemented, with the key features being workers relying on support from social insurance at only a low level because they are willing to bear the cost of retirement that is not paid for by social insurance and employment-based pensions, by working longer and accumulating wealth in individual accounts.

It should also be added that the continuing process of transition from DB plans to DC plans has been greatly misrepresented. It is not a transition from one form of pension to another, but a transition to more freedom for the retiree. DB plans may be desirable, but have been captured by political interest groups, and serve the purpose of regulating retirement age, regulating years of employment, regulating union membership and (in the case of social insurance DB plans) redistribution of income. The DB product cannot be purchased in an open market, but rather it comes in a tie-in transaction, with all the regulatory burdens imposed by government, and the move to DC may be, at least partly, in response to the undesirability of that tie-in.

Future reform

It can be seen, therefore, that the Invisible Pension Reform in the USA amounts to a reduction in the relative size of that part of the retirement system under significant government control, and expansion of the part functioning in a relatively free market. Reform proposals should embrace those trends. In particular, the following proposals should be adopted:

- All restrictions on employment of recipients of social security should be removed. To pay for the possible cost of this, future benefit increases earned by such employment activities can be reduced, simultaneously helping the financial standing of social security and increasing incentives to work.
- Regulation surrounding the design of individual accounts used for retirement should be simplified. There are many types of plans with individual accounts in the USA, and workers often do not understand their significance and relationships. One possible reform could be that a worker could have their defined-contribution plan funds placed in an employment-based account or in an Individual Retirement Account with completely equivalent tax treatment of the two transactions. The objective should be for all workers to have large and economically significant Individual Retirement Accounts.
- The final and key step should be to cut benefits in the social security system enough to make it financially sound again, while allowing the system of individual accounts to expand. The simplest means of achieving this would be to cut benefits in exchange for workers having a portion of their payroll taxes contributed to a Roth Individual Retirement Account (Roth IRAs receive the same tax treatment as originally designed social security benefits). If the cut is larger in actuarial present value than the funds contributed to Roth IRAs, the social security system will benefit, but workers will gain the freedom of having the desirable individual account.

Problem solved?

In conclusion, the pension crisis in the USA is currently being actively resolved, but only at the level of individual human action, not at the level of political human design. The big question is not: 'What can the government do to resolve the crisis?', but rather: 'What can the government do to not harm this naturally occurring resolution?' People work more and lobby less, at least in the context of their retirement income, if private arrangements are dominant. We should welcome and embrace that. If a political resolution is put forth, the key question to ask is: 'What lobbying groups will it create and why?' But we firmly believe that American people have found a way to tackle their retirement problem, and we should trust their actions.

No, the USA is not bankrupt: but it has some work to do.

References

Auerbach, A. J. and L. J. Kotlikoff (1990), 'Demographics, fiscal policy, and US savings in the 1980s and beyond', in L. Summers (ed.), *Tax Policy and the Economy*, Cambridge, MA: MIT Press.

Black, D. (1958), *The Theory of Committees and Elections*, Cambridge: Cambridge University Press.

Copeland, C. (2007), 'Labor-force participation: the population age 55 and older', *Employee Benefits Research Institute Notes*, 28(6), June.

EBRI (Employee Benefits Research Institute) (2007), *Fast Facts* no. 61, 11 September.

Feldstein, M. S. (1974), 'Induced retirement and aggregate capital accumulation', *Journal of Political Economy*, 82(5), September.

Feldstein, M. S. (1977), 'Social security and private savings: international evidence in an extended life-cycle model', *The Economics of Public Services: An International Economic Association Conference Volume*, Boston, MA: Harvard University Press.

Feldstein, M. S. (1997), 'The case of privatization', *Foreign Affairs*, 76(4), July.

Friedberg, L. and A. Webb (2005), 'Retirement and the evolution of pension structure', *Journal of Human Resources*, 40(2): 281–308, available online at http://works.bepress.com/anthony_webb/12, accessed 21 June 2008.

Hayek, F. (1988), *The Fatal Conceit: The Errors of Socialism*, ed. W. W. Bartley, III, Chicago, IL: University of Chicago Press.

Hutchens, R. (2007), 'Phased retirement: problems and prospects', *Issue Brief* Series 8, Center for Retirement Research at Boston College, June, available online at http://crr.bc.edu/images/stories/Briefs/wob_8.pdf?phpMyAdmin=43ac483c4de9t51d9eb41.

Kotlikoff, L. J. (2006), 'Is the United States bankrupt?', *Federal Reserve Bank of St Louis Review*, 88(4): 235–49.

Mueller, D. C. (1989), *Public Choice II*, Cambridge: Cambridge University Press.

Muldoon, D. and R. W. Kopcke (2008), 'Are people claiming social security benefits later?,' *Issue Brief* no. 8–7, Center for Retirement Research at Boston College, June, available online at http://crr.bc.edu/images/stories/ib_8–7.pdf.

Niskanen, W. A. (1987), 'Bureaucracy', in C. K. Rowley (ed.), *Democracy and Public Choice*, Oxford: Basil Blackwell.

Smith, Adam (1776), *An Inquiry into the Nature and Causes of the Wealth of Nations*.

Social Security Administration (1997), *Report of the 1994–1996 Advisory Council on Social Security*, vol. I: *Findings and Recommendations*, 7 January.

Social Security Administration (2008), *Annual Report of the Board of Trustees of the Federal Old-age and Survivors Insurance and Disability Insurance Trust Funds*, available online at www. socialsecurity.gov/OACT/TR/TR08/trTOC.html.

Tullock, G. (1987), 'Public choice', *The New Palgrave: A Dictionary of Economics*, vol. 3, pp. 1040–44.

Tullock, G. (1989), *The Economics of Special Privilege and Rent-seeking*, Boston, MA, and Dordrecht, Netherlands: Kluwer Academic Publishers.

Tyler, S. (2008), *Cowen on Monetary Policy*, EconTalk.org Podcast no. 69, 17 March.

United States Congress (1974), *Employee Retirement Income Security Act*, 29 US Code Chapter 18, available online at http://finduslaw.com/employee_retirement_income_security_act_erisa_29_u_s_code_chapter_18.

Von Mises, L. E. (1920), 'Economic calculation in the socialist commonwealth', reprinted in F. A. Hayek (1935), *Collectivist Economic Planning*, London: George Routledge & Sons, pp. 87–130.

5 PENSION CREDIT AND PERSONAL ACCOUNTS – THE PRACTICAL IMPACT OF MEANS TESTING IN THE UK
Deborah Cooper

Introduction

Saving requires forgoing consumption now so that at some future point the proceeds of that saving can be used to improve the quality of life. Specifically, retirement saving is intended to replace lost income after retirement and so, if savers are penalised through extra taxes or lost social security benefits because they have saved, we can expect levels of saving to be reduced. If people do save and they lose the benefit of that saving as a result of the tax and benefits system, then they will be worse off than anticipated throughout their retirement unless they are able and prepared to work for longer than they had planned.

Governments throughout the world recognise the special nature of retirement saving because its role as income replacement substitutes for social security provision the state might otherwise be expected to provide. In many cases they attempt to provide incentives for retirement saving by giving it preferential tax treatment, relative to other forms of saving. To ensure that retirement savings are used in the way governments intend, savings vehicles that attract tax breaks generally have restrictions on how they are accessed – for example, minimum payment ages and compulsory annuitisation.

These issues are particularly acute in the UK. The level of

pension provided by the state is low relative to that available in many other similar countries (see, for example, Turner, 2006); means-tested benefits for those above state pension age are a relatively high proportion of state benefits; and average levels of saving are low (see, for example, de Serres and Pelgrin, 2003).

Those people who find themselves eligible for means-tested benefits in retirement will find the value of any pension savings they have made effectively eroded as a result of the Pension Credit (the core means-tested benefit that has applied in the UK since 2003). As a result of saving they lose entitlement to means-tested benefits. We can think of this loss of benefits as reducing the effective rates of return from saving (which can happen to such an extent that the effective return is negative). Of course, the state does not literally confiscate savings but it removes means-tested benefits to which the individual would have been entitled had they not saved.

A series of reviews of retirement provision in the UK have criticised the balance between private saving, state 'accrued' pension provision and means-tested benefits, and questioned its sustainability. As a result, the Pensions Act 2007 and the Pensions Bill, which, at the time of writing (early 2008), was under debate in Parliament, establish a new model for pension saving. This chapter considers whether the proposed reforms address the weaknesses that have been identified with the provision of means-tested benefits. This chapter is UK-specific in that the specific incentives quantified are those that arise from the UK system. Clearly, any quantification of the problems caused by means testing must be country-specific. The general principles, however, apply across many other countries where means-tested benefits are widespread.

Background to state pension accrual over the past 60 years

Since 1978 the UK state pension scheme has been a defined-benefit mixture of a flat-rate benefit and an earnings-related benefit. The flat-rate benefit, the Basic State Pension (BSP), was introduced in 1948 as part of Beveridge's social security reforms. Initial intentions were that it would meet most people's 'basic needs', although from the outset it was unlikely that it achieved this objective. Until 1979, however, it more or less retained its value as a proportion of earnings, for those able to accrue full entitlement. In the last twenty years of the twentieth century, the BSP was increased no faster than retail prices. So, relative to those in work and in the absence of other income, its purchasing power was diminished.

After much debate about the level of pension the state should deliver, an earnings-related benefit was introduced from 1978. Originally called the State Earnings Related Pension (SERPS), it provided earnings-related accrual on earnings between a level of earnings called the Lower Earnings Limit (LEL – £4,524 in 2007/08) and a level called the Upper Earnings Limit (UEL – £34,840 in 2007/08). The LEL was more or less the same as the BSP, so, having provided for 'basic needs' via the BSP, SERPS stepped in to ensure state pensions helped replicate standards of living prior to retirement. SERPS accrual originally targeted a pension of 25 per cent of earnings between the LEL and UEL; from 1988 this target was reduced to 20 per cent and the eligibility conditions for full entitlement were made more stringent.

Individuals with alternative provision, regarded as equivalent to SERPs in total value terms, were allowed to contract out of SERPs and pay lower National Insurance contributions (or receive a rebate of contributions). The combination of BSP and SERPs could therefore be regarded as the minimum level of compulsory provision with BSP being provided by the state and SERPs (or something equivalent) being provided by either the state or the private sector, depending on individual circumstances.

In 2002 SERPS accrual was replaced by the State Second Pension (S2P), which extended the flat-rate pension for those on pay up to what is described as a 'Lower Earnings Threshold' (LET – £13,000 in 2007/08). To some extent this recognised that, because the BSP had been revalued at a rate less than the rate of increase in earnings for over twenty years, it was no longer credible to claim that it financed a basic living relative to those in work. Consequently, flat S2P accrual would supplement BSP – effectively a new flat-rate pension was brought in to add to BSP (though the two pensions had completely different accrual and indexing rules).

S2P could not, however, immediately address the apparent poor value of BSP because it was based on an accruals system – the changes would help only those retiring many years hence. The eligibility and revaluation rules for BSP and SERPs had resulted in a high proportion of people not being eligible for a pension that was sufficient to prevent them relying on the Minimum Income Guarantee, the means-tested benefit that preceded the Pension Credit. The Minimum Income Guarantee (MIG) had 100 per cent withdrawal rates, so that for every £1 of income with which an individual provided themselves, over the means-tested limit, the government would take away £1 of means-tested benefit. There was, of course, no point in the poor saving and the government was criticised for imposing high benefit withdrawal rates on the elderly poor.

Reform of means-tested benefits

A system of means-tested benefits, known as Pension Credit, was then introduced, which imposes a 40 per cent benefit withdrawal rate on the income from retirement savings, and this basic system remains intact today. The position now is that, for every £1 of extra income from savings, 40p of means-tested benefits are lost until an individual reaches the point at which tax is paid. Although this is an improvement on the MIG, it still left a strong disincentive effect on saving for those people who think they might be eligible for means-tested benefits once they reach state pension age (see Figure 4). The earlier system made it not worthwhile at all for a smaller number of people to save. The reformed system provides better incentives for those people at the expense of dragging a larger number of people into the means-tested net because Pension Credit continues to be paid to a much higher level of income.

The features of Pension Credit causing this pattern are:

- Anyone aged over the women's state pension age (currently 60), and with an income (ignoring Pension Credit) that is less than the saving credit threshold (approximately full BSP), will be eligible for 'guarantee credit', which tops income up to the appropriate minimum guarantee. The net effect of this is 100 per cent marginal tax rate on any income from savings.
- Anyone over the state pension age that applies to men (currently 65), and with an income (ignoring Pension Credit) above the saving credit threshold and less than the appropriate minimum guarantee, will receive guarantee credit and some savings credit. The net effect is a 40 per cent marginal tax rate on their income from savings.
- Anyone over the state pension age that applies to men,

Figure 4   **Pension Credit and marginal tax rates**

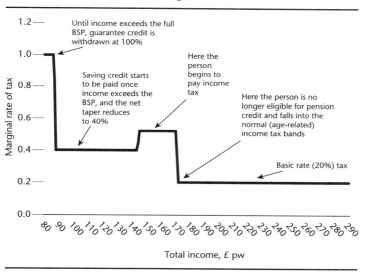

and with an income (ignoring Pension Credit) above the appropriate minimum guarantee and less than the Pension Credit threshold, will also be eligible for some savings credit.

Ignoring the rules that apply between ages 60 and 65, Pension Credit is designed so that most people who have saved will be better off in retirement than an equivalent person who did not save. The person who did not save might, however, experience a higher standard of living measured over their entire lifetime. The situation is considerably more complex for people who are also eligible for housing benefit and council tax benefit, with the rates of benefit withdrawal being potentially considerably higher (see Booth and Cooper, 2005).

Pensions Act 2007

The large number of people eligible, and forecast to become eligible, for Pension Credit led to serious soul-searching about the best way to provide retirement benefits for people in low-to-middle-income occupations. Following various investigations and reviews, the Pensions Act 2007 has heralded a major reform in state provision, imposing material shifts in the balance of cost and risk-sharing between employees, employers and the government. The Act has the following commitments:

- the restoration of the earnings link for BSP;
- an increase in the state pension age;
- a weakening of the eligibility conditions for full BSP and, to a lesser extent, S2P;
- the capping of the salary on which S2P accrues in nominal terms (a measure brought forward to the 2009/10 tax year in the 2007 pre-Budget report);
- the establishment of 'Personal Accounts'.

The full detail of how Personal Accounts will be designed and delivered has not been considered yet. The main features are set out in the Pensions Bill currently being debated in Parliament, but a lot of the detail will be left to rules and regulations drafted by ministers. Very broadly, employers will have to auto-enrol employees who are paid more than a threshold which is expected to be about £5,000 per annum (in 2007 terms) into a qualifying pension scheme, which will include Personal Accounts. Provided employees do not opt out, they and their employer will have to make contributions to the scheme. Personal Accounts will be a money purchase retirement savings arrangement, operated under trust but established by the government, and the contributions will be invested in investment funds.

The net effect of these reforms is:

- the level of 'defined-benefit' pension which the state is providing will be lower for medium-to-high-paid employees, but higher for those on low earnings;
- most employees will have some money purchase retirement savings, and so will be subject to investment market risks.

Because of the quasi-compulsory nature of auto-enrolment, Personal Accounts are being held up to scrutiny, particularly in the context of Pension Credit. The concern is that, if people do not get 'value' from their Personal Accounts because of means testing, this will undermine their effectiveness as a mass-market savings tool and/or create a new pensions mis-selling scandal (see, for example, Steventon et al., 2007, and Chris Grayling's speech in the House of Commons debate on the Pensions Bill in January 2008[1]).

How the Pension Credit affects the value of savings

One way of measuring the effect of the high marginal tax and benefit withdrawal rates imposed by the Pension Credit is to see them as eroding the rate of return the saver has received. The following tables show the effect the Pension Credit has on returns to saving, under the current state pension regime, for individuals on different levels of pay who are accruing S2P. The net returns

---

[1]   www.chrisgrayling.net/speech/2000801-pensions-bill.htm.

are calculated after deducting from the accumulation of the saving, the means-tested benefits that the individual loses as a consequence of saving. In each case, the individual is assumed to contribute 8 per cent of their pay for the number of years assumed in the table. The percentage return in the left-hand column is the gross average compound return received on saving over and above increases in average earnings; the percentages in the body of the table are the net returns achieved on saving after allowing for the loss of Pension Credit. Table 6 shows the position for an individual earning roughly median earnings and Table 7 shows the position for somebody earning 60 per cent of that level.

Table 6 **Pension Credit: return on saving for someone earning £25,000 per annum**

	Number of years' saving			
Return	10	20	30	40
2%	–8%	–3%	–1%	0%
4%	–6%	–1%	2%	3%
6%	–4%	1%	4%	5%

Table 7 **Pension Credit: return on saving for someone earning £15,000 per annum**

	Number of years' saving			
Return	10	20	30	40
2%	–8%	–3%	–1%	0%
4%	–6%	–1%	1%	2%
6%	–4%	1%	3%	5%

Where the net return is negative, the extra income achieved by the individual who has saved does not even represent a return of the capital value of the saving (after deducting the means-tested benefits from which the individual has lost).

Tables 6 and 7 illustrate that even people on relatively high levels of pay risk having the value of their savings eroded by means-tested benefits, particularly if they are unlucky with their investment decisions (that is, if the gross rate of return was low).

Personal Accounts

The new legislation both introduces Personal Accounts and changes the basis upon which the state pension is calculated. Personal Accounts are not significantly different in principle from voluntary saving through defined-contribution schemes under the pre-existing regime. The important change is that the minimum amount of compulsory state pension provision that individuals will have will be higher.[2] Personal Accounts can therefore be seen to be building on a higher base of income, making it less likely that individuals using them will be enmeshed in the means-tested benefits net.

Nevertheless, several commentators have recently pointed to the circumstances that might lead to people ending up with poor returns from Personal Accounts. Though most people will get some benefit from saving, certain groups are still at risk of obtaining negative returns from saving after allowing for the loss of means-tested benefits. These include people who will be more than midway through their working lifetimes when the

---

2   This arises from the linking of the BSP to earnings, the increase in the value of S2P for low earners and the prohibition on individual contracting out so individuals have to be contracted in to the state pension arrangement that provides a guaranteed return.

government's reforms come into force, and single people who are eligible for housing benefit in retirement.

It should be noted that, in the government's own published research, and that of the Pensions Policy Institute, on this topic, it has been assumed that the employer contribution to Personal Accounts is effectively a 'free gift' to the employee. While it will not be possible for an individual to opt out of Personal Accounts in return for a salary increment, it is surely inconceivable that the equilibrium level of wages will not be lower after employers take into account the contributions they are required to make to Personal Accounts. If the requirement to contribute does not reduce salaries for relevant employees, it may affect the level of employment. So the estimates in published research understate the problems of means-testing post-reform. The net returns to saving indicated in Tables 8 and 9 (opposite) assume that all the saving is effectively made by the employee.

Separately, the Pensions Policy Institute (PPI) and the Department of Work and Pensions (DWP) have also estimated the proportion of people likely to be eligible for some form of Pension Credit in 2050. Their estimates are 28 per cent (DWP) and 44 per cent (PPI). These estimates rely on a number of more or less subjective variables, so there is little value is disputing which one is more 'correct'. The important things to note are that, on the measures used in Tables 8 and 9, around one tenth of people could be eligible for guarantee credit only, and so could experience a 100 per cent marginal tax rate on any saving they have made; and around one third of people are likely to have the value of their saving reduced by Pension Credit, with perhaps one fifth experiencing negative rates of return on their saving after allowing for the withdrawal of means-tested benefits. The restoration of the earnings link for BSP will, however, take those people with full (or nearly full) working lifetimes out of means-tested benefits.

Tables 8 and 9 show that even an individual on a low income will receive a positive rate of return on their saving after allowing for the withdrawal of means-tested benefits if they have, more or less, a full working history. This is true even if they obtain a relatively low rate of return from Personal Accounts. The risks rest with low-income people with less than a full working history. In particular, it can be seen that an individual who has only a twenty-year working life receives a considerable reduction in their return to saving as a result of the loss of means-tested benefits. This is particularly so for those on low incomes.

Table 8 **Personal Accounts: return on saving for someone earning £25,000 per annum**

	Number of years' saving			
Return	10	20	30	40
2%	−8%	0%	1%	2%
4%	−6%	2%	3%	4%
6%	−3%	5%	6%	6%

Table 9 **Personal Accounts: return on saving for someone earning £15,000 per annum**

	Number of years' saving			
Return	10	20	30	40
2%	−8%	−2%	1%	1%
4%	−6%	1%	3%	4%
6%	−4%	4%	5%	6%

Comparison with the first set of calculations, presented in

Tables 6 and 7, shows that the reforms are likely to reduce, but not eliminate, the circumstances in which people get low net returns on their saving or, equivalently, lose part of their savings from being entrapped in the means-tested benefit net.

The proposed reforms should result in higher retirement incomes for those on low to medium incomes who did not previously have access to employer-sponsored saving. This presupposes that employees will remain opted in to Personal Accounts (or their employers' 'qualifying scheme'). If they do, and they have a long enough working history, then they can expect to receive higher retirement incomes than they would have done otherwise, assuming they receive adequate returns on their savings.

Those who choose to opt out of Personal Accounts will be worse off in retirement. They are also likely, however, to be worse off in work than they would have been had the reforms not taken place, because their employers are likely to reduce average wages to pay for the contributions they will be making to employees who remain opted in. We have not allowed for this in our calculations.

Purpose of means testing

Personal Accounts are intended to give low-to-medium-paid people access to 'affordable' retirement saving. Auto-enrolling employees into Personal Accounts, however, just to claw back a proportion of their savings through means testing, appears a questionable policy. From the above analysis, and modelling of individual scenarios in other papers, it is clear that a substantial minority of people could be in receipt of Pension Credit, though there is an improvement for many people. Does this undermine the main aims of the reforms?

Many of the reforms being implemented via the Pensions Act 2007 are intended to limit the risk that large proportions of the Personal Accounts 'target group' will be eligible for means-tested benefits in retirement. The following points are worthy of note, though they are not discussed further in this chapter:

- Preventing contracting out on a money purchase basis and increasing compulsory state pension provision for the low-paid deals to some extent with the risk that the low-paid will suffer from poor investment returns. It should be noted, however, that this has been achieved by increasing state pension provision in response to an earlier increase in means-tested benefits. Unlike many of the other authors of this monograph, this author is comfortable with such a reform, but it directly militates against stated government objectives of increasing private funded pension provision to 60 per cent of total pensioner income. Indirectly, however, removing the disincentives to save might increase privately provided retirement income at the same time as it increases state-provided retirement income.
- Reducing the period over which full entitlement to BSP accrues and providing credits for those with certain absences from paid employment help limit the risk that the state pension will be an insufficient underpin for private saving.
- Increasing state pension age allows people (slightly) longer to accumulate their savings while limiting the impact of the increase in state provision on the state budget.
- There remain considerable complexities and uncertainties in the system, which may have the effect of reducing private saving because people will be uncertain about whether rule

changes will reduce the value of their saving after allowing for taxes and means-tested benefits. In particular, the state is now providing two pensions that are both calculated using completely different sets of rules but which both broadly fulfil the same purpose of providing a basic income in retirement.

Conclusion

Means-tested benefit provision is aimed at providing income for the very poorest families or households, in an effort to target state resources at people who have slipped through the pensions net. Inevitably, this includes people who have found it difficult to provide a pension for themselves. There seems to be a general consensus in the UK that state pension provision should depend to some extent on working history. Given this starting point, and since failure to complete a working lifetime is not entirely under the individual's control, it may seem inevitable that some means-tested benefits will be provided by the state. The existence of means-tested benefits should not, of itself, by regarded as a failure of the system of provision in the UK.

Once more than a certain number of people are eligible for means-tested benefit, however, the system is surely failing, as it implies either that means-tested benefits are being provided to people whose income does not merit it or, for one reason or another, large numbers of people are not providing themselves with an adequate income in retirement. Currently, DWP estimates that about 45 per cent of people above state pension age are eligible for Pension Credit. The change to retirement saving being introduced by the Pensions Act 2007 seems likely to reduce this proportion. State pension is no less complicated than it was before, however, and the 'value proposition' the Pension Credit poses for many people on low-to-medium earnings has not altered. There is a material risk that quasi-compulsory savings will not deliver real returns after adjusting for the loss of mean-tested benefits. This seems a poor result for a pensions reform process that began in earnest with a White Paper entitled *Simplicity, security and choice: Working and saving for retirement* (published by the Department for Work and Pensions in 2002), and it demonstrates the dilemmas facing many high-income democracies that struggle to balance a number of conflicting policy objectives. Simultaneously, there is democratic pressure to provide an income in retirement to those who have no pension provision. If this income is universal and at a high level then it leads to a higher, and possibly unsustainable, tax burden. If the income is provided on a means-tested basis, then it leads to disincentives to save. The more specific policies are designed to overcome both these objections, the more complex the whole system of retirement income provision becomes, without necessarily adequately achieving any of the desired objectives. A relatively simple problem of shifting consumption across lifetimes has become mired in complexity.

References

Booth, P. M. and D. R. Cooper (2005), *The Way out of the Pensions Quagmire*, Research Monograph 60, London: Institute of Economic Affairs, London.

De Serres, A. and F. Pelgrin (2003), 'The decline in private saving rates in the 1990s in OECD countries', *Economic Studies*, 36, available online at www.oecd.org/dataoecd/22/15/33638821. pdf.

Steventon, A., C. Sanches and C. Curry (2007), 'Increasing the value of saving in Personal Accounts: taking small pension pots as lump sums', PPI Working Paper no. 58.

Turner, A. (2006), 'Pensions challenges in an aging world', *Finance and Development*, 43(3), available online at www.imf.org/external/pubs/ft/fandd/2006/09/index.htm.

6 LONG LIVE LONGEVITY
Alan Pickering

Increased longevity is perhaps the most valuable gift with which any of us could be blessed. This is certainly the case for people who are enjoying good health and living in developed economies. Sadly, the picture is much more mixed in other parts of the world. While lifestyle, frame of mind and environment mean that some people who are materially poor are living longer than their more affluent peers elsewhere, life expectancy is in retreat in some territories owing to the scourge of HIV. The productive heart is being ripped out of some nations with economic consequences that are both deep-seated and long-lasting.

In the UK, life expectancy is increasing faster than either the medics or the statisticians anticipated. Again, the blessing is by no means even-handed in its application. Life expectancy is increasing, however, in most socio-economic groups and in most parts of the country. But the pace of change varies according to a number of factors, such as occupation, location and size of pension. Even in the UK, however, there are groups in our society whose life expectancy looks like being even shorter than that of their parents and, in some cases, grandparents. Lifestyle, often self-inflicted, has a major influence, since many of those occupations that were traditionally associated with premature death are no longer located in the UK.

Much of the media and political commentary suggests that

the phenomenon of increased longevity is a bad news story. While increased longevity presents us with new challenges, such challenges are surely much more benign than those faced by our contemporaries in other parts of the world where life expectancy is in retreat. Nevertheless, increased longevity in high-income countries gives rise to policy challenges.

One-dimensional response

In the years immediately following World War II, old age and absolute poverty were synonymous. Indeed, very few people above pension age were comfortably off and, by and large, the longer people lived, the poorer they became. Today, the picture is much more complicated. There is a significant proportion of our retired population that has a higher standard of living than that enjoyed by millions of working-age people. Few generalisations can still be made, although absolute poverty is most prevalent among older pensioners. For this, there are many reasons, perhaps the most significant being the poor economic status of elderly women, reflecting either their widowed status or their lower incomes, and hence lower savings opportunities, while in employment during earlier decades. Indeed, female employment was often the exception rather than the rule in parts of our society during certain phases of the twentieth century. Those women who were in work often lost their jobs first as a result of the 'last in first out' principle during downturns.

Because increased longevity exacerbates diminishing purchasing power in retirement, it has traditionally been assumed that the single, if not simple, answer has been to increase the proportions of employment-generated incomes that are saved by today's workers in order to increase their affluence when they become tomorrow's pensioners. Such a premise is not merely simple but simplistic. Increased savings alone cannot bridge the retirement poverty gap. Those who could afford to save more were often already saving enough. Those who received modest incomes found it impossible to make ends meet in the short term. For them, clarion calls to save more had a hollow ring. To demonstrate how difficult it is for interventionist policymakers, however, there are many folk on low incomes who are able to behave thriftily despite, and on occasions because of, their straitened circumstances.

The challenge of longevity has required a holistic approach to policymaking which the British-style government frustrates rather than facilitates. Policy is simultaneously piecemeal, prescriptive and event-driven. None of these characteristics makes for sensible policy proposals in the face of rapidly improving longevity.

That's not the way to do it

When Labour came to power in 1964, it did so on the basis of a detailed manifesto. While the National Plan to which this manifesto gave rise may have been too much 'big government' for some, certainly policies had been worked out before the election and provided the new ministerial team with some benchmarks against which to measure actions taken when confronted by the unforeseen. During the 1970s and 1980s, Conservative governments came to power either with an overarching philosophy or a set of policies that had been reasonably thought through. Nowadays, the art of politics seems to be oriented around being successful in elections without spelling out either philosophy or policies in advance of those elections. This means that government is soon

driven by the evil trilogy of incoherence, prescriptive intervention and the knee-jerk reaction to the 'someone must do something about it' syndrome. The legislation that emerges is a recipe
for disaster as it is based on the fallacy that politicians and their
parliamentary draughtsmen know everything about everything.
This prescriptive approach inevitably produces bad laws which
have unintended consequences. The charge is not one of malevo-
lence but naivety.

Doing politics better

In a democracy, diverse opinions should be welcomed and not
shunned in the pursuit of consensus. Neither consensus nor
reliance on the technocrat is a desirable alternative to robust
debate, which is influenced by both philosophy and experience.
This combination should then be translated into a manifesto that
should be put before the electorate. Provided that all of those who
seek office are simultaneously honest with the electorate, those
who produce a clear outline of their intentions should never again
risk being accused of inadvertently writing the longest suicide note
in history. Perhaps one area of consensus to which all our parties
should aspire is the provision of honest 24/7 news media. Being
honest and adult with the electorate should surely pay dividends
both for our political class and, more importantly, for the society
they wish to serve.

Having secured office, an incoming government should buck
the recent trend by sponsoring legislation that is based on principle and not prescription. Prescriptive laws breed laziness and
blunt economic drive. Those who advocate non-prescriptive legislation are often accused of undermining the certainty that society

and various stakeholders need. If prescriptive laws produced such certainty, why is there so much interpretive litigation? Anyway, life is neither certain nor risk-free.

Sadly, some of those who are the most vociferous critics of non-prescriptive legislation are the professional classes on which our society depends in many ways and who receive a premium for their professionalism. If this premium is paid for the application of a tick-box mentality, it is a premium being paid on false pretences. Any professional worthy of the name should welcome an opportunity to apply professional judgement in their chosen field where Parliament has done no more than provide principles that are outcome-based and not process-driven. In such a world, there will still be some need for regulators since there is an asymmetry of knowledge between providers and consumers in many aspects of society. This asymmetry cannot be dealt with adequately by the simple application of the principle of *caveat emptor*. A proportionate, risk-based regulator with a light touch has a role in ensuring that those with power and knowledge treat customers fairly.

What has all this got to do with longevity?

The principles just enunciated are essential if we are to have a legislative framework within which society can come to terms with the implications of longevity. Different people will be affected in different ways. There will be a variety of solutions which individuals will need to apply on a mix and match basis. None of us know whether a super-drug or a super-bug will eventually reign supreme. All the government can do is create a framework within which employers and employees, commercial providers and their customers can arrive at solutions that are determined in the work-place or the marketplace rather than in Parliament.

There will not be a 'one size fits all' solution. We will not be able to foresee future events and must not allow such events to produce specific policy responses which are so often both counter-productive and produce outcomes that are worse than the disease. What is more, when it comes to longevity and pension planning, we must place a greater emphasis on wealth creation than on wealth distribution. So often, it is the latter which is debated ad nauseam. Unless we can create wealth in the first place, debating how it might be distributed is an inane academic pastime.

Three basic policies should be at the heart of our reaction to increased life expectancy. First, we need a labour market that is blind to age. Second, we need a basic state pension that deals with absolute poverty. Third, we need an environment where market savings solutions will be to the fore, with such a market being lightly regulated on the basis of outcomes and not processes. This policy framework may be more prescriptive than that proposed by other authors in this monograph. Nevertheless, it is qualitatively different from what exists at present. What I propose is a prin-cipled framework that gives individuals the opportunity to take action that is appropriate to their specific circumstances – circum-stances that cannot be foreseen in advance. That is quite different from a policy framework based on detailed planning to resolve particular and specific problems that governments perceive as important.

Labour market reform

The job-for-life culture never existed to the extent that many might suggest. Many people in the private sector often changed jobs either of their own volition or as a result of economic circumstances. To the extent that we do have greater job mobility today than we did in the past, the change may be one of degree rather than one of principle. Additionally, people may be changing jobs at different ages than in earlier decades.

Perhaps the biggest change in our labour market is not the rate of employee turnover but employer turnover. While individual longevity may be increasing, corporate longevity may be declining quite rapidly. While the transient nature of corporate presence may be a macroeconomic benefit, it does have certain microeconomic consequences.

We need a labour market that is blind to age so that workers of all ages can maintain gainful employment. This is the most significant contribution to the defusing of the demographic time bomb. If workers are to remain employable, it is not just lifelong earning that must be on offer but lifelong learning too. Whether people work for a single employer or a multiplicity of firms on a concurrent or consecutive basis, we need to ensure that top-up training is readily available. While there may be a place for legislation that outlaws the worst aspects of ageism, it is hearts and minds which we must win. Workers who have been made redundant several times must not be allowed to lose self-esteem. Retraining is essential before the rot of desolation sets in. Employers must play their part in helping indigenous older workers refine their skills even when it may be much easier to employ overqualified young immigrants for whom attitude is not a problem but an asset.

This may require limited intervention, but the principal reform will involve older workers being allowed to mix and match work and retirement pay and pension as never before: pensions, tax, labour-market and social-security regulations must not inhibit this. If young people can respond to an unexpected financial crisis by taking on extra work, why should pensioners not expect to take advantage of similar opportunities if they want to supplement their pension? It should be possible for pensioners to dip in and out of the labour market for as long as they are able and for as long as they have a need.

Such a modern and flexible approach to employment may cause us to revisit our attitude to volunteering. There will always be a role for volunteers. These days, however, when reference is made to getting work done in the voluntary sector, it often suggests that the work can be done on the cheap or for nothing. If our new ageless approach to employment is to succeed, structured work must remain an economic activity. If those who undertake this work do not need the money, let them give it away. If they give away their labour, they will make it even more difficult for marginal employees to gain the work they need if our economy and theirs is to prosper.

State pension system

I would suggest that there is not an efficient market solution to dealing with absolute poverty in old age. This is an area where the taxpayer collectively can provide a foundation upon which all else can be built. I do not see any need either for state pension provision to be funded. If funding of a state pension system were to lead to assets that were state directed or state controlled then the assets in which a funded state scheme invests might not be used as wisely as would be the case if markets and not politicians were responsible for capital allocation.

The UK state pension system provides one of the lowest levels of income replacement in the world. For this, we should not be praised for prudence but criticised for inefficiency. There is a gap of more than £30 per week between the level of the Basic State Pension and the amount which Parliament determines is a minimum subsistence level in retirement. Millions of workers cannot afford to close this gap through saving while in employment. For large proportions of our population it does not, therefore, pay to save given the level of taxes and the withdrawal of means-tested benefits that result from their saving. This is not healthy. What is more, the fact that workplace or market-place pensions are used to fill the state poverty gap means that these private arrangements are regulated as if they were part of the welfare state. This over-regulation and consequent undue prescription have resulted in the demise of much that was good about our pension system.

Parliament should be free, from time to time, to define what is meant by 'old age' and 'absolute poverty' when it comes to the state pension age and the state pension level. While the present government is moving in the right direction, it is not being bold enough in either case. We need a much bigger basic state pension if our economy is to work efficiently. For such a state pension to be affordable, state pension age will need to increase more rapidly than is currently being proposed. If a rapid increase in state pension means that some socio-economic groups miss out on some state pension, the loss of such pension is nothing when compared with the premature loss of life. For these groups, it is increased life expectancy and not the early payment of a state pension which should be a policy priority.

Private saving for retirement

Neither tax policy nor social policy have been particularly helpful in creating an environment in which employers and employees, savings institutions and their customers can plan sensibly for those periods when income from savings rather than from employment will shoulder the burden of individual economic sustainability. While tax policy has traditionally helped defer the payment of tax until the pension income is drawn down, the associated regime has been unduly restrictive. It assumed that people joined a pension scheme to save tax rather than to save for retirement, and the tax authorities develop regulations to try to stop this. As a consequence, there are perverse effects, particularly on lower-paid people who missed out when tax incentives were offered on a 'use it or lose it' basis associated with individual tax years. What is more, the use of tax advantages to incentivise the take-up of particular government savings initiatives has complicated the environment and increased the extent to which it was tax incentives and not the suitability of a particular savings vehicle which influenced take-up. Many tax-favoured savings schemes have been regressive in nature. Those who could save most money often saved most tax as well.

Fortunately, the present tax regime in the UK is much more sensible. Limits on pension saving are principally lifetime limits rather than annual limits. What is more, the limits are set so high as to have little or no effect on the vast majority of workers, who can now save for retirement what they want, when they want and how they want.

Social policy is, to some extent, moving in the opposite direction. On the one hand, there is a realisation that the layer-cake approach to prescriptive imposition on those employers who voluntarily signed up to risk-sharing pensions has diminished the extent to which employers are any longer willing to share such risks.[1] Employers are being asked to honour promises to which they never voluntarily signed up. Pensions paid under private company arrangements were determined in Parliament and not in the workplace. To its credit, government is at long last revisiting this counterproductive feature of social policy. At the same time, however, it is proposing to introduce so-called Personal Accounts, which will be a state-sponsored defined-contribution pension plan that will operate from 2012. Through the principle of auto-enrolment, the default position for most workers taking up employment after 2012 will be the inclusion in government-sponsored Personal Accounts into which employers will be obliged to contribute unless their employees opt out or unless the employer provides an alternative pension vehicle which meets certain minimum standards.

Here is not the place to describe in detail Personal Accounts nor highlight their flaws. It is sufficient here to point out the contradiction between tax and social policy. Tax policy recognises that saving through a pension may not be a sensible default option for every worker at every stage in his or her career. Social policy, through the manifestation of personal accounts, is a throwback to the 'one size fits all, use it or lose it' approach to the pensions tax framework, which has been so clearly discredited.

What we need is an environment in which employers and employees can freely determine what sort of remuneration package makes sense. It is at the level of the workplace that

---

1   Specifically, regulations that have been developed ostensibly to reduce the risk faced by members of defined-benefit schemes have led to the demise of these schemes which, in turn, has required individuals to use more risky pensions vehicles.

decisions should be taken on the extent to which there should be a pension element within that remuneration package. If such a pension element includes employer risk-sharing, this risk-sharing should be rewarded by society and not penalised through the government imposition of further features and further guarantees, which, although technical in appearance, are financially burdensome in nature.

The market for savings products should not be distorted by tax incentives either. Savings products should sell on their merits. Inefficiencies should not be masked by tax privileges.

In the past, when it came to savings and pensions, the workplace and marketplace were in competition. Such competition was corrosive. In future, the workplace should increasingly be the marketplace for savings opportunities of all forms. In this way, we can blend individual need with the economies of scale. Such scale can be increased by acknowledging that the individual needs of similar groups of workers may be similar but not necessarily identical.

Financial literacy is the key

In addition to providing work for older workers and savings opportunities for workers of all ages, the workplace will be an ideal environment in which to increase financial literacy. We do not need to create a population that has certificates in do-it-yourself personal finance. We do need, however, a population that understands when it makes sense to save, when to borrow and when to invest. Furthermore, such a holistic approach should include an appreciation of when working longer might be more attractive than saving more.

None of this is rocket science. We need to restore the politicians' faith in the electorate and the electorate's trust in politicians. The relationship between politician and electorate should then be governed by principle-based legislation implemented by professionals who have respect for their profession and self-confidence in their ability to ply their trade without being told what to do. In such a world, regulators would have a light-touch role to ensure that customers are treated fairly in those aspects of the marketplace where there is an inevitable asymmetry of knowledge. When it comes to finance, however, this asymmetry can be ameliorated if not eradicated by supplementing the inherent virtue of thrift with some contemporary knowledge of how this principle might be applied. Above all, the debate about pensions and longevity should focus first on wealth-creating opportunities and only then on wealth distribution. We cannot distribute what we have not first created. Remember, when we save, we are not freezing loaves of bread but staking a claim on the wealth that will be created by future generations of workers, some of whom may not yet be born.

PART TWO – PENSIONS AND PUBLIC POLICY IN MIDDLE-INCOME COUNTRIES AND EMERGING ECONOMIES

7 THE DETERMINANTS OF REFORM SUCCESS – AND FAILURE – IN EMERGING ECONOMIES

Eugen Iulian Mihaita

Introduction

There is a growing literature on the political economy of pension reform and on the appropriate timing, speed and tactical sequencing of fundamental reforms (Tommasi and Velasco, 1995; Bönker, 2002) but there is still little literature focused on the political economy of pension reform. James and Brooks (2001), Müller (1999, 2001), Orenstein (2000) and Pierson (1999) are the main contributors on this subject.

The political economy of pensions is of utmost interest given the multitude of actors involved, such as pensioners, governments, pension institutions (both public and private), trade unions and employers' associations. The number of interests directly affected makes the reform of old-age security a sensitive matter. As a result, pension systems have long been difficult to reform, even if nowadays old-age security is considered a top priority in most countries of the world.

Pension reform models and the importance of international financial institutions

While many developed OECD countries show reluctance to reform pensions radically, an increasing number of Latin American and central and eastern European countries (CEECs) have opted for full or partial privatisation of their pension systems. This is truly a remarkable change. It not only reflects a fundamental shift from collective inter-generational old-age support (the pay-as-you-go (PAYGO) inter-generational contract) to individual responsibility, but also a change in the social contract, as the state retreats and promotes the market as the main provider of retirement benefits.

In 1981, under the military dictatorship of General Pinochet, Chile was the first country in the world to attempt to defuse the fiscal time bomb represented by the government-run PAYGO pension system. At the end of 2004, almost all qualifying Chilean workers had their own pension saving accounts affiliated to the new private pension funds, whose total assets had grown to over $60 billion (63 per cent of GDP), at an average annual rate of return of approximately 8.9 per cent per year (FIAP, 2006). Pension reform has helped the introduction of further structural reform in Chile, reinforced political stability and partially depoliticised the economy (Devesa-Carpio and Vidal-Meliá, 2002). The new fully funded private system has been implemented in the neoclassical belief that it will increase long-term national saving and help deepen capital markets, thus spurring long-term growth and decreasing the role of government and of public spending. So far, Chile has been one of the fastest-growing economies in Latin America.

Spurred by its success, variations of the Chilean reform have been introduced in Peru, Argentina, Colombia, Uruguay and other Latin American countries (see Table 10). The main common feature present in all these subsequent reforms is the mandatory private pension fund pillar, which is either competing with, substituting for or complementing the public PAYGO pillar.

Depending on this relation, the new pension systems have been labelled 'parallel or selective', 'substitutive private' and 'mixed' (Mesa-Lago, 1997).

Table 10 **Latin American pension reforms**

Country	The public pillar	The private pillar introduced	Reform type
Chile	Phased out	1981	Substitutive
Peru	Traditional PAYGO, alternative	1993	Parallel
Argentina	Traditional PAYGO	1994	Mixed
Colombia	Traditional PAYGO, alternative	1994	Parallel
Uruguay	Traditional PAYGO	1996	Mixed
Bolivia	Closed down	1997	Substitutive
Mexico	Closed down	1997	Substitutive
El Salvador	Phased out	1998	Substitutive
Costa Rica	Traditional PAYGO	2001	Mixed

A key example of reforming to a mixed system has been that of Argentina, which combined a thorough reform of the public PAYGO scheme with the introduction of private pension fund administrators (AFJPs), keeping all the workers in the mandatory public scheme but allowing them to redirect part of their pension contributions to one of the AFJPs and the private pillar. The most important differences from the Chilean model are the following: the comparatively slow building up of the mandatory private pension fund pillar, the impossibility of completely opting out of the public pension pillar, the maintenance of the employers' contribution to co-finance the public pillar and the replacement of interest-bearing recognition bonds with a compensatory pension arrangement to deal with acquired pension entitlements (Arenas de Mesa and Bertranou, 1997).

The significance of the Chilean case resides not only in developing a substantially new concept for reform but also in putting a long-existing liberal reform theory into practice and establishing a precedent. The Chilean model gained international prominence when the World Bank published *Averting the Old-Age Crisis* (1994), a report that tried to establish the guiding criteria for the World Bank policy on pensions. Besides stirring international public debate on the subject of pensions, it has marked the fall from grace of the International Labour Organisation (ILO) social security model, the rise to dominance of private pension provision, and has pushed the World Bank to the forefront of the pension policy arena. Since then, the World Bank has been actively involved in pension privatisation programmes throughout the world, starting with Latin America and eastern Europe. Drawing heavily on the Chilean and Argentinian precedents, the World Bank developed and now recommends its own version of the mixed system – the 'multi-pillar' model.

It can be argued that pension reforms in the CEECs gained focus only after the Latin American pension reforms became well known globally – direct diffusion effects from Latin America into CEE were weak in the beginning. The local debates taking place in CEECs had been triggered by forecasts of population ageing and the wave of pension reforms in Latin America, and, consequently, reflected the international controversy over pensions. Even if it cannot be entirely said that the CEECs have had a positive attitude towards privatisation, at least they have always shown distrust in the public sector – a legacy of their communist past which has helped privatisation in general (Cangiano et al., 1998). Before the international financial institutions took an interest in the Chilean model, however, and started putting it on the agenda of international pension discourse (through publications and conferences sponsored by the World Bank, the IMF, etc.), the CEECs were looking to the EU for models. They were not looking at Latin America, which was seen as being a less-developed region and an improbable ground for generating adequate models. Müller (2001) argues that, preoccupied with the concerns of EU accession, CEECs were slow to recognise the lack of an EU mainstream pension model. Given the heterogeneity in old-age provision in the EU, the accession negotiations contained nothing on reform models. In fact, administrative reform as a whole was not required by the *acquis communautaire*, everything being left for decision at member-state level. As a consequence, the post-enlargement EU pension landscape is even more diverse than the pre-enlargement landscape.

The international financial institutions[1] have been the most influential factor in the privatisation of pension systems. Their involvement in both regions' privatisation efforts has been extensive, through all forms of technical assistance, financial assistance and involvement of consultants in national policy offices. For Latin American and CEE governments, on the domestic front, this support has been instrumental in overcoming opposition to privatisation, while on the international scene it signalled the governments' commitment to openness and neoliberal reform (Kay, 2000).

---

1   In Latin American countries like Argentina, Colombia, Peru and Uruguay, pension privatisation campaigns mainly had the support of the World Bank and the Inter-American Development Bank (IDB), while in CEE support came from the World Bank and the IMF (Kay, 2000; Orenstein, 2000).

Policy legacies in the two regions

Although inferences from the two groups of countries are not a novelty, and despite the large number of papers dealing with the Latin American pension reform experiences, little literature is to be found on the subject of area-specific comparisons.[2] It is clear from Tables 11 and 12 that the social security systems of the Latin American front-runners of pension reform – i.e. Chile, Argentina and Uruguay – had more features in common with the high-income OECD and eastern European countries than with other Latin American countries: wide coverage (Table 11), high levels of public spending on pensions (Table 11) and alarmingly high dependency rates (Table 12).

The similar financial burdens faced by countries in the two regions are not coincidental. First, pension systems in both regions are of Bismarckian tradition,[3] with similarly high contribution rates and benefit levels. Second, Table 11 shows similarly large discrepancies between the system and demographic old-age dependency ratios in the Latin American pension reformers and all the CEECs,[4] which are caused by identical factors – low

2   Thus, Müller (2001) can be singled out as particularly focused on old-age security reform comparisons between the two regions.

3   The first mandatory scheme of social insurance on a national scale was initiated in Germany by the chancellor at the time, Otto von Bismarck, who introduced successively sickness insurance (1883), accident insurance (1884) and old-age and invalidity pensions (1889). The schemes were focused on employees, were financed by mandatory contributions, and pension benefits were linked to individual contribution and earnings history. They were publicly managed but allowed for the involvement of trade unions and employers' associations (tripartite). By 1920, the model had become the main pension provision scheme throughout Europe. Between 1920 and 1930, comprehensive social insurance schemes had also been adopted in Latin American countries – Argentina (1921), Uruguay (1922), Chile (1925), etc.

4   Kazakhstan is included as a former Soviet Union country.

Table 11 **Coverage of pensions and pension-related public expenditure as a percentage of GDP, mid-1990s**

Country	Contributors/ labour force (%)	Contributors/ working age population (%)	Pension spending/ GDP (%)
Uruguay	82	78	15
Chile	70	43	5.8*
Argentina	53	39	6.2
Costa Rica	47	35	3.8
Colombia	33	27	1.1
Mexico	30	31	0.4
El Salvador	26.2	25	1.3
Peru	20	16	1.2
Bolivia	11.7	9.4	2.5
Slovenia	86	68.7	13.6
Czech Rep.	85	67.2	9
Hungary	77	65	9.7
Estonia	76	67	7
Slovakia	73	72	9.1
Poland	68	64	14.4
Croatia	66	57	11.6
Bulgaria	64	63	7.3
Latvia	60.5	52.3	10.2
Romania	55	48	5.1
Kazakhstan	51	44	5
High OECD	90.4	80.2	10

Sources: Palacios and Pallares-Miralles (2000) and author's calculations
*Chile's spending on pensions peaked at 10 per cent in 1984 (Kay, 2000)

Table 12 **Dependency ratios, mid-1990s (percentages)**

Country	Pensioners/ contributors (System ratio)	Population 60+/ population 20–59 (Dependency ratio)	Pensioners/ population 60+	Pensioners/ total population
Uruguay	70	34.5	151.8	25.8
Argentina	64	27	104.6	13.8
Bolivia	40	16.2	32.8	2
Peru	31	14.3	34	2.3
Chile	24.3	17.5	108.2	10.4
Costa Rica	14	14.5	35.9	2.5
Mexico	12.5	12.9	26.1	1.6
Colombia	11	16.1	19.3	1.5
El Salvador	8.6	14.3	14.3	0.9
Bulgaria	81	38.5	133.5	27.5
Hungary	78.1	35.7	142.2	27.5
Lithuania	69.2	32.3	129.4	22.5
Kazakhstan	66	18.9	164.3	16
Latvia	65.9	34.5	134.3	25
Croatia	61.7	37.6	90.1	19
Estonia	60	33.3	137.7	25
Slovenia	58.9	31.3	127	22.2
Romania	58.3	32.3	88	15.1
Slovakia	57	27.8	146.8	22
Poland	53.7	29.4	116.1	18.2
Czech Rep.	53	31.3	139.8	24.2
Russia Fed.	–	30.3	151.1	25.1
High OECD	46.77	34.44	102.49	19.74

Sources: Palacios and Pallares-Miralles (2000) and author's calculations

retirement ages, loose early retirement and disability provisions and weak administrative capacity. Hence, they shared the same policy legacies: high implicit debt, decreasing contributor base, many privileged groups and extensive evasion. Additionally, many countries in both regions suffered from poor indexation and had poorly developed and regulated capital markets (Mihaita, 2006).

It is these policy legacies which have proven pivotal in the outcome of the pension privatisation efforts. The large implicit pension debt helped bring radical pension reform to the top of the political agenda, but, at the same time, it constrained the degree of funding and privatisation achieved as the large transition costs implied were strongly resisted by bureaucrats and pensioners (James and Brooks, 2001). In Argentina and Uruguay, where, as in most CEECs, the coverage has been very high, the reform ended up as a mixed type. On the contrary, in Bolivia and El Salvador the implicit debt was much smaller and substitutive pension reform was feasible. While in Latin America all three types of reform have been followed (substitutive, parallel and mixed), in central and eastern Europe the multi-pillar model has been the strategy of choice (see Table 13).

Table 13 **The central and eastern European pension reforms**

	Mandatory public pillar	The private pillar	Reform type
Kazakhstan	Phased out	1997	Substitutive
Hungary	Traditional PAYGO	1998	Mixed
Poland	Notional defined contributions	1999	Mixed
Bulgaria	Traditional PAYGO	2000	Mixed
Latvia	Notional defined contributions	2000	Mixed
Lithuania	Traditional PAYGO	2002	Mixed
Romania	Traditional PAYGO	2004	Mixed

Political economy lessons

Old-age pension systems are a strong case of institutional sticki-ness in that they have always displayed strong path-dependency effects, especially in relation to PAYGO schemes.[5] PAYGO systems build long-term expectations and, when extensive and matured, they are highly resistant to radical reform. Mature PAYGO systems with high implicit debts involve large populations of pensioners and older workers with generous rights acquired. These groups resist reform if they fear that their pension promises would not be kept under the new system. Further, mature PAYGO systems with large implicit debts also imply path dependencies in entrenched governmental bureaucracy. The entrenched bureau-cracy that has accumulated power and employs a large number of workers, and unions, has participated in the running of the old system and would see its role diminished after the reform (James and Brooks, 2001). Even when undergoing moderate reforms (incremental cutbacks and parametric adjustments), pensions are framed by past commitments and specific institutional arrange-ments (Müller, 1999; Pierson, 1999). Thus, in many developed and developing countries, a radical and quick change towards fully funded systems is not considered a serious option because of transition costs and the political prospect of many 'losers' for many years to come.

As a result, many political scientists and economists explain the feasibility of radical reform on the basis of the presence of strong, authoritarian regimes and vigorous political leaders. Chile and Kazakhstan passed substitutive pension reforms, the first

---

5   Multiple veto points and 'path-dependent' processes that lead the reform agenda
     towards incremental or moderate adjustments to the existing arrangements
     (Pierson, 1999).

because of its dictatorial regime and the second because of its presidential system, which dismissed the parliament as an institutional veto actor. Argentina was the first country to implement fundamental reform through the democratic process (Vittas, 1997) and the collapse of its old pension system served as a warning against procrastinating reform – at the time of reform, the system was bankrupt,[6] pensioners being paid only fractions of their entitlements (Quiesser, 1999).

James and Brooks (2001) argue that the inclusion of a broad range of interests in the reform process leads to less radical pension reforms owing to unstable government coalitions, credibility problems and unreliable 'veto partners'. In Argentina[7] and Uruguay, as in Hungary, Poland and Romania, the result was the adoption of mixed reforms as these countries have parliamentary democracies in which governments are formed by coalitions, giving partisan actors and civil society interest groups a much greater role in policy outcomes. Among the interest groups that opposed pension system privatisation were trade unions, pensioners' associations and privileged beneficiaries of the pensions system. In Mexico, a Chilean-style reform was annulled by public protest and strikes after the government failed to consult public sector unions. In order to implement a national pension reform, Mexico had to exempt all public sector workers (ibid.). In Uruguay, an alliance between a left-wing political coalition, labour unions and pensioners managed to defeat government efforts to reform for ten years – between 1984 and 1994 (Kay, 2000). In

6   Between 1989 and 1994, hundreds of thousands of workers sued the government in order to recoup previously made benefit cuts and won. According to Kay (2000), payouts were often 70–82 per cent of a worker's former salary.

7   Argentina ended up with a mixed type of reform, even though it was aiming to replicate the Chilean model (Tommasi et al., 1999; Vittas, 1997).

Argentina, Hungary and Poland, trade unions had strong ties with the governing parties, which proved ambivalent in terms of reform. On the one hand, these ties were helpful in softening opposition; on the other, they ensured the political presence of the trade unions and forced pension reformers to negotiate and make concessions.[8] In Romania, however, trade unions have played only a minor role – mostly supporting the reform and only occasionally intervening in order to obtain positions in the monitoring of the new system.

The tremendous resilience shown towards pension reform is also evident in the electoral incentives associated with pension programmes. In democracies, voters are crucial players. Huge segments of electorates rely on the state for their income and pensioners are probably the largest single-issue constituency, a highly concentrated interest group whose power increases as the population ageing process progresses. Also, many other age groups sympathise with the elderly, who have certain expectations regarding their own benefits or feel that reform may indirectly negatively affect them. Besides, voters present a 'negativity bias', more likely to react strongly against potential losses than support potential gains. Thus, the political risks associated with pension reform are enormous, as the voters rebel against unpopular initiatives.

Regarding winning over the support of existing pensioners and older workers, it can be observed that, in all the reform cases, efforts have been made to assure them of secure and improved pension rights and to exempt them from the new systems. Financing the transition deficit at least partially with debt has also

8   Among these concessions was allowing trade unions to own pension funds (James and Brooks, 2001).

helped in neutralising their opposition (for most of the existing pensioners, tax financing would have no effect either). Also, given that the benefits of the radical reform are subject to uncertainty and would be observable only in the long run, the policymakers publicised them more heavily to the younger generations – the countries that have privatised their systems to a larger extent had a younger population (James and Brooks, 2001).

The importance of political leadership must also be stressed: the need for courageous, committed individuals who succeed in expressing a coherent neoliberal vision on pension reform is essential (Müller, 2001). Carlos Menem, Dominico Cavallo (Argentina), Sanchez de Lozada (Bolivia), Lajos Bokros (Hungary) and Andrzej Baczkowski (Poland) are personalities without whom fundamental reform packages would have been impossible to push through.[9] For example, in Romania the lack of strong leadership (and parliamentary debate) caused a four-year delay in the adoption of private pensions.[10]

Related is the issue of the tactical packaging of reforms – Schmähl and Horstmann (2002) mention the 'reform package illusion', where series of necessary but non-radical reform steps have been bundled together under the label of 'fundamental

9   Interestingly, in these four countries the governing parties that implemented the reforms had antecedents of left-wing or populist actions. Also, Rocha and Vittas (1999) point out that in Hungary the centre-left-leaning coalition government that had designed and implemented the pension reform was succeeded in 1998 by a centre-right-leaning coalition that demonstrated little support for the reform – evident in its efforts to maintain the initial low contribution rate to the private pillar instead of raising it.

10 Private pension funds were rushed through as a government ordinance by the centre-right coalition government at the end of its mandate in 2000. After the elections, the new centre-left government swiftly annulled all previous private pensions initiatives and revisited them only in 2004, at the end of their mandate.

reform', which has been more easily accepted, while Müller (2001) underlines the idea that the political costs of reform can be lowered by increasing its complexity. Both country groups resorted to 'bundling up' unavoidable and politically sensitive reforms to the PAYGO pillar with the very visible introduction of individual pension fund accounts. In this way, reformers highlighted the gains and shaded the envisaged cutbacks. A similar technique was used in Argentina – only it was used the other way around. Opposition against radical pension reform was softened by keeping the first pillar as a public PAYGO scheme, the embodiment of such concepts as solidarity and redistribution, which offered a universal basic pension of about 30 per cent of the average covered wage, thus helping to enhance the social acceptance of radical pension reform (Vittas, 1997). Maintaining large parts of their old PAYGO system also helped to appease opponents of pension reform such as the bureaucrats and unions involved in running the old system (James, 1997). The World Bank multi-pillar model's public–private mix with a risk diversification feature made it easier to 'sell' the transition problem to interest groups (Disney et al., 1999).

In these ways, in most Latin American and CEE economies the drawbacks related to pension privatisation (such as the major issue of transition costs, the effects of portfolio restrictions, etc.) were successfully shielded from public debate (Müller, 2001). Thus, public faith in the strengths and advantages of the new system may be shaken when ignored financial burdens start showing. Various government guarantees (minimum rates of return specified, fluctuation reserves, state benefits, etc.) have, however, been employed to allay workers' fears of downside investment risk in the fully funded pillars.

Provisional assessment of reforms

An accurate evaluation of the effects of the pension reforms will be possible only once the new systems have matured. So, at least until a generation has passed, only provisional inferences can be made. So far, as Table 14 shows, using GNP growth as a proxy for the returns under a PAYGO system, it seems that the private pension funds have outperformed this measure.

Table 14 **Comparative performance of the fully funded schemes**

Country	Real historic rate of return (until Dec. 2000), %	Annual growth of GNP per capita (1989–99), %
Argentina	11.11	4.1
Bolivia	11.10	1.8
Chile	10.90	6.0
Colombia	7.84	1.6
El Salvador	12.88	2.9
Mexico	9.47	1.1
Peru	5.30	3.3
Uruguay	9.13	3.4

Source: Devesa-Carpio and Vidal-Meliá (2002)

The picture becomes less clear, however, when administration costs and transition costs are taken into consideration. In a recent study on the outcomes of pension reform in Latin America, Mesa-Lago (2006) concludes that increasing the employees' share of the (now higher) contributions, and rising administration costs and premiums, have contributed to the continued growth of the informal sector and have created disincentives for compliance among the self-employed. As a result, on average coverage has suffered. While Devesa-Carpio and Vidal-Meliá (2002) argue that, in Chile, current and forecasted pensions have high replacement rates, with benefits around 50 per cent higher than under the old system, Mesa-Lago (2006) does not find sufficient evidence to generalise this outcome.

Full criticism of pension reforms is beyond the scope of this chapter. In the author's opinion, however, many failings have to do with the half-measure changes adopted as part of 'moderate' reforms. There are restrictions imposed on individual pension fund choice, investment preference and the pension account decumulation. There are confining regulations on pension fund portfolio investment, minimum profitability rules and strong moral hazard/asymmetric information effects.

Conclusions

Retirement pension schemes are (probably) the most complex and multidimensional social arrangements to be found in modern societies, influencing public finance, national saving, labour and capital markets. Many Latin American and CEE economies have required rapid and comprehensive restructuring of their pension systems for both macro- and microeconomic reasons. For them, social security reform, economic restructuring and economic growth options have been closely linked.

There are many parallels between the Latin American and CEE groups of countries: large amounts of state control, poorly developed financial markets, and the Bismarckian tradition of social insurance with high benefit levels and high contribution rates, low retirement ages, loose early retirement and disability provisions and extensive evasion. The combined analysis of the two groups of countries confirms the postulates of the political economy of pension reform, highlighting the importance of the international financial institutions, leadership and authority in combating the moderating influences of policy legacies, institutional stickiness and deliberative and democratic decision-making forums.

References

Arenas de Mesa, A. and F. Bertranou (1997), 'Learning from social security reforms: two different cases, Chile and Argentina', *World Development*, 25(3): 329–48.

Bönker, F. (2002), *The Political Economy of Fiscal Reform in Eastern Europe*, Cheltenham: Edward Elgar.

Cangiano, M., C. Cottarelli and L. Cubeddu (1998), 'Pension developments and reforms in transition economies', IMF Working Paper no. 98/151, Washington, DC: International Monetary Fund.

Devesa-Carpio, J. E. and C. Vidal-Meliá (2002), 'The reformed pension systems in Latin America', Social Protection Discussion Paper Series no. 0209, Washington, DC: Social Protection Unit, Human Development Network, World Bank.

Disney, R., R. Palacios and E. Whitehouse (1999), 'Individual choice of pension arrangement as a pension reform strategy', Institute for Fiscal Studies Working Paper Series no. W99/18, London: Institute for Fiscal Studies.

FIAP (Federación Internacional de Administradoras de Fondos de Pensiones) (2006), *Statistics Section*, available online at www.fiap.cl, accessed May 2007.

James, E. (1997), 'New systems for old age security – theory, practice, and empirical evidence', Policy Research Working Paper no. 1766, Washington, DC: World Bank.

James, E. and S. Brooks (2001), 'The political economy of

structural pension reform', in R. Holzmann and J. Stiglitz (eds), *New Ideas about Old Age Security*, Washington, DC: World Bank.

Kay, S. J. (2000), 'Recent changes in Latin American welfare states: is there social dumping?', *Journal of European Social Policy*, 10(2): 185–203.

Kritzer, B. E. (2000), 'Social security privatization in Latin America', *Social Security Bulletin*, 63(2).

Mesa-Lago, C. (1997), 'Social welfare reform in the context of economic-political liberalization: Latin American cases', *World Development*, 4: 497–517.

Mesa-Lago, C. (2006), 'Private and public pension systems compared: an evaluation of the Latin American experience', *Review of Political Economy*, 18(3): 317–34.

Mihaita, E. I. (2006), *Pension Reform in Central and Eastern Europe: Implications and Simulations for Romania*, Unpublished PhD thesis, Nottingham Trent University.

Müller, K. (1999), *The Political Economy of Pension Reform in Central-Eastern Europe*, Cheltenham: Edward Elgar.

Müller, K. (2001), 'The making of pension privatisation: Latin American and East European cases', Paper presented at the 'Political Economy of Pension Reform' workshop, World Bank and International Institute for Applied Systems Analysis (IIASA), Laxenburg, Austria, 5 April.

Orenstein, M. A. (2000), 'How politics and institutions affect pension reform in three postcommunist countries', Policy Research Working Paper no. 2310, Washington, DC: World Bank.

Palacios, R. and M. P. Pallares-Miralles (2000), 'International patterns of pension provision', Social Protection Discussion Paper no. 0009, Washington, DC: World Bank.

Pierson, P (1999), 'The politics of welfare state restructuring in affluent democracies', Wiener Inequality and Social Policy Seminar Series, Fall 1999, Multidisciplinary Program in Inequality and Social Policy, Harvard University.

Quiesser, M. (1999), 'Pension reform: lessons from Latin America', OECD Policy Brief no. 15, Paris: OECD.

Rocha, R. and D. Vittas (1999), 'Pension reform in Hungary: a preliminary assessment', Private and Financial Sectors Development Unit Working Paper no. 2631, Washington, DC: World Bank.

Schmähl, W. and S. Horstmann (2002), 'Transformation of pension schemes in comparative perspective', in W. Schmähl and S. Horstmann (eds), *Transformation of Pension Systems in Central and Eastern Europe*, Cheltenham: Edward Elgar.

Tommasi, M., J. Bambaci and T. Saront (1999), 'The political economy of economic reforms in Argentina', Centro de Estudios para el Desarrollo Institucional (CEDI) Working Paper no. 28, Fundación Gobierno y Sociedad & Universidad de San Andrés.

Tommasi, M. and A. Velasco (1995), 'Where are we in the political economy of reform?', Paper presented at Columbia University Conference on 'Economic Reform in Developing and Transitional Economies', New York, May.

Vittas, D. (1997), 'The Argentine pension reform and its relevance for eastern Europe', Policy Research Working Paper no. 1819, Washington, DC: World Development Sources, World Bank.

World Bank (1994), *Averting the Old-Age Crisis: Policies to Protect the Old and Promote Growth*, Washington, DC: World Bank.

8 TWO TIGERS: ONE FIT, ONE FAT CAT – PENSIONS IN HONG KONG AND SINGAPORE[1]

Oskari Juurikkala

Introduction

Two 'Asian tigers', Hong Kong and Singapore, are famous for their low taxes and business-friendly economic policies. One aspect of this is their policy towards old-age security: neither country has adopted publicly funded pay-as-you-go pensions, but old-age security is provided as a combination of traditional family support and personal savings. This makes Hong Kong and Singapore important case studies for other countries that are struggling to keep their pension systems afloat, or the emerging economies, which are hoping to respond to the challenge of rising life expectancies.

Yet the Hong Kong and Singapore models differ from each other drastically. One has chosen a path of greater freedom, while the other has covertly favoured heavy intervention. This chapter charts the past and present pension policies in these two countries and argues that Hong Kong is a good model for other countries to follow, whereas Singapore serves as a warning example of the pitfalls that should be avoided.

---

1   This chapter is included in Part Two, rather than in Part One, because it deals also with the development of pensions from an earlier stage in the economic development of Singapore and Hong Kong.

History and basic information

Hong Kong and Singapore are both unusual countries in their political histories and dynamisms. They were both at one point British colonies, which is reflected in their civil service, law and educational systems. They are both peculiarly small in size and poor in natural resources, which brought about opportunities as well as distinct challenges.

Many commentators in the 1960s considered these newly independent countries as hopeless cases, which were doomed to failure, but Hong Kong and Singapore unexpectedly raised their material living standards and lifted themselves out of the cycle of poverty. The main cause of that external success seems to have been their unabashedly free market policies: low taxes and open trade with the rest of the world.[2]

Family-based old-age security and provident funds

In terms of old-age security, the two countries share many features. Although in the Western world formal pension systems are the mainstay of old-age security, this is actually not the case in most parts of the world. Likewise, in Hong Kong and Singapore the role of traditional family support is strong and is almost as important as in present-day LDCs, where most people are outside any kind of formal pension arrangement.[3]

In Singapore, as many as 90 per cent of individuals over 60 years of age live with at least one of their children (Chan, 1997). There are many who do not have formal pension incomes,

---

2   See, for example, Simon (1996).
3   On informal old-age support, see generally World Bank (1994: 61–5) and Chapter 11 in this monograph.

especially older women. Although it is often claimed that the traditional family system is being eroded, Singaporean data does not support that conclusion. Even those who do participate in formal pension arrangements receive additional support from their relatives. The situation is similar in Hong Kong, where the great majority of those of working age support their parents financially. It is also common that parents support their children in return, and siblings support each other (Wilding, 1997).[4]

Yet the two countries differ markedly when it comes to their formal pension policies. Their historical conditions were similar, but they reacted in different ways. In the 1950s, both received the same orders from the British crown to establish formal pension arrangements known as 'provident funds'. This referred to an arrangement whereby workers in formal employment must contribute a fixed proportion of their salary into a government-operated savings fund. Savings accumulated in the provident fund are invested – mostly in government bonds – and individuals can access their savings when they reach a specific minimum age. A share of the funds can be used earlier for purchasing a house and other specified assets.

Officials in Singapore did as they were told, and established the Singapore Central Provident Fund. Those in Hong Kong did not obey – providentially so, as will be shown below.

Singapore's Central Provident Fund

Singapore established its Central Provident Fund (CPF) in 1955.[5]

---

4 Wilding (1997: 566) has data on the 1990 Social Indicators Study.
5 The CPF website is www.cpf.gov.sg/. Other sources relied on include Ng (2000), Ramesh (2000) and Asher (1995).

Participation was obligatory for most employees, excluding such groups as the self-employed and the higher-ranking civil servants, who still have a non-contributory pension scheme funded out of tax revenue. The fund originally played a modest role in helping workers to save: the minimum total contribution rate was just 10 per cent of salary (5 per cent from both employer and employee).

Soon after the independence of Singapore in 1965, the CPF gained a more prominent role in Singaporean politics and society. First, the government began to raise the minimum contribution rates every year, so that in 1984, when the high point was reached, most employees were required to contribute as much as 50 per cent of their net salary (25 per cent each from employee and employer) into the fund. These rates were subsequently reduced and at the time of writing they stand at 34.5 per cent (20 per cent from the employee and 14.5 per cent from the employer). The level of this compulsory savings rate explains why Singapore officially has the highest savings rate in the world.[6]

The CPF was not an ordinary savings vehicle, however. It was closely tied to politics. On the one hand, the government wished to raise the proportion of funds going into retirement financing. On the other hand, the government broadened the scope of the CPF; originally meant for old-age security, it soon became a tool for a range of social and political purposes. A large proportion of the savings can today be used for buying a home, purchasing insurance and paying for the university education of one's children. A significant portion of personal savings is earmarked

---

6   As a point of comparison, the forced retirement savings system in Chile demands compulsory contributions of 10 per cent of wages. Even in Western countries with very generous public PAYGO pension systems, contribution rates are normally not more than 20 per cent.

for medical expenses. Finally, funds can be transferred among family members: for example, children can support their elderly parents out of their own CPF savings.

The CPF is not an ordinary pension system: it is an alternative to the welfare state. It advances the acquisition of 'merit goods' while promoting individual and familial self-reliance. Consequently income taxes are very low in Singapore, and most citizens actually pay no income tax whatsoever. On the surface, it appears as if the government has nothing to do with welfare issues, but in reality it plays a major role in a covert manner.

Modest intervention in Hong Kong

Hong Kong received similar orders in 1954 to establish a provident fund. The British colony was at the time struggling with a range of more pressing challenges, such as a heavy stream of immigrants from mainland China. Therefore the pension scheme was not implemented, and although it returned to the agenda once in a while, resistance from the local business community and the strongly laissez-faire ideology prevalent among the British civil service in Hong Kong stopped the plan from moving ahead.

The government did start various welfare programmes. For example, it initiated housing support for the elderly. The Hong Kong government also funds state education, and there are fully tax-funded healthcare facilities. The preference has always been, however, to keep the costs of welfare provision to a minimum, and to actively encourage family-based social security and voluntary community initiatives (Jacobs, 1998).

As the government kept its hands off old-age security for several decades, pensions in Hong Kong followed a natural evolutionary process (Pai, 2006). Traditionally, it was the family which provided old-age security, just as in other countries and cultures. From the 1970s onwards, larger companies established occupational pension schemes for their workers, although there was no specific regulation of those schemes until 1993. By that time, around 30 per cent of Hong Kong workers were participating in a pension scheme.

In more recent years, the government decided to take a more active stance in old-age security. There is now a Comprehensive Social Security Assistance Scheme, which provides a wide range of benefits to those who have no other source of support. The Social Security Allowance Scheme also gives a flat-rate allowance to the severely disabled and other elderly with special needs. But most importantly, the government in 1995 enacted the Mandatory Provident Fund (MPF) system, which became effective in 2000.[7]

Hong Kong's MPF system is superficially similar to Singapore's CPF. The MPF covers all full-time and part-time workers, as well as the self-employed, between the ages of 18 and 65. There are some minor exemptions, such as certain civil servants (for whom there is a final salary pension scheme) and domestic employees. Presently around two-thirds of workers participate in MPF schemes. This means that the system has substantially increased pension coverage: before the MPF, just one third of the labour force had pension savings; now a total of 85 per cent of workers in Hong Kong have some sort of pension.[8]

---

7 The MPF website is www.mpfa.org.hk/eindex.asp. Detailed information can also be found in Pai (2006).

8 Some 19 per cent belong to other schemes, and 11 per cent are exempted. There is only a small 4 per cent who should have joined the MPF system but have not done so: see Pai (2006). Still, an interesting question is why the MPF was adopted. Clearly, social concerns played a role; although aggregate savings rates were very

A closer look, however, reveals significant differences in the design of the systems in Singapore and Hong Kong, as the next section demonstrates.

Comparing Hong Kong and Singapore

Hong Kong was lucky in not adopting the provident fund system too early. The provident fund system is not a prudent and efficient set-up: in many other former British colonies, such as Nigeria and India, the provident fund system has been struggling to fulfil its purpose with dignity; it has provided low rates of return, poor service and mismanagement of funds.[9] Singapore has arguably fared better, but this seems to be thanks to the good legal and institutional infrastructure in the country which fosters business and investments – not to any aspect of the pension system as such, as is shown in more detail below.

Contribution rates: freedom versus compulsion

The most distinct advantage of the Hong Kong system is freedom. In Hong Kong, there were originally no forced savings whatsoever. Even now the compulsory levels are relatively low. The minimum contribution rate to the MPF system is 10 per cent of salary (5 per cent from both employer and employee). This is subject to further

---

high in Hong Kong before the MPF, there were groups that did not save much, and which might have benefited from better financial discipline imposed from above. But another possible reason for the MPF system was the support from the growing pension fund industry, which benefited handsomely from the system of compulsory savings. Pension funds are still lobbying for increases to the compulsory savings rate: see Gadbury (2004).

9   On India, see, for example, Goswami (2002); on Nigeria, see Silver et al. (2007).

limits: those who earn less than HKD 5,000 per month need to contribute only 5 per cent. Also, the maximum salary on which contributions are calculated is HKD 20,000 per month, so that the maximum monthly contribution is just HKD 2,000.[10]

By contrast, the CPF in Singapore plays an intrusive and interventionist role in society. As mentioned earlier, compulsory contribution rates rose rapidly in the first decades of Singapore's independence, up to a high point of 50 per cent of net salary. Although the rates have been reduced recently, they are still very high in comparison with other countries. One might, of course, argue that compulsion is not bad as such: after all, the money still belongs to the people. But this system has given rise to a vast fund of money that is channelled to the government and has become an important source of political power – and political risk. Such risks have manifested themselves in serious ways in countries such as Nigeria, so the identification of this risk is not mere theoretical speculation.[11] Second, CPF savers in Singapore are not getting adequate returns on their savings, as is shown next. A system that involves compulsion blunts competition (or in the case of the Singapore system more or less extinguishes it), thus ensuring that money is not well invested.

Rates of return: market versus government

The level of returns is another major difference between the Hong Kong and Singapore pension systems. The level of rates of return is

---

10   As of May 2007, these figures translate roughly as follows: lower limit £320/€470 per month, upper limit £1,300/€1,900 per month, and the maximum monthly contribution £130/€190 per month.

11   See, for example, Silver et al. (2007) and the references therein.

one of the most important issues when it comes to pension policy. A small difference per annum will make a substantial difference in total wealth over a period of 30–40 years. In most market-based pension schemes, the annual real returns (i.e. investment returns over and above consumer price inflation) exceed 5 per cent. This is also expected in Hong Kong, so that contributions of just 10 per cent of salary should yield a pension of around 30–40 per cent of final salary.

In Singapore, the returns seem less promising. It is difficult to calculate comparable figures, because CPF savings are often used for purposes other than retirement, so that the strict replacement ratio (pensions divided by pre-retirement salaries) is not a good measure of success. One study estimates, however, that the income at retirement of Singaporeans is just 20–40 percent of final take-home pay, even after 35 years of saving at a 40 per cent rate.[12] If this resembles the reality even closely, it means that low returns to savings have a significant negative impact on people's retirement wealth.

In any case, there is also direct evidence that the rates of return on investments are low in Singapore's CPF: they are barely positive in inflation-corrected terms. Technically speaking, the funds in the CPF are mainly invested in government bonds; that in itself is troubling, because it usually implies low rates of return and poor portfolio diversification. But in Singapore, CPF balances are not remunerated even at the level of return on government bonds: rather, the interest on CPF accounts is calculated in a purely administrative fashion, as a weighted average of the twelve-

12   The figures are from Fernandez (1994), quoted in Ramesh (2000). The simulation analysis of McCarthy et al. (2002) shows that the real replacement rate in 2001 was roughly 28 per cent for the base case.

month deposit and month-end savings rate of the four major local banks, subject to a minimum of 2.5 per cent. For many years, this has translated into a real return of approximately zero; the average for the past twenty years has been just 1.3 per cent, assuming that official inflation figures are reliable.[13]

Fund management

Reasonable rates of return are usually achieved through fund management and diversified investment portfolios of real investments (equities, real estate, corporate bonds and so on). In order to obtain market-based returns, one must normally let markets run the system. In Hong Kong, this has been the consistent policy of the government. Before 2000, old-age security was a purely voluntary affair, and those who set up pension schemes were free to employ the best instruments and service providers available.

The new system does not replace the earlier practice, but is built on top of it. In fact, pension savings in Hong Kong are not administered by the government at all, but are instead held in the legal form of private trusts. Employers may set up their own MPF schemes, or they may use one of those offered by financial institutions. There are presently a wide variety of schemes, and government does not attempt to reduce their number or impose strict regulations.

As a result, the government plays no role in the system other than setting the rules on compulsory contributions, and certain

---

13   See Asher and Nandy (2008: 53, Figure 2). These authors further point out that Singapore's official consumer price inflation figures may be understated, which implies that the real rate of return on CPF balances is even lower, potentially negative (ibid.: 52, note 16).

investment guidelines. Rates of return are based on the best that the markets can offer, and individuals have full freedom to decide – and access to information on – how their savings are to be invested.

In Singapore, things are rather different. The government plays a central role in administering the funds, with poor results. Already the fact that CPF savers receive returns based on short-term interest rates – below what one could earn on the market risk-free – suggests that there is something strange going on.

And indeed there is something strange about the system. The CPF is not an ordinary pension fund at all: it is a complex tool of social policy managed by the government, and it is operated according to its own rules. The savings are technically invested in government bonds, but given that the Singapore government has enjoyed a long period of budget surpluses, the additional income received from CPF savings has been channelled further to such opaque bodies as the Singapore Government Investment Corporation (GIC), which manages one of the largest investment funds in Asia.

Less personal and familial freedom ordinarily comes with more extensive powers of government. In Singapore this is very much the case: as the CPF began to be used for social engineering, it lost its original function as a servant of the people and became a tool of political manipulation. The current set-up is not just financially unfair, but gives rise to substantial political risk, which may manifest itself when a change of regime sooner or later takes place. There is no public information about how the significant amount of money is being used, because the GIC's investment portfolio is a state secret. It is generally believed that the funds are invested overseas; in addition to GIC, however, the government invests its surplus funds through Temasek Holdings, which own major stakes in many of the largest corporations in Singapore. Some of these investments may be perfectly beneficial to the citizens and CPF savers, while others may do more to further the personal interests of politicians (even if not necessarily personal or financial).[14]

Freedom to invest

Also important are investment regulations. In Hong Kong, a light and sensible approach has been adopted even after 2000. MPF schemes have a great deal of freedom in choosing their investment strategy, and they can take advantage of almost all different assets classes and use derivative instruments to hedge risks.

There are some basic regulations, of course. These include, for example, the requirement that 30 per cent of funds must be invested in HKD-denominated assets; employer-sponsored schemes may not hold more than 10 per cent of their own shares; the portfolio must be diversified, so that any single entity may take up to 10 per cent of total assets; and to limit undue speculation, only 5 per cent of funds may be invested in warrants. The Mandatory Provident Fund Schemes Authority (MPFA) of Hong Kong oversees the system.[15]

---

14 John G. Greenwood criticised the CPF for diverting funds to economically un-productive public projects twenty years ago, writing at a time when Singapore was suffering from a major depression: 'There can be little doubt that this is what has happened in Singapore, where – admittedly with unusually high rates of contribution to the CPF – there has been an over-investment in public sector goods contributing directly to the recent downturn in the Singapore economy.' See Chau et al. (1987: 68).

15 There are also various other safeguards in place. For example, trustees of MPF schemes must take professional indemnity insurance, and there is a statutory Compensation Fund (in case the indemnity insurance does not suffice to cover

Singapore too has taken slow but sure steps towards greater freedom to invest. That path, however, has been influenced by government interests. The first relaxation of investment rules took place in 1968, when CPF savers were allowed to use their account balances to purchase government flats. In 1978, a part of savings could be invested in the Singapore Bus Service, a government company. In more recent years, the CPF has been moving towards greater freedom of investment, but the liberalisation path shows the difficulty of reforming a badly designed system.

At present, Singaporean workers are entitled somewhat freely to invest 80 per cent of their account balance, over and above a minimum balance determined by the CPF Board. In practice, however, it seems that under 20 per cent of total savings are invested in securities, which means that good investment returns cannot be attained. A major reason for so little market investment is over-regulation: those who wish to invest in securities must deal with complex and cumbersome regulatory procedures, which are likely to deter anyone who otherwise takes no active part in the financial markets. In addition, the minimum account balance includes other investment items such as housing and education, so that most people could even in theory invest just a small proportion of their savings.[16]

---

losses to beneficiaries). In addition, each MPF scheme must offer its beneficiaries a Capital Preservation Fund, which is invested in bank deposits and high-grade debt securities; the net rate of return (after administrative fees) of the Capital Preservation Fund must at least equal the current bank savings rate.

16 See Ng (2000) for details on the liberalisation process, and investment rules and behaviour.

Lessons and challenges

In recent years, there has been a growing interest in 'individual account' pensions, which are, in effect, compulsory savings.[17] Pension policy in Hong Kong and Singapore can give many lessons on such approaches. While savings-based pensions are probably better than conventional pay-as-you-go pensions, they are not the remedy to every problem, and the devil is in the detail of the system. It is important to give people real freedom over their lives and decisions, not simply introduce substantial compulsory savings with tight rules and regulations about how the savings are invested. A system must be genuinely market-based, not simply based on market rhetoric.

Paths of development

An interesting question is why Hong Kong and Singapore adopted such different paths. It seems that one reason for Hong Kong's hands-off approach was that the British ruled the country until 1997, and one of their challenges was to keep the local Chinese inhabitants happy. That was coupled with a fiercely family-centred local culture, which preferred informal welfare provision and viewed the government with distrust. The Confucian culture of the Hong Kong Chinese nurtured a strong work ethic as well as an ethic of voluntarism, which expected social and political stability from government, but nothing more (Wilding, 1997).

Culturally, Singapore shares many features with Hong Kong. It has, however, been ruled by the rather family-centred People's Action Party (PAP) since 1959. The strongly Chinese ethnicity and

---

17   The World Bank has played an important role in furthering this interest. See generally World Bank (1994).

orientation of the country further enabled the PAP to take a more active role in society. It favoured families and voluntary initiatives, but in contrast to Hong Kong with its British laissez-faire civil servants, Singapore was ruled with the Confucian ideal of a strong, centralised state.

The current situation in Singapore highlights the path-dependence of political and social development. The pension savings system is presently being reformed and liberalised on the surface, but the fundamental aspects remain to be changed. This is natural, because in the first decades of Singapore's independence, the CPF became an important tool of social engineering. This had social and political consequences, which are difficult to reverse. It may well have been that the scheme was used by the PAP to centralise power and wealth in the hands of the elite. The importance of the CPF to Singaporean power politics is, however, still largely unexplored and poorly understood.

The dilemma of democracy

It may be relatively easy to say what kind of pension policy would be optimal in theoretical terms; it is often much harder to implement that policy in practice. This is a further challenge to advocates of market-based pensions. Pay-as-you-go schemes are democratically attractive, because they effectively give a windfall to the current and next retiring generations, at the expense of grandchildren and beyond who cannot vote. The short-term demands of the electorate also make it difficult to reverse unsustainable policies (Galasso, 2006).

It is sad yet surprising to note that the most successful, market-based pension reforms were adopted in less democratic countries. This is not to say that their systems are perfect, or that democratic countries could not do the same, but it is a challenge (see the chapter by Booth). To some extent, it has been argued that one of the reasons for the rapid expansion of Singapore's CPF was popular demand, and indeed today there are pressures for a more extensive welfare state (Ramesh, 2000).

Conclusion

Pension history in Hong Kong and Singapore can give several lessons for countries that desire reform but are unsure of the desired direction. The development of pension systems in these two small Asian tigers highlights several factors:

- path-dependence and the importance of a good start;
- the value of markets and the risks with government-managed funds and levels of compulsory saving that are too high; and
- the interplay of pension design and broader politics: policymakers should pay great attention to the overall scheme of things, but the details matter too, as they determine the development path in the longer term.

References

Asher, M. G. (1995), *Compulsory Savings in Singapore: An alternative to the welfare state*, Dallas, TX: National Center for Policy Analysis, available online at www.ncpa.org/studies/s198/s198.html.

Asher, M. G. and A. Nandy (2008), 'Singapore's policy responses to ageing, inequality and poverty: an assessment', *International Social Security Review*, 61(1): 41–60.

Chan, A. (1997), 'An overview of the living arrangements and social support exchanges of older Singaporeans', *Asia-Pacific Population Journal*, 12(4), available online at www.unescap.org/esid/psis/population/journal/1997/v12n4a3.htm.

Chau, L. C. et al. (1987), 'Symposium on Central Provident Fund', *Hong Kong Economic Papers*, 1987(18), available online at http://sunzi1.1ib.hku.hk/hkjo/view/12/1200121.pdf.

Fernandez, W. (1994), 'State welfarism, Singapore-style', *Straits Times*, 18 September, p. SR6.

Gadbury, J. (2004), *Retirement Income Policy in Hong Kong*, Hong Kong Investment Funds Association, available online at www.hkifa.org.hk/eng/newsevents_kpr_051304.aspx.

Galasso, V. (2006), *The Political Future of Social Security in Aging Societies*, Cambridge, MA: MIT Press.

Goswami, R. (2002), 'Old age protection in India: problems and prognosis', *International Social Security Review*, 55(2).

Jacobs, D. (1998), *Social Welfare Systems in East Asia: A Comparative Analysis Including Private Welfare*, CASEpaper 10, Centre for Analysis of Social Exclusion, London School of Economics, available online at http://sticerd.lse.ac.uk/dps/case/cp/Paper10.pdf.

McCarthy, D., O. S. Mitchell and J. Piggott (2002), 'Asset rich and cash poor: retirement provision and housing policy in Singapore', *Journal of Pension Economics and Finance*, 1(3): 197–222.

Ng, E. (2000), 'Central Provident Fund in Singapore – a capital market boost or a drag?', in *Rising to the Challenge in Asia:*

A Study of Financial Markets, vol. 3: *Sound Practices*, Asian Development Bank, available online at www.adb.org/Documents/Books/Rising_to_the_Challenge/Sound_Practices/sing-cpf.pdf.

Pai, Y. (2006), *Comparing Individual Retirement Accounts in Asia: Singapore, Thailand, Hong Kong and PRC*, Social Protection Discussion Paper no. 0609, World Bank, available online at http://siteresources.worldbank.org/SOCIALPROTECTION/Resources/SP-Discussion-papers/Pensions-DP/0609.pdf.

Ramesh, M. (2000), 'The politics of social security in Singapore', *Pacific Review*, 13(2): 243–56.

Silver, N., E. Acquaah and O. Juurikkala (2007), 'Savings in the absence of functioning property rights', *Economic Affairs*, 27(1).

Simon, J. L. (1996), *The Ultimate Resource II: People, Materials, and Environment*, 2nd edn, Princeton, NJ: Princeton University Press, available online at www.juliansimon.com/writings/Ultimate_Resource/.

Wilding, P. (1997), 'Social policy and social development in Hong Kong', *Asian Journal of Public Administration*, 19(2): 244–75, available online at http://sunzi1.1ib.hku.hk/hkjo/view/50/5000138.pdf.

World Bank (1994), *Averting the Old Age Crisis: Policies to Protect the Old and Promote Growth*, Washington, DC, available online at www.worldbank.org/pensions.

9 MUTUALITY, THE MIXED ECONOMY OF WELFARE AND THE INTRODUCTION OF THE OLD-AGE PENSION IN BRITAIN
David Gladstone

Introduction

This chapter explores the introduction of the Old Age Pensions Act in 1908 and the tradition of mutuality – represented by the Friendly Societies – which it replaced.

The fact that state-provided old-age pensions began only a century ago prompts the question of how older people survived financially before their introduction. This question became especially important during the nineteenth century, for two reasons. First, because Britain was the first industrial nation, in which a growing proportion of the increasing population were waged labour. How did they survive – especially relative to the rising living standards of many working-class people in the later nineteenth century – when they were no longer part of the labour market because of the often interconnected conditions of frailty, ill health or old age? The second reason is the increasing number of those surviving into older age, especially towards the end of the century. Whereas the population aged over 65 was 830,800 in 1851, by 1901 it had increased to 1.51 million.

Financial survival was thus an issue for individuals, compounded by changing labour market conditions and increased longevity. Those same factors were also at work in placing the financial circumstances of older working people on to the political agenda, especially in the period after 1878, when alternative schemes of old-age pensions were proposed and debated.

The mixed economy of welfare

Until comparatively recently, historians of the nineteenth century highlighted the role of the Poor Law and of philanthropy in discussing the survival strategies of those outside the labour market. While not in any way challenging the importance of those agencies, more recent historical research has indicated a more comprehensive network of survival strategies used by those at risk from financial uncertainty and vulnerability.

Older people were among those at risk, as the 'social explorers' of the late nineteenth century noted. Though Booth and Rowntree both highlighted the issue of low pay for workers with large families, their research also illustrated 'how many old people at the beginning of the twentieth century still patched together pitiful incomes, often supplemented by inadequate poor relief' (Thane, 2000: 213). Low pay was also 'the major constraint on working class saving ... to provide for such eventualities as old age' (Kidd, 1999: 163).

For older people outside the labour market, as for other 'at risk' groups, the struggle for survival was constructed from an 'economy of makeshifts': a rich, varied and not always adequate tapestry in which family support, neighbourly assistance, strategies of self-help, mutual aid and commercial insurance played an important role alongside charity and philanthropy and the provisions of the state-provided Poor Law. Cumulatively, the interplay of these agencies – formal and informal – constitutes what is nowadays referred to as the mixed economy of welfare.

It is clearly beyond the scope of this chapter to review and discuss each of these strategies and the often important interrelationship between them. Instead, it will focus on the role of the Friendly Societies, which, historians are agreed, were 'by far the most important of the voluntary associations concerned with the promotion of thrift and self-help in the nineteenth century' (Gosden, 1973: vii), not least in providing financial support to older people. There is less unanimity, however, about the number of adult males who were members of the societies. In part, this reflects the paucity of data and the difficulty of interpreting what is available. Many, especially the smaller local societies, remained unregistered for most of the nineteenth century, while those societies that were registered did not always supply membership data. Recent research based on national and local sources, however, suggests that around 40 per cent of the adult male population were Friendly Society members.

Friendly Societies and support for old age in the nineteenth century

With their emphasis on support and sociability, the Friendly Societies were, in many respects, the successors of the medieval guilds and their tradition of mutuality.They originated in the late seventeenth century, but the number of local and independent societies increased during the later eighteenth and early nineteenth centuries. From mid-century onwards, however, the strength of the movement lay with the affiliated orders: a central organisation to which individual lodges or branches could affiliate. This emergent structure was largely the result of the accountability imposed by registration under successive Acts of Parliament. But there were also benefits of scale in the new organisation. 'It was possible to spread the risks and the costs across several branches and so provide benefits over a wider geographical area' (Kidd, 1999: 113). This was especially important when members were migrating in search of work.

The growth and expansion of the movement have been attributed to several factors, though primacy is usually given to the transition from an agrarian to an urban economy and society, in which market relations and the relative anonymity of town life stimulated their growth. In that environment: 'it was not so much a question of advancing levels of poverty; indeed wage rates and real incomes were generally higher in the towns than in the countryside. Rather, it was a matter of declining levels of social security' (ibid.: 112).

In addition, the national system of financial support – the Poor Law – came, in the 1834 Amendment Act, to embody the harsher deterrent principles of less eligibility and the workhouse test. Anticipation and experience of the Act led to a considerable surge in the number of Friendly Societies during the 1830s and 1840s and of those seeking to join. It is worth noting *en passant* that there was considerable similarity in middle- and working-class attitudes. The latter criticised the New Poor Law for punishing 'the distressed rather than alleviating distress' (Cordery, 2003: 52); the former saw it as a means not only of reducing their own liabilities as ratepayers but also of creating an independent, self-reliant working class. Independence has recently been defined as a central core of Victorian manliness (Tosh, 2005). One public aspect of such independence lay in demonstrating a distance from the Poor Law, something that the friendly societies with their system of contributions and benefits were able to provide.

A recent characterisation brings together changing conditions in the labour market and welfare support in describing the
average Friendly Society member as a 'migrant who had been
absorbed successfully into an urban labour market but had to
purchase insurance as a substitute for the customary prerequisites
and poor relief which had supplemented the rural wage' (Gorsky,
1998: 503).

What the societies offered their members has been summed up
as sociability and support (Cordery, 2003: 40): 'to earn freedom
from a fear of penury and a pauper's burial and the ability to enjoy
unhindered recreation with their friends' (ibid.: 75), especially at
the club or lodge nights often held in a local public house. Insurance, the pooling of risks – and the payment of regular weekly
contributions ranging from sixpence to one shilling – were the
means by which members could safeguard themselves against
'The vicissitudes which could so easily overtake working class life,
and, in particular, those presented by a period of illness, by old
age, or by death itself, with its accompanying funeral expenses
and loss of money for dependents' (Finlayson, 1994: 24).

The actuarial balance between risks, contributions and
benefits was obviously central to good financial management.
In the first half of the nineteenth century the absence of reliable
actuarial tables created problems for the small local societies,
and presaged the growing importance of the affiliated orders.
At the end of the century financial concerns were of a different
order. Growing funds and increasing membership were offset by
increasing life expectancy and higher sickness rates, which meant
that more members 'too old to work ... too young to die' were
in effect drawing 'virtual' retirement allowances in the guise of
extended sickness benefits. 'Because the payment of such "virtual

pensions" had not been calculated into the tables actuaries used, the societies had neither predicted nor prepared for their expense' (Cordery, 2003: 132–3) and the societies that attempted to introduce superannuation schemes in the 1880s and 1890s not surprisingly found their members unwilling to pay additional contributions. By the end of the nineteenth century the financial difficulties of the societies were 'largely as a result of trying to cater for an ageing constituency' (Finlayson, 1994: 138). One graphic illustration is provided by the fact that between 1846 and 1848 and 1893 and 1897 the percentage of Oddfellows (one of the leading affiliated orders) aged over 65 increased twenty-three-fold (cited in Cordery, 2003: 130).

In addition to benefits, contributions were also an important part of the equation: 'The survival of each friendly society depended on its calculation of the risks insured against, and no society wanted to elect to membership someone regarded as a "bad risk" either on grounds of health or income' (Kidd, 1999: 112).

To ensure regular payment of contributions some societies imposed a minimum wage clause, prohibited new members joining above a certain age, and excluded those who worked in irregular trades. As a consequence, membership of a Friendly Society became one of the defining characteristics of working-class respectability in Victorian England and represented 'the badge of the skilled worker' (Johnson, 1985: 55). Not only were those engaged in casual labour excluded from membership, women also were in a minority, especially in the affiliated orders, and women-only societies became increasingly rare in the second half of the century. It is perhaps not altogether surprising, therefore, that women's organisations were prominent among those campaigning in support of a state old-age pension scheme.

The issue for the Friendly Societies, especially in the final quarter of the century, concerned not only exclusions, however. It was also about the competition for members from trades unions (which offered a wider workplace agenda as well as welfare benefits), and the increasing importance of commercial insurance and other methods of small savings, such as the Post Office Savings Bank. Such a competitive environment had a double impact on the Friendly Societies. On the one hand, new members were needed to help pay the benefits created by the increasing longevity of older members. On the other, existing 'virtual' pensions among the societies' existing membership made it difficult to introduce lower contributions for new members.

At the beginning of the twentieth century, therefore, the paramount issue for the Friendly Societies concerned present disbursements and future membership, both of them the interrelated consequence of the increased longevity of the insured population. It was thus against the background of their own buoyant membership, but also of increased demands on their resources, that a majority of the Friendly Societies reluctantly came to accept the introduction of the state-provided old-age pension in the first decade of the twentieth century.

'The first step in a journey': the introduction of old-age pensions in 1908

When they were introduced in 1908, state-provided old-age pensions were a non-contributory and means-tested benefit administered by Customs and Excise and paid through post offices. Haldane, the Secretary of State for War in the Liberal government that introduced the old-age pensions legislation, described the measure as 'the first step in a journey ... which it is our bounden duty to enter upon' (cited in Harris, 2004: 160). With the advantage of hindsight, there can be no doubt that the 1908 Act was but the first step on a journey that has encompassed much subsequent legislation, and changing administrative and financial arrangements. More recently the pensions debate has been set within a growing political concern at unprecedented life expectancy during the twentieth century, the impact of the inter-generational contract between those not working and those who are (with its important consequences for the funding of the state pension system) and the adequacy of the state pension itself.

In this section, we locate the Act of 1908 in its social, political and intellectual context. Why was it that Haldane spoke of the Old Age Pensions Act not only as the 'first step in a journey' but one 'which it is our bounden duty to embark upon'? Why did the Liberal government finally espouse the idea of a tax-funded pensions scheme rather than one based on insurance contributions? What difference did the introduction of the old-age pension make to the 'economy of makeshifts' that characterised the lives of many of the labouring poor a century ago?

The 1908 Act in context

After a decade in power the Conservatives were replaced in 1906 by a Liberal government in a landslide election victory. Though social reform was not specifically an election issue, the Liberal government was to carry through an impressive programme of social legislation which in many respects laid the foundations for the creation of the classic welfare state during and after World War II. In addition to the Old Age Pensions Act of 1908, those measures included the introduction of school meals and school medical inspection, a wide ranging Children's Act (also passed in 1908), and the introduction of health and unemployment insurance in 1911. These measures represented a significant redefinition of political Liberalism itself. Whereas for much of the previous fifty years it had been synonymous with low taxation and with fostering individual responsibility, the New Liberalism of thinkers such as T. H. Green found political expression in the activities of rising Liberal politicians such as David Lloyd George and Winston Churchill. Their commitment to state-sponsored collective action for the public good exercised through the increasingly important social policy departments of central government thus represented both a new departure and a significant break with the ideological past.

This changing ideological and political climate is one explanation for the introduction of old-age pensions in 1908. But other factors also need to be explored. One of these is the old-age pensions component in the social insurance programme introduced by Bismarck in Germany during the 1880s. As Searle (2004: 372) has noted, while 'visits to Germany formed an indispensable part of the education of all Edwardian social reformers … the British did not blindly imitate earlier German achievements'. Nowhere was this more apparent than in the matter of old-age pensions. Whereas the British scheme of 1908 was funded through taxation on a means-tested basis, German pensions were contributory and income-related. It would be later in the twentieth century when the British and German schemes came to share those features in common.

At the outset, however, they were based on different principles. Thane (2006: 78–9) has attributed this difference to the different motivations that underpinned the two systems: 'Bismarck's desire [was] to win the loyalty of key groups of German workers to create a counter-attraction to the growing lure of socialism by demonstrating that the liberal state could provide income security in old age, sickness or disability.'

By contrast, in Britain the movement for old-age pensions focused on the high levels of poverty among older people, as revealed by the late Victorian social investigators such as Booth and Rowntree, and the inadequacies of the Poor Law. Both of these, Thane contends, affected women in particular. It was this issue of gender poverty which favoured a tax-funded scheme rather than an insurance-based system, since very few women could afford to pay regular insurance contributions. As Thane (ibid.: 80) notes, 'two thirds of the first state pensioners were female'.

The debate about old-age pensions: 1878–1908

The Old Age Pension Act was the culmination of 30 years of social investigation, political debate and government inquiries into the conditions of the aged poor, culminating in the Royal Commission on the Aged Poor (1895):

> The Report crystallised the widespread awareness and concern at the end of the nineteenth century about the aged poor as a distinct social group and a growing sense of awareness that they deserved, and that the country could afford, a new, more secure and less degrading form of public support than in preceding centuries. (Thane, 2000: 193)

That critique applied especially to the operation and working of the New Poor Law, which had been introduced in 1834. Despite the fact that the majority of necessitous older people were receiving outdoor relief by the end of the nineteenth century instead of having to submit to the stigmatising Poor Law workhouse, it was accepted, even by the Permanent Secretary at the Local Government Board, that the amount customarily given as relief (between 2*s* and 3*s* 6*d* per week) was inadequate to live on. It is in the context of inadequate relief, therefore, that the late-nineteenth-century debate about alternative methods of guaranteeing financial security in older age has to be considered.

Three alternative solutions were actively canvassed. Two of these – those associated with Canon Blackley and Joseph Chamberlain – were based on the payment of insurance contributions. The third, proposed by the Liverpool merchant and social investigator Charles Booth, was for a non-contributory pension financed out of taxation.

Despite the accumulation of empirical evidence concerning the extent of destitution among older people, both the insurance and taxation schemes had their opponents and critics. Gilbert (1966) argued that contributory schemes such as those that Blackley and Chamberlain advocated were opposed by the vested interests of the Friendly Societies, which, through a liberal interpretation of sick pay, were already providing what amounted to old-age pensions to their older members. More recent historical scholarship has suggested that such an interpretation overestimates the unanimity among the very diverse grouping of Friendly Societies. Some, striving to maintain their independence and business, were anti-state. Others, increasingly concerned at the rising costs of the growing numbers of aged members and the more competitive environment in which they found themselves, saw benefits in the introduction of some form of state pension. In that, they were allied with the growing and expanding labour movement, which also supported Booth's proposals. That scheme, too, had its critics, however: largely on the grounds of the costs involved in paying for pensions without contributions.

The impasse between the two alternatives led to a flurry of government committees to discuss the issue during the 1890s, but no action ensued. In the event, Chamberlain's public recognition in 1899 that he now regarded contributory pensions as impracticable because of the inability or unwillingness of the working classes to purchase deferred annuities left only Booth's tax-funded scheme as a serious contender. Concurrently, it also received powerful support from extra-parliamentary action organised through the National Committee of Organised Labour for the Promotion of Old Age Pensions (NCOL). That interest group created a powerful caucus that moved the issue up the political agenda at the beginning of the twentieth century on the basis of Booth's scheme: a state pension financed out of taxation.

Debate about the 1908 Act

Recent historical research has explored the discussion that took place about the precise details of the Bill and the ensuing debate in both Houses of Parliament. A number of points of significance emerge.

First, the rejection of a contributory insurance scheme because of the impossibility of including the lower-paid. Despite that, insurance had a powerful advocate in the youthful William Beveridge and his support for the German model in his articles in the *Morning Post* (Harris, 2006). Second, although the Friendly Societies were not unanimous in their support, the larger societies had come to acknowledge the advantages to them of a non-contributory scheme. Third, the NCOL continued its campaign for pensions to be introduced at age 65, restricted to British citizens, and with a higher limit on the means test. Fourth, given the emerging consensus in favour of Booth's scheme, not least in Parliament, Fraser (1984: 153) seeks to explain why it was not until they had been in power for two years that the Liberal government presented their Old Age Pensions Bill. He suggests that it was the by-election reverses that the Liberals suffered at the hands of the incipient Labour Party in 1907 which led them to action. 'Political action chimed with social concern to make 1908 an appropriate moment to introduce pensions.' Finally, a number of significant amendments were made to the Liberal government's Bill during its passage through Parliament. Labour succeeded in obtaining a review of the clause that denied pensions to those receiving poor relief after 1 January 1908 (as a result of which this clause was abolished at the end of 1910). Meanwhile, the Conservatives successfully obtained a sliding scale on the means test by which full pensions would be paid to old people with incomes up to £21 per year with reductions in the weekly rate for those with incomes between £21 and the upper limit of £31 10s. Backbench opposition succeeded in overturning the government's proposal that the 5s weekly pension should be paid only to a married couple at the rate of 7s 6d. While the government's plan to introduce pensions at the age of 70 was a defeat for the NCOL campaign, payments were to be restricted only to British citizens, as they had proposed.

Old-age pensions represented 'the first big breach in the Poor Law' (Collins, 1965) and 'an important step in the development of central state welfare services' (Johnson, 1996: 238). They were, however, subject not only to a test of financial means but also (until 1919) of character eligibility (denying pensions to criminals, drunkards and malingerers) designed to promote personal independence and family obligations. In addition pensions were not paid until the age of 70, at a time when the average mortality occurred some twenty years earlier. Furthermore, their level was far from generous. Five shillings, the amount of the full pension, represented about one fifth of the average labourer's wage and 'would just about feed and clothe a parsimonious couple ... What was given made it easier for the poor to arrange their income over time, what was withheld forced them to do so' (Vincent, 1991: 41). Old-age pensions may have guaranteed greater financial security. They did not entirely supplant other methods of assistance that made up the economy of makeshifts of the older poor: family support, community and mutual aid, philanthropic and charitable help.

Costs and responsibility: the legacy

Despite that, pensions were popular: especially since they entailed no sacrifice (such as financial contributions) on the part of their beneficiaries. Almost 100,000 more qualified for the old-age pension in its first year than the Treasury estimate of 572,000; and in 1911, when the exclusion of those receiving poor relief was abandoned, the number of qualifying people had reached almost 1.1 million. These two factors created extra costs which, since the scheme was non-contributory, had to be met by the Treasury. It has been suggested that it was these extra costs which made insurance a more attractive proposition to fund the sickness and unemployment schemes introduced in the National Insurance legislation of 1911, since contributions from employers and workers limited Treasury liability. The result, as Harris (1993: 218) notes, was that the British welfare system was 'almost by accident' committed 'to two wholly different prototypes of citizenship and social welfare for the rest of the twentieth century': means-tested benefits funded out of general taxation, on the one hand, and contractual social insurance, on the other.

Politically, the introduction of old-age pensions generated a concern with their costs, just as critics of the non-contributory scheme feared that it would. The supplementary amount of nearly £1 million to finance the first year of the scheme was a significant precursor of the more current debate about the future funding of pensions. So too was the criticism that old-age pensions represented the replacement of traditional Liberal values, manifested by the mutual and private provision of the nineteenth century, by a progressive transfer of responsibilities from the individual to the state. That too, in the context of family responsibilities for the care of older people, has been a continuing theme in policy debates over the past century. In each of these ways, therefore, the legacy of the introduction in 1908 of old-age pensions for 'the very old, the very poor and the very respectable' (Thane, 2000: 225) is about more than financial support. It also crystallised the debates about the state and other providers, independence and control, self-reliance and state action that have been the essence of wider social policy discussion over the ensuing century.

References

Collins, D. (1965), 'The introduction of old age pensions in Great Britain', *Historical Journal*, 8(3).

Cordery, S. (2003), *British Friendly Societies 1750–1914*, Basingstoke: Palgrave Macmillan.

Finlayson, G. (1994), *Citizen, State and Social Welfare in Britain 1830–1990*, Oxford: Clarendon.

Fraser, D. (1984), *The Evolution of the British Welfare State*, London: Macmillan.

Gilbert, B. B. (1966), *The Evolution of National Insurance in Great Britain*, London: Michael Joseph.

Gorsky, M. (1998), 'The growth and distribution of English friendly societies in the early nineteenth century', *Economic History Review*, 51(3).

Gosden, P. H. (1973), *Self Help: Voluntary Associations in the 19th Century*, London: B. T. Batsford.

Harris, B. (2004), *The Origins of the British Welfare State*, Basingstoke: Palgrave Macmillan.

Harris, J. (1993), *Private Lives, Public Spirit: A Social History of Britain 1870–1914*, Oxford: Oxford University Press.

Harris, J. (2006), 'The roots of public pensions provision: social insurance and the Beveridge Plan', in H. Pemberton et al. (eds), *Britain's Pensions Crisis: History and Policy*, Oxford: Oxford University Press.

Johnson, P. (1985), *Saving and Spending: The working class economy in Britain 1870–1939*, Oxford: Oxford University Press.

Johnson, P. (1996), 'Risk, redistribution and social welfare in Britain from the Poor Law to Beveridge', in M. Daunton (ed.), *Charity, Self Interest and Welfare in the English Past*, London: UCL Press.

Kidd, A. (1999), *State, Society and the Poor in Nineteenth Century England*, Basingstoke: Macmillan Press.

Searle, G. R. (2004), *A New England: Peace and War 1886–1918*, Oxford: Clarendon.

Thane, P. (2000), *Old Age in English History*, Oxford: Oxford University Press.

Thane, P. (2006), 'The "scandal" of women's pensions in Britain', in H. Pemberton et al. (eds), *Britain's Pensions Crisis: History and Policy*, Oxford: Oxford University Press.

Tosh, J. (2005), 'Masculinities in industrializing society: Britain 1800–1914', *Journal of British Studies*, 44(2).

Vincent, D. (1991), *Poor Citizens: The state and the poor in twentieth century Britain*, Harlow: Longman.

10 CHINA'S NEW GREAT WALL
Meng Li and Nick Silver

Introduction

It is sometimes convenient to divide countries into two categories
when thinking about pension reform. The industrialised nations[1]
generally have a large proportion of their population near to or
past retirement age, combined with large formal retirement provision. Underdeveloped countries are typically characterised by a
high proportion of young people, and a very low participation in
any form of formal savings vehicle. Most of the countries in the
first category have high GDP per capita, and most in the second
have a low GDP per capita.

There is one major exception to this rule – important, as it
contains nearly a fifth of the world's population. China has a
rapidly ageing population, low pensions coverage and currently a
low – though rapidly growing – GDP per capita. China's old-age
dependency ratio will be greater than the USA's by the 2030s,
but it is much poorer than most developed countries when they
reached China's current demographic state. For example, Japan
had a median age of 33 (China's current median) in 1980 and a
GDP per capita of US$15,600 compared with China's current
US$4,800 (Trin, 2006). And by 2030 China will have 500 million[2]

---

1   Including the countries of the former Soviet bloc.
2   Authors' calculation based on data from Lutz et al. (2005).

people past its current retirement age, the same as the *entire* current population of the European Union.

We begin by looking at the scale of the demographic transformation facing China in the context of the world economy. We then describe the current pensions system that will have to cope with this transformation, and then we discuss the need for further reform.

The demographic transformation

The Chinese population currently stands at 1.3 billion,[3] which is the largest in the world. China has seen growth of GDP per capita of 9.4 per cent per annum since 1989.[4] The demography of China sheds light on two major features of the world economy; first, the apparently limitless supply of rural labourers migrating to the city and entering the labour markets, a stream that is already faltering, pushing up wages. Second, China's savings surplus, which has been instrumental in causing flows of capital to a small number of industrialised countries and reducing international real interest rates.

As in many other countries, better healthcare in China has led to a decrease in mortality and an increase in life expectancy. Someone born in China today can expect to live for 72 years – this means an average 'life extension' of approximately 32 years compared with a Chinese person born in 1950. Life expectancy is predicted to increase to 85 by mid-century (Reuters, 2007).

China's recent history has, however, aggravated the 'demographic time bomb'. Chairman Mao's policies encouraged

---

3   www.cia.gov, 28 December 2007.
4   IMF working paper, 2007.

Figure 5   **Chinese population, 1950–2010**

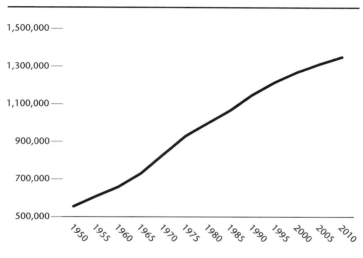

Source: http://esa.un.org/unpp/p2k0data.asp

population growth and led to an explosion in population: from 582.6 million in 1953 to 1,300 million today. This was dramatically reversed in 1979 with the introduction of the 'One Child Policy' (Kynge, 2006), which has led to population growth levelling off – see Figure 5.

The uneven age distribution is shown in Figure 6 overleaf. This shows a high population density between ages 30 to 50, with a much lower population below age 30 and above age 60. Figure 6 also shows the imbalance between males and females – for example, there are a quarter more boys than girls up to age four. We would expect this to result in a high and increasing proportion of people over retirement age starting in about ten years' time.

Figure 6   **Population distribution by age and sex in China, 2004**

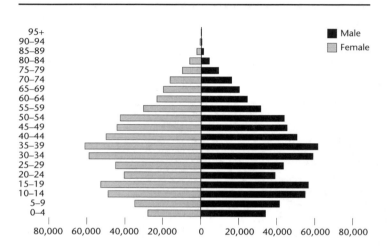

Source: China Statistical Yearbook (2006). Population figures in thousands.

Young Chinese people face what has become known as the 4–2-1 problem – a current worker (and single child) will be supporting two parents and four grandparents, as well as saving for their own retirement. The important statistic is the ratio of people of working age to people of post-retirement age, as the former will have to support the latter in some way. Figure 6 would lead us to expect that this ratio will dramatically increase as Mao's baby boomers begin to retire. The effect will be exacerbated by the low fertility rate[5] and high proportion of males to females. This ratio is graphed in Figure 7 (p. 244).

5   1.3 (calculated from 2000 census in Lutz et al. (2005)).

A sophisticated population model of China was developed which shows the anticipated numbers in different age groups in the years from 2000 to 2050. The model was based on a recent survey derived from a 2000 census (Lutz et al., 2005). For each age, the starting population plus net migrants less deaths gives the number in the population, one year older, at the end of the year. To this number births are added. Age is defined as completed years at the last birthday. The number of births in the year is the average number of women at each single year of age during the year multiplied by the fertility rate applicable to them during that year. The total number of births in a year is divided between the sexes in the ratio of 117 males to 100 females, in line with recent experience.[6] Mortality is assumed to improve at 1.0 per cent per annum and we have ignored migration. We have used a fertility rate of 1.7 births per annum.[7]

Figure 7 uses 60 as the age for calculating the support ratio. Currently a low retirement age is prevalent in China, partly because of the high working population. The retirement age for men is 60 and 55 for women. Those in managerial positions are allowed to work an extra five years but some workers (mainly manual) retire as early as 50 (45 in the case of women). In reality workers will undoubtedly have to work longer, but whatever retirement age is chosen, there will be a dramatic lowering of the support ratio.

Figure 7 also graphs the support ratio in the UK for comparison purposes.[8] The UK was chosen as being a typical 'developed'

6   The current ratio is 116.9, with estimates ranging from 113 to 123; Lutz et al. (2005).

7   This is a hugely controversial subject; the official figure from the 2000 census is 1.23, but estimates range from 1.2 to 2.3; Lutz et al. (2005).

8   We have applied a similar methodology for the UK using the UK's Government

Figure 7 **Chinese and UK support ratio, 2004–50***
Working age population/population over 60

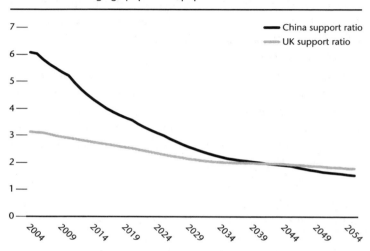

*The mortality assumption implies that life expectancy will increase to 80 by mid-century, which is conservative compared to a recent study by the Chinese government which concluded that it will be 85 by this date; Reuters (2007).

economy; some countries, such as Japan and Italy, have worse support ratios while some, such as the USA, have slightly younger populations and hence better ratios. The result is dramatic – like other developed countries the UK is a country widely regarded as facing a 'demographic time bomb'. Yet China's situation will worsen far more rapidly, the support ratio overtaking the UK's in the 2030s.

There are three major implications of Figures 6 and 7:

Actuarial Department (GAD) data. A full description of the method for UK projections can be found in Booth (2008).

- Labour supply in China will shrink relative to the total population.
- China's high savings rate is rational given a rapidly ageing economy. As the population ages, the savings rate should decline in line with standard economic theory (Misoulis, 2008).
- China will face a rapid transition from a young to an aged population and may have insufficient savings and an insufficient tax base to support its population, unlike many of the developed nations, where wealth has been accumulated before labour force decline set in.

China's pension system – from iron rice bowl to empty accounts

Having outlined the scale of the challenge facing China owing to its rapidly ageing population, we now look at the current pensions system, with a view to assessing how it is likely to cope with the onset of mass retirement. The system is highly complex and is better understood in a historical context. We therefore start with a brief history of the Chinese pension system before moving on to an analysis of the current arrangements.

The iron rice bowl – 1952 to 1984

The iron rice bowl system of cradle-to-grave work and social security was introduced by the 1951 Regulations on Labour Insurance: workers were guaranteed a job for life and a pension to match. The pension was part of a lifetime association with State Owned Enterprises (SOEs) and Collective Owned Enterprises

(COEs). A country-wide pooling system was introduced in 1952 administered by subsidiaries of the All China Federation of Trade Unions (ACFTU), with a 3 per cent contribution from workers leading to a 50–70 per cent defined-benefit replacement ratio. The system built up surpluses as China had a predominantly young population with a low life expectancy. Interestingly, the system was only for urban areas – the majority of the population who lived in rural areas were excluded (Salditt et al., 2007).

During the Cultural Revolution (1966–76) the system was abandoned and pension funds were eroded and embezzled. Pension payments had to be met solely by enterprises' current revenues (Holzmann et al., 2000).

From 1977 onwards, the adoption of 'iron rice bowl' jobs in SOEs and COEs saw a reinforcement of the 'cradle-to-grave' ethos. For example, a worker was not only guaranteed lifetime employment, but also one of their children was allowed to take the same job when the worker retired. The replacement rate increased to 75–80 per cent. Eligibility for a pension was reduced from the previous 25 years to ten years of work. The reforms created incentives for early retirement for the then current workforce, in an attempt to create vacancies for returning youth who had spent the Cultural Revolution in rural areas (Hu, 2006).

Significantly, none of the pension reforms covered the rural workers in China (80 per cent of the population by the end of the 1970s; ibid.). These workers had to rely on informal community or family ties.

Further reforms, 1985 to 1996

As a result of these reforms and higher life expectancy,

expenditure on pensions increased rapidly after 1978. From 1986 SOE employees and employers had to contribute up to 3 per cent and 15 per cent respectively of wages towards pension. Contributions were paid into funds run by Collective Insurance Agencies (CIAs) (Salditt et al., 2007).

The 1990s were characterised by the government experimenting by allowing some regions to test different systems. These resulted in two approaches: the emergence of funded systems and the integration of local systems at national level. Attempts were also made to broaden coverage into rural areas with the Basic Plan for Old Age Social Insurance in the Countryside (ibid.).

1997 reforms – the three-pillar system

Regulations such as the No. 33 State Council Resolution on Pension Reform for Enterprise Employees (1991) and the 1995 State Council circular on deepening the reform of the old-age pensions system were attempts to shift the system from a standard PAYGO system to a multi-pillar system. Most of the new regulation for reform was, however, akin to guidance, to grant local government the flexibility to tailor the regulations to their regions. The fragmented system meant that the resolution was mostly shunned. Not until Document 26 in 1997 did the government lay the foundations for the modern pension system.

The No. 33 Resolution called for contributions from individual workers. Employees should make contributions of not more than 3 per cent of their wages to the first pillar. The 1995 Circular No. 6 State Council Resolution of Deepening Pension Reform for Enterprise clearly focused on pillar 1A (PAYGO) and 1B (individual accounts). Both employees and employers were to contribute to pillar 1B.[9] The intended replacement rate was in the range of 60–75 per cent of salary, depending on the type of employment. The resolution encouraged the establishment of second and third pillars. The second pillar was enterprise-based and required contributions from both employers and employees, and the third pillar served as a complementary savings account with contributions from employees only. Both pillars were fully funded and all contributions were credited to individual accounts.

Workers who retired before 1997 are entitled to the old, 75–80 per cent replacement rate; workers who retired in 1997 or later but who enrolled before 1997 are entitled to the new benefits (a pension equivalent to 20 per cent of local wages and accumulations in their individual accounts), plus a supplementary 'transition pension' to compensate them for the years during which they did not contribute to the individual accounts. In practice, the effective replacement rate for the transition generation is estimated to be around 60 per cent (Sin, 2005) or higher (Chen, 2004). Moreover, the ranks of the transition generation were swelled by the early retirement and lay-offs associated with the acceleration of SOE reform after 1997, with SOE employment falling by one third (35 million workers) between 1997 and 2005. The legacy cost for the transition created a lasting problem in the pension system.

Urban pensions – the Chinese multi-pillar system

The multi-pillar system was first introduced in China in 1995. In 1997, the modern framework was fully established by Document

---

9   Employee contributions were 3 per cent while enterprise contributions were 11 per cent. For further discussion, see Hu (2006).

Table 15 **Three-pillar system**

	Pillar 1A	Pillar 1B	Pillar 2	Pillar 3
Status	Mandatory	Mandatory	Voluntary	Voluntary
Type	DB* & PAYGO	DB & PAYGO	DC† & fully funded	DC & fully funded
Contribution	17% from enterprises	8% from enterprises, 3% from employees, increasing by 1% every two years until it reaches 8%	From both enterprises & employees, with tax benefits of up to 4% for employers – though actual rate will differ in different provincial government areas	Individual contributing to his/her own pension account
Replacement ratio	20%	38%	n/a	n/a
Benefits	Only qualify if 15 years of contribution have been made. Replacement ratio indexed to rate between consumer price inflation and salary inflation	Monthly payout of 1/120	Lump sum or annuity	Lump sum or annuity

*DB = defined benefit
†DC = defined contribution

26. The Chinese pension system consists of three pillars (Table 15). The first pillar is run by the government and is the most basic system citizens subscribe to. The pillar is split into two distinct sections: pillar 1A, which is a pay-as-you-go (PAYGO) scheme, and pillar 1B, which is an individual pension account. Pillar 2 is enterprise based and requires contributions from both employers and employees. Pillar 3 serves as a complementary savings account with contributions from employees only.

Pillars 2 and 3 are voluntary arrangements: only the very well-off companies and employees have the material wherewithal to subscribe to them. Most of China is reliant on pillar 1. This system applies only in urban areas.

Further reforms since 1997

Since the establishment of the multi-pillar system in 1997, a series of reforms followed to define and rectify problems in the new system. The most important reforms dealt with separating the management of 1A and 1B and the development of pillar 2.

Document 42 and the Liaoning experiment

The pension system relied on the individual accounts of pillar 1B to supplement and stabilise the PAYGO pillar 1A. Pillar 1B accounts were often empty, however, as local governments took money from the individual accounts to fund any deficit in the pillar 1A PAYGO system. It is estimated that three-quarters of the 31 provinces in China have empty accounts (Hu, 2006).

To tackle this problem the central Chinese government implemented a pilot scheme of pillar management separation in

Liaoning. The resulting reform is called Document 42 ('The Pilot Programme for Improving the Urban Social Security System'), which extends the scheme to other provinces in China. Liaoning is a province in the 'rust belt' of China; once a great industrial hub, it contained 11 per cent of laid-off workers from State Owned Enterprises (SOEs) in 2001 and housed up to 7.2 per cent of all SOE retirees in 2004. The dependency was particularly large, as Liaoning has only 3.2 per cent of the overall population in China. Liaoning was chosen on the ground that, if pillar separation management could work there, it could work in areas with much smaller dependency ratios.

The separation of the management of pillars 1A and 1B was to ensure that funds were not getting illegally transferred. To this end, any deficit in pillar 1A was covered directly from the government budget. Tax breaks were also given to employers to encourage the creation of a supplementary pension system. Overall the experiment had some success by showing that the two funds can be managed separately and created more efficient operating schemes with different benefit formulae, but still showed major weaknesses with low coverage and uneven contribution rates across municipalities (Arora and Dunaway, 2007). But these schemes still heavily depend on government funding to cover the deficits of the system. By the end of 2005, the central government payment accounted for up to 80 per cent of the pension payment. The Liaoning experiment has been extended to cover 11 out of 31 provinces by 2001 (China Statistical Yearbook, 2006).

National Social Security Fund

A National Social Security Fund (NSSF) was established in 2000 after the Liaoning experiment to serve as a reserve for social insurance programmes and to cover the cash-flow deficit in the social pension. The NSSF was entitled to receive 10 per cent of the proceeds from equity sales of SOEs in initial public offerings (this practice was suspended in 2002). Lottery ticket sales serve as an additional source of revenue.

Enterprise Annuities

To attract more employees to set up occupational pensions, Document 42 introduced Enterprise Annuities, which are basically market management occupational pensions of pillar 2. Documents 20 and 23 went further to refine the policies. Enterprise Annuity schemes were to be set up by trusts and administered by an unbundled service provider that includes administrators, trustees, custodians and fund managers. Up to 30 per cent of funds can be invested in equities and linked products, with the rest residing in bank accounts and government bonds. Government involvement is limited to making sure firms are complying with the regulation, and in doing so they hope competitive market forces will yield high returns which will attract more firms to join.

More reforms were implemented in 2005/06 (see Table 16), altering how pensions are calculated. Major changes included a decrease of contribution rate for employees and employers for pillar 1B and changing incentives to encourage later retirement. For the first pillar, workers now gain an additional 0.6 per cent for each additional year of service (Sin, 2005). The second tier is funded solely by employee contributions of 8 per cent of wages. The total replacement rate from pillar 1 is therefore projected to

Table 16 **2006 reforms**

	Pillar 1A	Pillar 1B	Pillar 2	Pillar 3
Status	Mandatory	Mandatory	Voluntary	Voluntary
Type	DB & PAYGO	DB & PAYGO	DC & fully funded	DC & fully funded
Contribution	17% from enterprises	8% from employees	From both enterprises and employees, with tax benefits of up to 4% for employers – though actual rate will differ in different provincial governments	Individual contributing to his/her own pension account
Replacement ratio	20%	24.6%	2–12%	30–40%
Benefits	Only qualify if 15 years of contribution have been made. Benefit increases by 0.6% for every additional year worked after retirement age	Monthly payout of 1/120	Lump sum or annuity	Lump sum or annuities
Management	Government	Market	Market	Market

be 59.2 per cent. The payments are adjusted according to an index combining local wage and price inflation.

Rural pension scheme

There is a separate pension system in the rural areas of China. Its operating system is different as it is voluntary with vague operating instructions left to the discretion of local governments. Named the 'Provisional Rural Pension System', it had a coverage rate of only 9 per cent in 2003 (Hu, 2006), increasing to 12 per cent in 2007 (Arora and Dunaway, 2007). The rural population is 60 per cent of China's total population, so that a low coverage of rural workers implies a low coverage of the population as a whole. The level of 100 RMB (£8) per month is not really sufficient for a basic pension, even though the rural cost of living is lower than that of the city.

The Chinese government seems to be more concerned with reforms of the urban pension system than of the rural system.[10] Farmers are seen to have a 'fallback' with their land and extended family, whereas urban workers can rely only on financial assets in their old age.

Problems with pension provision in China

Much of the criticism levelled against the Chinese system is that its coverage is low. Critics then go on to suggest ways in which

---

10 There were five major regulation reforms from 1991 to 2004, with many more supplementary changes. Only two reforms to the rural system have been announced since 1995.

coverage can be improved.[11] But people are choosing not to join the 'compulsory' system because of a lack of trust in the system and the government and lack of suitability for their personal circumstances. We outline below some of the specific features of the Chinese system which make it a particularly poor model.

Highly regressive and highly subsidised

Even after the new pension reforms, there is still a low coverage rate for urban workers (48 per cent in 2005) and an even lower coverage rate for rural workers (12 per cent in 2005) (Arora and Dunaway, 2007). Migrating workers have particular incentives to evade the pension system because fifteen years of employment are required to qualify for a pension, whereas the average time a migrant worker stays in one job is three years. Furthermore, the fragmented governance in different provinces means that funds cannot be easily transported between regions (workers are allowed to take only their accumulation in pillar 1B with them – this accounts for about 5 per cent of their payroll, while another 15 per cent is kept by the local government for the social pool).

Urban workers are overwhelmingly wealthier than rural workers and likely to be wealthier than migrant workers – official figures show that the disposable income of an urban worker is over three times that of a rural worker, on average.[12] Approximately 60 per cent of the population is rural (China Statistical Yearbook, 2006), so most pensions are concentrated in the much wealthier 40 per cent of the population. This is supported by the fact that pensions have varied between 65 and 90 per cent of GDP

11   For example, Zhang (2007) and Salditt et al. (2007).
12   www.hemscott.com/news/latest-news/item.do?newsId=57266947508029.

Figure 8   **Ratio of contributors to pensioners**
Contributors/pensioners

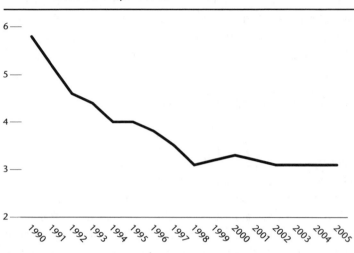

Source: Data from Zhang, 2007

per capita over the last six years. This is much higher than in all other regions of the world, the OECD average being 50 per cent (Salditt et al., 2007). This implies that people receiving pensions are likely to be much richer than the average.

Richer individuals are likely to benefit more from pensions as richer people tend to live longer than poor people, and urban dwellers live longer than rural dwellers.

There was an annual funding gap – averaging RMB44 billion (0.4 per cent GDP) – between 1993 and 2003 (Trin, 2006). While this seems small at present, considering the low coverage of the scheme and the rapid future worsening of the support ratio, it is likely to increase significantly. This is paralleled by a worsening ratio of contributors to retirees – reducing from 6 in 1990 to 3 in 2005 (see Figure 8).

The subsidy from the government is estimated as 15 per cent of annual pension benefits (Zhang, 2007). The annual subsidy figure is somewhat misleading, as we have seen from the demographic data above that the pensions system is not in a steady state and costs are set to progressively rise because there is no pre-funding. The sum of the present value of all accrued benefits, or implicit pension debt (IPD), was estimated to be 141 per cent of 2001 GDP (Salditt et al., 2007) – a huge burden on future taxpayers.

Thus the government is effectively subsidising the wealthiest section of the population when this is the very group of people best able to support itself, while the poorest sections of society are outside the system.

Empty individual accounts – unattractive and lack of credibility

The pension system is characterised by low returns and lack of portability – discouraging participation and discriminating against migrant workers. A more serious problem is a well-founded lack of trust – officials have been making up the deficit in state-level basic accounts by using individual accounts' savings. This has led to so-called empty individual accounts. Low trust has been exacerbated by incidents such as the Shanghai pension fund scandal, as a result of which two senior Communist Party officials were jailed for illegal investments of funds.

Problems with investment in rural areas are similar to those in the city, with the main focus being on investment in government bonds and discouragement of in-house investment. Another problem, however, is the 'management by government', where funds are borrowed by local governments to meet short-term finance deficits. The borrowed funds are repaid with a predetermined return in the future. In theory, this practice is not permitted, but with the fragmented nature of the government system, such practices are quite common.

Conclusion

China's demographic transformation has the potential to cause major changes in the world's economy. The apparently infinite supply of new workers will cease, or perhaps go into reverse. The so-called excess savings[13] are not excess at all but entirely rational for a country with a rapidly ageing population. The country can be expected to dis-save when a large proportion of the workforce retires. If we accept that these two phenomena contribute towards low interest rates and low wages, then they could be reversed as the population ages.

The Chinese pension system is the conduit through which China will dis-save. It will come under unprecedented strain owing to the country's rapidly changing demographic situation and because most of the savings are effectively undertaken by the government (Wolf, 2007).

In the Chinese pension system's favour, the contribution rate is relatively high, which means that contributors and employers are at least being charged for their pensions.[14] The recent reforms being undertaken are a step in the right direction – separating the administration of the different pillars was an urgently required reform which will hopefully remove part of the vulnerability to

---

13   Currently 50 per cent of GDP (Wolf, 2007).
14   Although for a sustainable system an 'accruals' basis is required (Booth, 2008).

corruption. We can still infer, however, that the pension system as it stands will deliver high, unaffordable pensions to the relatively wealthy for their long retirements, and no or low pensions to the poor. It is characterised by explicit or implicit corruption. The current system has the potential to turn the ageing population challenge into a crisis.

We can apply the lessons learnt from other countries to the Chinese situation. Even though China is not a democracy, the PAYGO system will give rise to powerful interest groups which the government will not wish to antagonise. The obvious conclusion is for China to avoid a PAYGO system before a tipping point is reached. While coverage is low, and most of the population are not yet near retirement, it is probably the country's best chance to reform.

Reform should start outside the pension system. China is a rapidly growing economy with substantial potential long-term investment opportunities. To improve the climate for long-term savings, the government needs to implement reforms to enforce property laws, increase transparency of institutions and stamp out corruption. Financial markets should be fully opened to overseas investors and domestic savers should be able to freely invest internationally. This will empower people to make their own savings decisions and remove the need for state involvement.

In many countries, rural areas rely on the extended family system. This will be placed under strain in China, however, owing to the 4–2-1 problem described above. But unlike in most other developing countries, micro-insurance is widespread in China,[15] and this could be scaled up and savings products developed.

---

15   Through the All China Federation of Trade Unions (ACFTU) (Roth et al., 2007).

Thus, China does not need a pension blueprint but the liber-alisation of financial markets from which sustainable systems of income replacement in retirement can evolve. The systems that should be allowed to evolve will be different for people in different areas of the country, with different employment profiles and different levels of income. This is as it should be. The desired working patterns and opportunities for family support are so varied that it would be wholly inappropriate to impose a system of retirement income provision on a country that comprises around 15 per cent of the world's population – even if the financial and legal infrastructure were sufficient to support a uniform, formal pensions system.

References

Arora, V. and S. Dunaway (2007), *Pension Reform in China: The Need for a New Approach*, IMF Working Paper 07/109.

Booth, P. M. (2008), 'The young held to ransom – a public choice analysis of the UK state pension system', *Economic Affairs*, 28(3): 4–10.

Chen, V. (2004), 'A macro analysis of China pension pooling system', PIE Working Paper.

China Statistical Yearbook (2006), China Statistics Press.

Deutsche Bank (2005), *China & India – a visual essay*, Deutsche Bank Research, October.

Holzmann, R., I. MacArthur and Y. Sin (2000), *Pension Systems in East Asia and the Pacific: Challenges and Opportunities*, World Bank Social Protection Discussion Paper 14.

Hu, Y.-W. (2006), 'Pension reform in China – a case study', Brunel University.

Kynge, J. (2006), *China Shakes the World*, London: Phoenix.

Lutz, W., Q. Ren, S. Scherbov and X. Zheng (2005), *China's Uncertain Demographic Present and Future*, Princeton, NJ: Princeton University Press, available online at http://iussp2005.princeton.edu/download.aspx?submissionId=51192.

Misoulis, N. (2008), 'Demographic effects to economic growth and consequences to the provision of pensions', *Economic Affairs*, 28(1): 29–34.

Reuters (2007), 'China's life expectancy to jump', 12 February.

Roth, J., M. McCord and D. Liber (2007), *The Landscape of Microinsurance in the World's 100 Poorest Countries*, MicroInsurance Centre.

Salditt, P., P. Whiteford and W. Adema (2007), *Pension Reform in China: Progress and prospects*, OECD Working Paper 53.

Sin, Y. (2005), 'China: pension liabilities and reform options for old age insurance', Working Paper no. 2005–1, World Bank.

Trin, T. (2006), *China's Pension System*, Deutsche Bank Research, February.

Wolf, M. (2007), 'Big test for the "great convergence"', *Financial Times*, 17 October.

Zhang, W. (2007), 'Further reforms of China's pension system: a realistic alternative option to full funded individual accounts', *Asian Economic Papers*, 6(2): 112–35.

PART THREE – PENSIONS AND PUBLIC POLICY IN LOW-INCOME COUNTRIES

11 OLD-AGE SECURITY IN LESS DEVELOPED COUNTRIES: FORMAL VERSUS INFORMAL PROVISION
Oskari Juurikkala

Introduction

Pension systems around the world are undergoing major reforms. Less-developed countries (LDCs) face a situation very different from that of the affluent world. Many commentators argue that LDCs need more extensive formal pension schemes – private savings accounts as well as governmental pay-as-you-go schemes – as life expectancies increase.

Countries such as India, China and Nigeria have either attempted or are contemplating major reforms in their pension landscape, often with the assistance of the World Bank. Reform needs are clear: existing schemes are underfunded and badly administered. In India, for example, the pension scheme for public sector employees is so indebted that it is beginning to crowd out other public services. China is suffering from similar problems, and Nigeria has a record of repeatedly failing to deliver pension promises.

The World Bank is pushing for private sector solutions, but there are major difficulties with these in practice. The institutional capacity in most LDCs is not sufficient for operating large-scale pension funds, especially when capital markets are underdeveloped or non-existent. Private sector pensions may also create large administrative costs, and give rise to fraud and corruption.

This chapter argues that these proposals are heading down the wrong track. They assume it is necessary to choose between one of two options: the government or formal market-based pension schemes.

Instead of formal schemes, more importance should be attached to informal sources of old-age security, particularly the traditional family. It is shown below that the family is not only the most important source of security in LDCs, but it is also the most reliable, efficient and adaptable. Pension policy should support family provision – as well as other types of informal security – and also focus on building up a stable institutional framework with the rule of law and well-defined property rights so that there can be a longer-term movement towards formal pension provision as the sophistication of these economies develops.

Family support and informal old-age security

Informal old-age security – particularly the traditional family system – is the main source of protection for elderly people in LDCs. This was recognised by the influential World Bank study, *Averting the Old Age Crisis* (World Bank, 1994). In India, for example, about 90 per cent of individuals are outside formal pension schemes (Goswami, 2002). In many African countries, the percentages are higher still (Barbone and Sanchez, 1999).

In practice, the term 'informal old-age security' can mean a number of things. Most commonly, it denotes children taking care of their elderly parents or close relatives. But there are also support systems built around local communities, informal clubs, kinship networks, patrons, and religious and other non-governmental organisations.

Informal support systems also vary from culture to culture. In African countries, the extended family system is the prevalent source of old-age and other social security. Non-family systems, such as tribal networks, are also important. Old-age support from siblings is more common than in Asia.

In Latin America, formal pension systems are more developed than in other LDCs. The family continues to be very important for the poor, however, both urban and rural. Moreover, public pension schemes are experiencing difficulties, so that people may need to fall back on informal support.

In Hindu and Muslim cultures the family support system is old, strong and practically intact, according to the World Bank study. In these cultures, well over 75 per cent of the elderly live with their children. This practice is not confined to rural areas, as even in urban Mumbai more than 80 per cent of the elderly live with their children. Muslim and Hindu cultures reinforce the traditional family system, because parents usually control property, inheritance, marriage age and the choice of marriage partner.

Finally, China has some of the strongest family systems in the world. This is rather surprising, because the communist system deliberately sought to destroy the traditional family, particularly during the Cultural Revolution. The government broke up families, imposed forced abortion and infanticide and frequently tried to turn children against their parents. Nevertheless, Chinese families are still strong today, and many children feel obliged to care for their parents in old age, especially in rural areas.

The World Bank study mentioned above reached three important conclusions with respect to informal old-age security. Each of them has powerful implications, yet it appears that they have been missed, ignored or forgotten by many pension reform experts. The rest of the chapter will examine each of these propositions in detail. The conclusions are as follows:

- The traditional family is the most important source of old-age security, and it continues to be so.
- The family system has clear benefits: it solves informational and behavioural problems that plague formal systems.
- Mandatory formal pension programmes can crowd out informal security, which implies that governments should think carefully before imposing formal programmes.

No evidence of breakdown

The first issue is whether the traditional family system is able to cope with the process of modernisation. In theory, there is no reason why it should not. There is, however, only a limited amount of quantitative evidence of the current state of informal support systems. Some of it is summarised in the World Bank study cited above (1994: 61–5). According to this evidence, the traditional family system is alive and well.

The main body of evidence is based on questionnaire results from a large set of countries, both economically developed and less developed. In low-income countries, almost all of the elderly live among family members. Their main sources of income and support are their own work and their family. In addition to housing and financial support, children around the world provide non-financial support such as help with household work and in emergencies.

Cross-sectional data shows that filial support for elderly

parents is less common as countries develop economically. That does not necessarily imply, however, that the family system is breaking down, but rather that retirees in high-income countries have a large pension and private savings, so that they do not need direct support from their children.

It is clear that family support is particularly strong in LDCs, as one would expect. But non-financial assistance from children is very common even in high-income countries like the USA, where the vast majority of elderly individuals receive a large pension. Many children also give financial support to their elderly parents. It is also not uncommon for elderly Americans to live with their children or family – as many as 13 per cent of Americans over 65 do so. Living with children is particularly common in Japan, even though that country has high incomes and a mature formal pension system. It is true that in many developed countries expectations have changed and parents do not expect as much support as in the past. But the reason for this is simply that direct support from the family is not needed when countries and families become more affluent.

Some counterarguments

Despite this clear evidence, several authors promote wider formal pension coverage on the ground that the family system is breaking down. This assumption can be found in numerous papers, as a standard starting-point of discussion. Yet very few authors give any tangible evidence to support it. In fact, the present author has yet to find a single piece of such evidence. It *may* still be the case that traditional family arrangements will face harder times in the future, but in view of clear empirical evidence to the contrary, we cannot take it as given, because important decisions depend on it and they should not be taken on the basis of gut feeling.[1]

Certainly, there is limited empirical knowledge of the issue, and in any case it is not easy to measure the state of the traditional family system because support within families is provided outside the context of market transactions and therefore goes unrecorded. There are, of course, practical arguments as to why the family should be coming under greater strains than before. Shah (2005) argues that labour mobility is a major challenge. In the traditional family system, parents live with their children; but now children often find work in distant locations, so the traditional pattern becomes harder to follow.

But this argument undermines the flexibility and adaptability of the family support system. The traditional system is more than living with one's children. Children can – and do – support their parents from a distance too. Moreover, parents can move with their children, and family ties are wider than those within the nuclear family.

Responses to rising longevity

Another challenge comes from rising life expectancy. This puts pressure on the family system because parents will need more

---

[1] To give just one example of the bias in favour of formal pension schemes: Palacios (2003) argues that 'already some analysts cite growing strain in family support systems', but strangely enough, he does not cite a single name or reference to support his statement. Instead, he defends the view by arguing that the family is coming under greater strains owing to low fertility rates. This is not evidence, and it also reveals a simplistic understanding of family support systems: they are normally combined with savings and part-time work in old age. Moreover, under extended family arrangements, it is not necessary for all individuals to have children of their own.

support in old age. Other variables that tend to be correlated with longevity will, however, make it easier for families to provide for their aged. First, rising real wages and living standards are making it possible for people to save more during their working lives: whether or not this is in formal pension schemes. Also, higher earnings by children make it easier for them to support their parents. Second, the development of financial markets also fosters private savings which can gradually supplement provision made from current income.

In other words, even where the traditional family is under stress, support systems are resilient, flexible and adaptable. Higher incomes and more financial aid can replace the traditional way of living together – but this is a natural economic process and does not require the creation of a 'pension blueprint'. Although lower fertility rates mean that families have fewer children, this can be offset by the fact that lower fertility enables women to earn and also provide financial support to their parents too.

The benefits and weaknesses of family support systems

The second important conclusion of the World Bank study is that family provision for old-age security does have clear benefits. This is often forgotten. Indeed, it is often argued that formal pension plans are more efficient than traditional family arrangements. There is undoubtedly some truth in this contention. But a closer look reveals a more complex picture.

One benefit of family systems is that there is no need to define any specific 'old age', after which a person is entitled to benefits. In informal systems support is not based on age, but on inability to work and care for oneself. Family members and other close individuals know best what kind of support is needed and when.

This contrasts with many formal pension systems, especially publicly financed ones and pension schemes for public sector workers (Gruber and Wise, 1999, 2005). Formal schemes encourage people to retire too early and often provide limited flexibility with regard to retirement age. They often penalise economically those who could work longer.

Sometimes, of course, illness or disability prevents somebody from continuing to work. But that is another situation that informal systems can handle well; whereas formal schemes are struggling with the problem of disability retirement, families can provide for those who are disabled or ill and family systems are less prone to free-riding by those who are not genuinely ill.[2]

Flexibility and adaptability

Family and other informal support systems are, though, more prone to localised shocks, such as the unemployment, illness or death of a crucial individual. This can be alleviated by extended family arrangements, which function as a kind of risk-pooling device. When the support network goes beyond the nuclear family, vulnerability to localised risks is greatly reduced. Modern portfolio theory supports this: allocation of assets into just a few baskets brings about a significant reduction of risk.[3]

---

2   See generally Gruber and Wise (1998). An analysis of the problem in the UK context can be found in Blundell and Johnson (1998).

3   The classic study is Markowitz (1952). The diversification effect holds as long as the risks are not perfectly correlated. Of course, extended families may suffer from wider shocks such as droughts. Yet formal pension systems too are vulnerable to system-wide shocks.

The flexibility can be seen in the way in which, when a sudden need arises, more resources can be released for that purpose. In the USA, there was no formal social security or pension scheme when the Great Depression shook the country in the 1930s, yet there is no record of particular problems for the aged. Families and other informal support networks responded.

In formal schemes, it is difficult to target resources effectively to those who need them most. One method used is so-called 'means testing', which signifies that extra benefits are given to those with insufficient income and savings. Practically all experts agree that this has had disastrous consequences, in that it discourages work and thrift, and in the long term it exacerbates wealth inequality and poverty (Neumark and Powers, 1998, 2000). But in the absence of means testing, if you try to provide individuals with more support, you need to inflate the entire system. Moreover, it becomes difficult to cut down additional benefits once you have started giving them. Once again, formal systems struggle to distinguish between the deserving and undeserving poor and between cases of genuine need and free-riders.

It is very important to remember that informal systems do not need to operate in isolation. Even in the absence of any formal pension schemes, the elderly need not depend on their children alone. First, they can continue working, either full time or part time. They often work informally at the home of their children, as carers for their grandchildren, so that they are not merely a recipient of income and care but a provider of care too. Second, there are various other informal support networks. Even in currently affluent countries, mutual aid and fraternal societies played a major role in the past, looking after the sick, the unemployed and the elderly (see Bartholomew, 2006). Finally, people can save on their own – if not via pension plans, then using other, less sophist-icated instruments.[4]

Having a wide range of income and support sources is some-times seen as a negative thing – it is said that the system is too 'scattered'. But, in actual fact, there is nothing inherently wrong with that. Having diverse sources of old-age security gives rise to systemic heterogeneity, which makes individuals less reliant on specific institutions that can fail. Formality and sophistication are no sure guarantees of robustness and safety.

Difficulties with formal schemes

It is also important not to focus too narrowly on the character-istics of informal support systems, and to imagine that formal schemes are always without problems. That would be far from the truth. Formal schemes too are prone to risk, although these are of a different kind.

One common risk relates to insufficient funding. The Indian public sector pension scheme is a prime example. Some experts estimate that, just on account of central and state government employees, the implicit debt is over 50 per cent of GDP (Bhardwaj and Dave, 2005). The problem is not limited to India, however, as underfunding and under-accounting of debts within formal schemes are legion within developed countries too (see Record, 2006). It is possible that existing pension promises will become impossible to fulfil within the taxable capacity of both affluent and less-developed nations, although benefits may be undermined in subtle ways, such as higher rates of inflation. The individuals who

---

4 Often the biggest obstacle to private savings is the inflationary nature of modern paper money, which can be inflated by governments at will.

rely on these benefits must then find other ways of supporting themselves in old age.

One should note that funding problems are also found in the private sector. In countries with highly developed pension markets, such as the UK, defined-benefit pension plans are struggling with problems of underfunding. Arguably in the UK this is partly because of arbitrary government decisions relating to regulation (Silver, 2006). But there is always investment and longevity risk with any type of formal funded pension scheme. In LDCs, where financial markets are volatile and less developed, difficulties are even more likely.

Formal pension schemes – both public and private – are anything but easy to manage in the long term. They can give rise to significant administrative costs, and the institutional capacity in many LDCs is not sufficiently developed. Formal schemes are also prone to short-term political opportunism, administrative mismanagement and fraud in LDCs (Barbone and Sanchez, 1999). In Nigeria, for example, the payment of pension benefits has for years been subject to considerable delays and outright political plunder, and high inflation rates have tended to erode the real value of benefits (Silver et al., 2007).

It is interesting to note that, in fact, most individuals in LDCs are not looking to formal pension schemes for help with old-age security. In India, a recent Financial Literacy Survey established that financial knowledge in India is very low, and most people are not likely to want to participate in formal pension plans. They do not understand such systems well and therefore they would not trust them (Bhardwaj, 2003). In India, moreover, there is no tradition of investing in capital markets, so many people lack experiential knowledge.

It is also debatable whether formal institutions in LDCs are ready for the sudden growth of pension schemes. Indian financial markets were opened to competition only in the 1990s. Regulatory rules are still inflexible and underdeveloped, and most markets are shallow and illiquid (Deutsche Bank, 2007). Besides, there have been several scandals in the equity markets in the past, and many investors lack confidence in them (Hinz and Rao, 2003). These are not arguments against formal schemes in principle. They are arguments for allowing formal schemes to evolve naturally with other economic and social developments, and not trying to jump-start formal schemes where they are unlikely to prosper.

Widows and the challenge of culture

The family support system does, however, have at least two clear challenges. One is that it demands more from individuals, and there is clearly a risk that some elderly parents will be left without adequate care. This problem may be exacerbated by the trend for the young to move into cities in LDCs. They will, however, often provide remittances for older members of the family.

Another challenge is that, in some cultures, women are more vulnerable, and they depend on filial loyalty and extrafamilial support. Widows are a particularly vulnerable group. According to Dreze (1990), elderly widows in India face difficult constraints, such as restrictions on remarriage, patrilineal inheritance, difficulties in finding employment and lack of access to credit. Most widows are supported by their sons, but those without sons find it harder, and they can be treated harshly after their husband's death.

There is no easy answer to such problems. But in fact they are not necessarily eased by formal systems. For example, if women lack access to the labour market, they may be unable to save in formal pension systems. Culture is probably more important in this connection than the specific economic framework within which old-age security is provided. It is interesting to note that the covenant laws of the Jewish people make specific and concrete prescriptions on how one must look after and contribute to the needs of the poor and the vulnerable, such as widows, orphans and travellers (van Til, 2004). Similarly, the first Christians were known for their commitment to Christ's commandment of charity, and the early Church frequently arranged collections to support the needy, especially widows.[5]

The crowding-out problem

The World Bank study (1994) expresses concern that compulsory formal pension schemes may crowd out informal support. This is a major concern, because once informal networks are undermined they can be difficult to create anew.

Public PAYGO schemes

Publicly financed pay-as-you-go (PAYGO) schemes are particularly problematic in this respect. Several economists argue that they are an important cause of the stark declines in total fertility rates in affluent countries.[6] Pension systems do create incentives that discourage childbearing. Because a PAYGO system depends on the contributions of future generations, the negative fertility effect contributes to the insolvency of these very systems.

5   See generally Benedict XVI (2005: nos 22–4).
6   See Boldrin et al. (2005), Ehrlich and Kim (2007) and Juurikkala (2007).

Public PAYGO pensions discourage childbearing in two distinct ways. One is the substitution effect – or crowding-out problem. When there is no governmental pension scheme, many people rely on their children for old-age security. In LDCs, children are therefore seen as an economic resource, an 'investment' of sorts, in addition to many other reasons for having them. The imposition of a formal pension scheme reduces the economic benefit of having children, but the costs remain the same.

Exacerbating the crowding-out problem is the 'free-ride effect'. Public pension schemes are designed as if the entire nation were just one big family: all workers pay compulsory contributions, which are channelled to the entire generation of retirees. Families that have few or no children have the benefit of the tax receipts from those families that do have children. In a sense children become a public good: the benefits are shared among the community, but the costs of child-rearing are borne by the family.

Because of these problems, some economists advocate pension reforms that would link benefits to the number of children raised (see Demeny, 1987). One such reform in a UK context could, for example, divide National Insurance contributions into four equal components. As the pension system can be financed either by invested contributions today or children who pay taxes in the next generation, every child (up to four children) could lead to exemption from one component of National Insurance contributions. Such a reform would be simple and could replace other forms of state welfare provision for children which themselves distort behaviour, such as allowances for childcare.

Of course, there is no need to engage in such complex exercises if there is no PAYGO scheme that needs fixing. For LDCs, the better approach is to not develop universal PAYGO schemes, and to build instead on the oldest pay-as-you-go scheme in the world, namely inter-generational transfers within the family.

Compulsory savings

Private pension plans do not necessarily cause such crowding-out problems. Voluntary savings neither replace nor penalise the family: they merely offer an alternative. In practice, it is most likely that the majority of people would use a combination of saving and family support. A system should allow those who wish to rely primarily on saving to do so while also allowing those who wish to rely on the support of family to follow their desired course of action.

Compulsory pensions savings schemes may be problematic, however, as they institutionalise one particular type of old-age provision. Compulsory pensions savings in low-income countries can exhaust personal resources that families could otherwise allocate to education for children, developing a small business, current consumption or having more children.

A recent reform in Nigeria is a good example of this problem. The new pension system, enacted in 2004, is a savings scheme, which demands compulsory contributions of 15 per cent of gross salary.[7] The reform is undoubtedly a major step forward in comparison with the failing systems of the past, but the rate of compulsory savings would be rather high even in more affluent countries. In addition one should note that operating the reform is risky as the financial and legal infrastructure in Nigeria has not

7   See the website of the Nigerian government's National Pension Commission (www.pencom.gov.ng) for further information on the new system.

proven sufficiently enduring to protect the real value of pensions saving in the past.

The way ahead
Inconsistent advice from the World Bank

The World Bank, unfortunately, does not in practice seem to put much importance on the value of informal support systems. In *Averting the Old Age Crisis*, the Bank put forward an influential framework for pension reform – a framework that simply ignores informal support. The so-called three-pillar model builds on three types of old-age security: (1) a public scheme (either universal or means-tested), which has the goal of reducing poverty; (2) a mandatory savings scheme, managed by the private sector; and (3) voluntary private savings. Traditional family arrangements and other informal mechanisms stand out by their absence.

The three-pillar model seeks to plot a middle way between complete state and complete private provision. Thus there is some insurance against the financial risk of private systems as well as a minimum income guarantee for the very poor. In a similar fashion, compulsory savings are a way of reducing the risk that some individuals fail to save enough voluntarily. Even if aggregate private saving were sufficient, some individuals might act myopically and would need to be looked after by the state in old age. This is a particularly important issue if a means-tested PAYGO pension is used for this group, because means testing would actually encourage some individuals not to save privately. To be precise, in that case moral hazard, rather than myopia, can be the underlying problem.

Therefore both compulsory private and government schemes

do have an economic justification. The framework ignores the fact, however, that formal schemes may quite simply fail to deliver what they are supposed to deliver, especially within LDCs, whose very lack of development will often be caused by a lack of good governance, enforcement of contracts or the existence of secure property rights.

The three-pillar framework also makes no mention of informal support. This is particularly regrettable, because the study itself highlighted the value and relevance of traditional family and other kinds of informal old-age security. A more recent book by two World Bank authors extends the framework, as they realise that the three pillars alone gave an inadequate picture of old-age security options, particularly in LDCs (Holzmann and Hinz, 2005). But even then, informal security ends up as a fallback option.

There are many reasons why it is problematic to see informal security as a fallback option. First, the family system is more fundamental than the other options – it is more widespread and better functioning in LDCs than formal systems. Second, informal security can be more effective in certain respects, especially in reducing moral hazard and free-riding behaviour in countries with poor legal and financial infrastructure; it is more flexible, too, and capable of reinventing itself in the face of new challenges. And third, it is dangerous to view the family system as a mere default option, because this makes it vulnerable to public policies that crowd out families and other intermediate forms of association.

An alternative framework

There are not just two options for old-age security, provision through either the government or through savings. The third dimension, informal security through family mechanisms, is extremely important in LDCs. It is especially important that pension reform does not undermine this dimension. Indeed, pension policy should consider the protection of informal mechanisms as the first priority. There is a danger that an imperfect and unplanned system can be undermined by the imposition of a planned system that works well in theory but not in practice. Alternative forms of old-age provision should be allowed to develop naturally, along with the development of the financial and legal infrastructure, so that families can choose the appropriate mix of different forms of provision for old-age security. We should think in terms of at least the following five pillars of old-age security:

- family support systems;
- other informal systems and associations (including mutual aid societies);
- private savings (through financial markets or otherwise);
- charitable organisations;
- minimalist government schemes (e.g. through a minimum pension, or a compulsory savings provision).

These can be complemented by a sixth pillar of working through old age.

A combination of informal and formal support is more flexible and adaptable than formal systems alone. It is also more likely to function well in LDCs, where the institutional capacity is often insufficient for operating large-scale pension schemes, whether public or private. At the same time, it allows a smooth and natural – unforced – development of financial markets, which is necessary for the sustainable functioning of market-based pension plans.

Having a wide combination of sources of income security also gives rise to greater systemic *heterogeneity*. Each aspect has its limits and risks and the different aspects are not rivals but complements. Taken together, their heterogeneity increases the robustness and adaptability of the system as a whole.

Practical policy directions

In terms of practical politics, this framework yields a new set of policy directions. The first is that public policy should do everything possible to avoid crowding-out effects. For this reason, it is crucial to see governmental interventions as the very last resort. The compulsory nature of public pension systems means that they undermine the alternatives and, because of the fragile legal and financial infrastructure in LDCs, they give rise to long-term risks.

Second, one could complement informal systems in a targeted way. The World Bank's 1994 report suggests some practical possibilities. One is providing supportive healthcare services for those who care for their elderly parents or relatives. Another option is to give tax deductions to those who support their elderly parents. In practice, there may be some monitoring problems with such policies. But the direction is clear: government intervention should not seek to create new support systems, but simply to assist informal support systems and make their life easier.

Third and perhaps most important, one must help savings institutions and financial markets develop – not by imposing quasi-market schemes that in reality are hugely regulated and incapable of developing further. Instead, LDCs must focus on building up the basic institutional infrastructure that is necessary for the natural evolution of markets: secure and well-defined property rights, clear legal rules and so on.

Fourth, monetary stability is crucial for old-age security. This is already true of informal support systems. When governments seek to gain short-term income by printing money, they steal the property of ordinary people who do not know how to protect themselves against inflation. Even single-digit inflation rates can make a significant difference to private savings values if they are kept in coins, banknotes or in bank accounts – particularly if interest rates are regulated.

Conclusion

LDCs are standing at a cross-roads. On the one hand, they can try to follow the approach adopted in developed countries, and create wider formal pension schemes, both public and private. This path is likely to prove to be a mistake: public solutions are already unsustainable in LDCs, and the private sector in LDCs cannot realistically operate efficiently on a large scale giving guarantees over long time periods.

On the other hand, there is a more promising path. This is to focus on the informal support systems that are already doing well despite challenging circumstances. Governments should not undermine these systems by imposing unworkable formal schemes on the population, but should strengthen informal systems by reforming the broader institutional landscape, and perhaps by targeted assistance to families. In this way, private sector pensions can and will develop in a natural fashion when the time is ripe and appropriate institutions are properly developed.

References

Barbone, L. and L.-A. Sanchez (1999), 'Pensions and social security in sub-Saharan Africa: issues and options', World Bank, Africa Region Working Paper Series no. 4, available online at www.worldbank.org/afr/wps/wp4.htm.

Bartholomew, J. (2006), *The Welfare State We're In*, 2nd revised edn, London: Politico's.

Benedict XVI (2005), Encyclical letter *Deus Caritas Est*, Vatican : Libreria Editrice Vaticana.

Bhardwaj, G. (2003), 'The IIEF Financial Literacy Survey 2002', in A. Bordia and G. Bhardwaj (eds), *Rethinking Pension Provision for India*, Tata McGraw-Hill, available online at www.iief. com/rethink.htm.

Bhardwaj, G. and S. A. Dave (2005), 'Towards estimating India's implicit pension debt on account of civil service employees', Invest India Economic Foundation, available online at www. iief.com/Research/BhardwajDave2005_ipd1.pdf.

Blundell, R. and P. Johnson (1998), 'Pensions and labor-market participation in the United Kingdom', *American Economic Review*, 88(2): 168–72.

Boldrin, M., M. de Nardi and L. E. Jones (2005), 'Fertility and social security', NBER Working Paper no. 11146.

Demeny, P. (1987), 'Re-linking fertility behavior and economic security in old age: a pronatalist reform', *Population and Development Review*, 13(1): 128–32.

Deutsche Bank (2007), *India's Capital Markets – Unlocking the door to future growth*, Deutsche Bank Research, 14 February, available online at www.dbresearch.com/servlet/reweb2. ReWEB?rwkey=u1067195.

Dreze, J. (1990), 'Widows in rural India', Development Economics Research Programme DEP 26, London School of Economics.

Ehrlich, I. and J. Kim (2007), 'Social security and demographic trends: theory and evidence from the international experience', *Review of Economic Dynamics*, 10(1): 55–77.

Goswami, R. (2002), 'Old age protection in India: problems and prognosis', *International Social Security Review*, 55(2).

Gruber, J. and D. A. Wise (1998), 'Social security and retirement: an international comparison', *American Economic Review*, 88(2): 158–63.

Gruber, J. and D. A. Wise (eds) (1999), *Social Security and Retirement around the World*, Chicago, IL: University of Chicago Press.

Gruber, J. and D. A. Wise (2005), 'Social security programs and retirement around the world: fiscal implications. Introduction and summary', NBER Working Paper no. 11290.

Hinz, R. P. and G. V. N. Rao (2003), 'Approach to the regulation of private pension funds in India: application of international best practice', in A. Bordia and G. Bhardwaj (eds), *Rethinking Pension Provision for India*, Tata McGraw-Hill, available online at www.iief.com/pensions/CHAPTER4.pdf.

Holzmann, R. and R. Hinz (2005), *Old-Age Income Support in the 21st Century: An International Perspective on Pension Systems and Reform*, Washington, DC: World Bank.

Juurikkala, O. (2007), 'Pensions, fertility and families', *Economic Affairs*, 27(4): 52–57.

Markowitz, H. M. (1952), 'Portfolio selection', *Journal of Finance*, 7(1): 77–91.

Neumark, D. and E. Powers (1998), 'The effect of means-tested income support for the elderly on pre-retirement saving: evidence from the SSI program in the US', *Journal of Public Economics*, 68(2): 181–206.

Neumark, D. and E. Powers (2000), 'Welfare for the elderly: the effects of SSI on pre-retirement labor supply', *Journal of Public Economics*, 78(1/2): 51–80.

Palacios, R. (2003), 'Challenge of pension reform in India', in A. Bordia and G. Bhardwaj (eds), *Rethinking Pension Provision for India*, Tata McGraw-Hill, available online at www.iief.com/pensions/CHAPTER3.pdf.

Record, N. (2006), *Sir Humphrey's Legacy: Facing Up to the Cost of Public Sector Pensions*, London: Institute of Economic Affairs.

Shah, A. (2005), 'A sustainable and scalable approach in Indian pension reform', Ministry of Finance, New Delhi, available online at www.mayin.org/ajayshah/PDFDOCS/Shah2005_sustainable_pension_reform.pdf.

Silver, N. (2006), 'The trouble with final salary pension schemes', 14th IEA Discussion Paper, London: Institute of Economic Affairs, available online at www.iea.org.uk.

Silver, N., E. Acquaah and O. Juurikkala (2007), 'Savings in the absence of functioning property rights', *Economic Affairs*, 27(1): 71–75.

Van Til, K. (2004), 'A biblical/theological case for basic sustenance for all', *Journal of Markets and Morality*, 7: 441–66.

World Bank (1994), *Averting the Old Age Crisis: Policies to Protect the Old and Promote Growth*, Washington, DC.

12 PENSION PROVISION IN INDIA – CURRENT STATUS, PROPOSED REFORM AND CHALLENGES AHEAD

Sumita Kale and Laveesh Bhandari

Background

The provision of old-age security through a formal pension system has been in force in India since the middle of the last century. The pension programme, however, which is limited in scope and coverage, is fraught with financial distress, as has been the case with most government-provided services. Pension reform has been on the anvil for almost a decade now but with slow progress owing to resistance on both the political and labour-relations fronts. Though there are various schemes organised within the public and private sectors, the aim of covering all the working population in India calls for more concerted and comprehensive action from all stakeholders. Accessibility, affordability and sustainability are the critical criteria and, given India's demographic trends and organisational structure, it is quite clear that a 'one size fits all' programme will not work. Schemes targeted at different groups would need to be appropriately designed. Moreover, bearing in mind the diversity between regions and the federal structure of government, pension programmes in India need to be decentralised: they should be run at state level, with (perhaps) financial and technical support given by the central government. While debate on pension provision often focuses on the 'government versus market' issue, the characteristics of the Indian population and labour force make a case for effective regulation with sufficient choice for consumers. This chapter sets out the current situation in India and explores the various feasible strategies for pension reform.

The current situation

India's problem of providing security to its old people is a growing one as the number of persons of more than 60 years of age is estimated to increase from 71 million in 2001 to 173 million in 2026, with the share in total population rising from 6.9 per cent to 12.4 per cent (ORGCC, 2006). The burden of provision of financial security to old persons is becoming more severe over the years given increasing life expectancy, while other factors, such as higher health costs, changed consumption and saving patterns, decline in the joint family system, structural changes in the economy leading to job insecurity for some people, etc., compound the problem.

NSSO data (2004) reveal that as many as 65 per cent of the aged are dependent on others for their daily needs, and this problem is more severe for women, of whom 85 per cent are not financially independent. Traditionally it is expected that children will look after their parents in their old age and this is the perception even today. In an ADB survey of 2004, 58 per cent in urban areas and 72 per cent in rural areas expected children to take care of them when they were old. As a consequence, saving decisions during the earning periods are prompted by the requirements of providing security for the family, and the education and marriage of children, and only lastly by one's own retirement security. While a little more than 40 per cent were confident that their expectations would be realised, around 30 per cent were not so sure of this support, as they felt that their children 'might' look after them in old age.

Where access to credit is concerned, a similar picture emerges. The second-most important source of household credit across India (moneylenders being the most important) is loans from family and relatives (ADB, 2006). All other sources, such as banks, self-help groups, companies, etc., are less significant. The dependence on family and relatives is natural therefore in a setting where the financial sector has not spread widely enough because of the high costs and risks of including the majority of the population in the formal financial sector.

The implications for the state therefore are manifold, and the government sees social security for the aged as part of a package of policies to empower old people. Accordingly, the primary objectives of the National Policy for Older Persons, formulated in 1999, are concerned with encouraging individuals to make provision for their own as well as their spouse's old age, encouraging families to take care of their older family members, enabling voluntary and non-governmental organisations to supplement the care provided by the family, etc.

This concern for the aged has also led the government to introduce legislation under the Maintenance and Welfare of Parents and Senior Citizens Bill 2007. When passed, the law will make it obligatory for children and heirs to provide for their parents. It is of course unlikely that this Bill will ensure financial independence and security for old people in practice. The fact that there was a need for such a law, however, highlights the problems in a society where values are becoming more individualistic.

Yet, according to the Constitution of India, the state cannot shirk its responsibility of providing for the elderly. 'The State shall, within the limits of its economic capacity and development, make effective provision for securing the right to work, to education and to public assistance in cases of unemployment, old age, sickness and disablement, and in other cases of undeserved want.'[1] As a result, under the National Policy for Older Persons, various facilities have been implemented, such as strengthening primary healthcare for the aged, increasing coverage under the public food distribution scheme to the elderly (especially those who are marginalised), provision of financial security, and so on. The areas covered under the financial security aspect include the following:

• Proposing tax benefits and higher interest rates for senior citizen savings.
• Promotion of long-term savings in both rural and urban areas.
• Increased coverage and revision of old-age pension schemes for the destitute elderly.
• Prompt settlement of pension, provident fund, gratuity and other retirement benefits.

Provision of financial security should, however, account for the varied characteristics, and therefore needs, of the population, which can broadly be placed in four categories as follows:

1. Those who cannot save enough for their retirement.[2]

---

1   Article 41, Constitution of India.
2   Official poverty estimates for 2004/05 set a monthly consumption of Rs356.30 per month in rural areas and Rs538.6 in urban areas as the poverty line, according to which 301 million people fall under this basic level (GOI, 2007). In fact, the ADB survey data also showed that 23.2 per cent of the working population do not save, presumably because of low capacity to do so (ADB, 2006).

2. Those who can save but have no access to appropriate financial services.[3]
3. Those who can save and have access to financial services but are not concerned about retirement saving.
4. Those who are already saving for retirement as the above qualifications have been fulfilled.

From an administrative point of view, for pension plan design, it is useful to classify the labour force in two categories – those who are employed in the organised (formal) sector and those in the unorganised (informal) sector.[4] Both these categories will, of course, include people from all the four classifications mentioned earlier, but in varying proportions. It is much easier to spread the coverage of pension plans in the organised sector where book-keeping and records are formalised, where the government, employers and employees can work together to formulate plans to suit their purpose and a certain amount of enforceability can be guaranteed. But the bulk of the labour force works in the unorganised sector, where the first two categories (lack of saving capacity and lack of access to financial services) characterise the majority of people.

Financial security can be promoted in various ways. There are fiscal incentives, provident fund schemes like the Public Provident Fund, higher deposit rates for senior citizens, etc. There are also options for individuals to select private sector pension schemes,

3   The Reserve Bank of India estimates that 41 per cent of the Indian adult population (250 million people) do not have a bank account while 73 per cent of farmer households (65 million households) have no access to formal sources of credit (Thorat, 2007).

4   We use the terms organised and formal, and unorganised and informal, interchangeably.

such as those run by life insurance companies, the post office, mutual funds, etc. Such schemes would, however, cater to the needs of a minority of individuals in the country, above a certain level of education and income. The ADB survey in 2004 found that even within the organised sector, only 6.2 per cent of people were actively saving for retirement. Excluding government employees, 22 per cent of the respondents were not preparing for retirement or even expecting to retire; 64.5 per cent had not thought of retirement at all (though this number is 48.5 per cent for government employees).

There is thus a need in India for:

- Better information and awareness of the various savings options.
- Social insurance for the poorest of the poor.
- Accelerating financial inclusion to cover the marginalised and those who do not have access to financial services.
- Increased options for pension plans.
- Education about benefits for those who plan for the future through the market mechanism.

As is shown in the following section, for comprehensive coverage of the labour force there will have to be a judicious mix of government and market forces. But these forces will differ for those employed in the unorganised and organised sectors.

The unorganised sector

In India the challenge of providing financial security is compounded by the fact that 85.8 per cent of those employed work in the unorganised sector, to which the provident fund and other forms of formal pension provision are rarely applicable. For the estimated 304 million people in the unorganised sector (in 1999/2000), there are various central and state government pension schemes. All of these together, however, touch barely 21 million people (NCEUS, 2007). There are two main types of pension programmes:

- *Government cash transfers to the destitute.* Though technically such programmes are social assistance programmes, since most of the beneficiaries are workers in the unorganised sector, they are deemed to form a part of government initiatives for workers. For instance, the National Old Age Pension Scheme (NOPS) is the main central government scheme. This began in 1995 and is targeted at persons over the age of 65, who have little or no means of support from their own sources. The amount to be paid per month was initially Rs75[5], raised to Rs200 in 2005/06. In 2006, there were 0.73 million people covered through this scheme (ibid.). In general, audits of this scheme have been satisfactory (Srivastava, 2004), though apart from the administrative hurdles such as providing birth certificates to prove age, problems of fake beneficiaries, etc., one of the main problems was the irregularity in disbursements. States in which money was disbursed through the post office had a better (but not perfect) record of making available monthly payments. These are inadequate, however, to make any meaningful contribution to the destitute. Cash transfers

---

5   Rs100 represents about $2.50.

from the government in the past have often been criticised on grounds of poor implementation and high 'leakages'. The administrative machinery just does not exist to increase such transfers, even if the government had the financial ability to do so.

- *Pension programmes covering certain professions that are usually managed by Welfare Funds sponsored by the governments.* A board that has representatives from workers, employers and the government runs the Welfare Fund. Contributions from all three parties form the corpus of the fund, from which workers receive pensions after retirement. Central Funds include some mining operations, *beedi*[6] workers and cine workers. But the coverage of many of these programmes is not clear. 'As regards the extent of coverage of the various Welfare Funds administered by the Ministry of Labour and Employment, the Ministry vide letter No. Z-2005/17/05-W.11 dated August 10, 2005 has, *inter alia*, informed the Commission that "So far as number of workers actually receiving the benefits (along with amounts) is concerned, it is intimated that the actual number of workers receiving the benefits under different schemes are not maintained"' (NCEUS, 2007). Moreover, the scalability of such programmes is also quite low, since such boards typically are successful where the workers have become unionised. Most of the unorganised sector workers are unorganised themselves.

There are also numerous social security schemes run in various states. Kerala has the largest coverage, including 54 per

---

6   Local cigarettes made out of *tendu* leaf and tobacco.

cent of all informal sector workers in the state (ibid.), covering fishermen, hand-loom weavers and cashew plantation workers. Each scheme has separate features, however, and there is no uniformity in coverage, contribution patterns or benefits. Not only is the coverage of these programmes very low, the assistance given to the elderly is meagre. For instance, even in Kerala, the pension varies from Rs100 to Rs200 per month. At about $2.50 per month, Rs100 barely equals the amount required for the daily sustenance of a single individual. Unless the requirements of the majority of the workforce are addressed adequately, any pension reform programme will only touch the surface, lacking depth and utility.

It should be noted that the presence of the government in this sector does not of itself imply barriers to entry for private sector financial institutions. Even basic banking services have not spread deeply enough, however, despite government regulation that stipulates rural banking and priority sector credit for all banks.

The limited coverage of retirement saving in the unorganised sector is a consequence of three factors:

1. Lack of capacity to save, which is an outcome of the low incomes.
2. Lack of access to financial services, which is a result of the high cost of providing even basic banking facilities in the rural areas and to marginalised, low-income individuals with limited creditworthiness in urban areas.
3. Lack of recognition of the need for retirement saving. Though this is a universal problem, the lack of formal record-keeping and enforceability of regulations makes this a difficult challenge to overcome.

A non-market solution to these problems exists but is not sustainable in the emerging environment. Such a solution would involve the family continuing to take care of old-age security, and society enforcing these implicit contracts between the old and the young. Given that these traditional implicit contacts are slowly breaking down, many have called for the state to replace the role once taken by the family. Indeed, the Maintenance and Welfare of Parents and Senior Citizens Bill 2007 does seek to require citizens to take care of their destitute parents. The key question is whether the state can enforce such laws. In the past, whenever the state has attempted to enforce laws that impinge on individuals' social life, it has failed and withdrawn, or the government has been rejected at a subsequent election (for example, after sterilisation to control population in the mid-1970s).

This also strongly suggests that even if a market solution exists, it cannot be mandated and has to be voluntary in nature. The problem is that the bulk of the unorganised sector has wages that are so low that solutions necessarily require low transaction costs. Such low-cost pension schemes have yet to evolve in India. Neither do we find any experiments currently being tried to this end.

But going forward, the possibility for low-cost schemes does exist as technological innovation has succeeded in bringing down operating costs. For instance, financial inclusion through branch-less banking and the use of the mobile phone are increasingly being seen as profitable business opportunities for banks to access hitherto 'unbanked' areas and individuals. Moreover, as the economy grows, the unorganised sector is expected to shrink as it has the world over.

Below we discuss the reforms aimed at the unorganised sector currently being considered. We do not consider these reforms to be a significant improvement over the current situation. The key problems in the case of the unorganised sector are that government is unable to target its subsidies; a large proportion of workers are poor; and the requirements are very large relative to the ability of the government to fully subsidise contributions. This means that any kind of comprehensive and adequately funded pension system does not appear to be feasible in the near future for the unorganised sector. In such a situation the focus should be on enabling large and small institutions to provide a range of savings choices combined with investor education.

The organised sector

Even though the organised sector accounts for a minority of employees in the country, it has been well covered by pension programmes. These include the following:

1. Government employees, who form two-thirds[7] of the workforce in the organised sector, are eligible for an indexed defined-benefit pension plan, while contributing 6 per cent of their salary towards a provident fund scheme.
2. Under the Employees Provident Fund Union, workers in firms that employ more than twenty workers subscribe to the Employees Provident Fund (EPF), the Employees Pension Scheme and the Employee's Deposit Linked Insurance Plan. While the EPF is a defined-contribution plan giving a lump-sum amount at retirement, the EPS is in most cases a

---

7   Central government 3.5 million, state governments 7.5 million, quasi-government 6 million; total organised sector employment is about 27 million.

defined-benefit scheme providing an annuity after retirement. Workers save 25.67 per cent of their income through these three schemes combined.

3. Large firms in the public and private sectors have their own privately managed pension schemes for their employees.

Despite their being in the organised sector, however, awareness of benefits is very low in small firms (ADB, 2006). Just over 8 per cent of employees in private firms with ten to nineteen employees have accurate knowledge of benefits. The proportion of workers who are aware of the mandatory retirement coverage is 15.5 per cent among employees in private firms with twenty or more employees, while 51 per cent of state and central government employees have knowledge of their entitlements. There is also the added problem of multiple incidences of withdrawal from provident funds, as high as 64 per cent for Government Provident Funds (ibid.), showing that post-retirement needs are being ignored – or a low level of confidence in the funds.

Employees in the public sector do not have a range of choices in the mandatory pension schemes and often they prefer to withdraw and invest in higher-yielding assets. Second, they are under-informed and, as a result, make suboptimal decisions, even when they do have the freedom to choose. Lastly, the redressing of consumer grievances is quite poor in the established institutions as the institutions are monopolies – this further harms the cause of old-age security in general.

Current proposed reform

In 1999 the Ministry of Social Justice and Empowerment examined the need for pension provision for the elderly in India. The OASIS (Old Age Social and Income Security) committee set up for this purpose submitted its report in 2000, giving recommendations for pension reform to enable the financial empowerment of older persons (Oasis Foundation, 2000). The committee examined the constraints of public provision, which would raise the fiscal burden in the economy, and proposed a system based on contributions from workers.

The mainstay of the national pension system would be individual retirement accounts, with contributions made by individuals. According to OASIS calculations, low-contribution rates do not hinder the accumulation of adequate assets at retirement, provided such contributions are made regularly and consistently and the assets are managed efficiently by the managers. These accounts would have a high level of accessibility using the postal and banking systems that have branches across the country. Portability would have top priority, as the same account would continue across job and residence changes. To reduce costs, the government would set up a centralised depository to coordinate record-keeping and the administration of linking account holders, access points and pension fund managers.

To manage the pension funds, there should be six professional pension fund managers, each offering three styles of pension scheme with alternative investment strategies. Individuals would have the option to invest with any manager, in any scheme, and switch between schemes, etc., as long as a minimum contribution was made each year.

There were also recommendations to reform the existing Employees Provident Funds Organisation (EPFO), whose poor performance and financial stress have been a cause of much concern and conflict between the government and labour unions.

In line with the recommendations in the OASIS report, the New Pension Scheme (NPS) was designed – a defined-contribution pension system for all government employees, while those in the unorganised sector and the self-employed could opt for it on a voluntary basis. Regulatory guidelines were also prescribed in this report, and subsequently the Pension Fund Regulatory and Development Authority (PFRDA) was set up in 2003, to manage the NPS architecture. This is an interim authority, which will become a statutory regulator once the Pension Fund Regulatory and Development Authority Bill 2005 is passed in the legislature. So far nineteen state governments have issued notifications making the NPS applicable to future employees. All employees except those in the Indian armed forces and those who joined the central government before 1 January 2004 are registered under the NPS.

The PFRDA Bill 2005 is still pending in parliament, however, opposed vehemently by the parties of the left, who resist the move from the defined-benefit to the defined-contribution system, which they see as a takeover by private sector market forces. They demand a return to the old system for all employees.

The NPS is not without its limitations. The fact that individuals can choose only between the six pension fund managers selected under the NPS limits freedom of choice for the consumer. It would have been better to allow individuals to choose between any public or privately managed funds, with the government's role being only to regulate the fund providers. On the other hand, the NPS does not adequately address the issue of those who are financially illiterate: those who cannot choose between the schemes are, by default, placed in the plan whose portfolio has the maximum level of government securities and with the fund manager who had the highest returns the previous year. A better option would have been to place these individuals with funds that have the lowest administrative charges.

Pension reform for the unorganised sector has come in the shape of the 2007 draft Bill for providing social security in the unorganised sector, which looks at both agricultural as well as non-agricultural workers. Essentially it charts the responsibilities and organisational structure of social security programmes in the states but leaves the administrative details to be determined by the various players. But this Bill looks only at poorer workers,[8] with the possibility of defined-benefit and defined-contribution pension programmes depending on the income level of the workers. For those below the poverty line who cannot contribute towards a pension or provident fund, however, Rs200 per month has been proposed as the level of pension after the age of 60. National Boards for both categories of workers will oversee the management of the various schemes in coordination with the state-level boards. There is a crying need to consolidate the various schemes and reduce the administrative burden to optimise delivery to the beneficiaries, but progress on this front has been extremely slow so far. Again, as mentioned earlier, the amount to be provided is too meagre to have a significant impact on the lifestyle of a poor person.

---

8   Eligibity criteria proposed for agricultural workers are ownership of less than two
    hectares of land and for non-agricultural workers an income of less than Rs7,000
    per month in 2007 (NCEUS, 2007).

The way forward for India

Quite clearly, the main objectives of pension reform in India today are:

- to expand the coverage of the pension programmes within the labour force, most of which works in the informal sector; and
- to reform the existing pension plans, which have proved to be unsustainable for the government.
  This would involve:
- expanding access to financial services in the countryside;
- providing low-cost options to bring in the poorer sections of society;
- motivating individuals to plan for the future; and
- setting up pension plan programmes that are sustainable, keeping consumer interests as the focus, while simultaneously working to ensure financial stability in the economy.

During the last decade there has been significant liberalisation of the financial markets, while economic growth and financial stability have been the touchstone of the macroeconomic agenda. Since 1998, however, when pension reform first came on to the government agenda, the record of achievements has been mixed as the spotlight has mainly been on reforming the government programmes. The efforts of various stakeholders have culminated in the setting up of the PFRDA and the NPS, but legislation remains elusive at the centre and in many state governments. While opposition to the new system would like to revert to the old defined-benefit system, it must be emphasised that this is really not an option any more. Pay-as-you-go defined-benefit pension systems have been plagued with financial distress everywhere in the world, and studies have shown that, while it may be feasible to argue that a sound system can exist in theory, 'it is *practically* infeasible to enable them to run properly' (Dave, 2006). This is essentially because the political system is not capable of reacting to an evolving demographic and economic situation appropriately and speedily.

There has been no progress at all on reform of the EPFO. There are various structural flaws that need urgent modification and the 'Reinventing the EPFO Plan' formulated by the organisation itself includes the following issues that need to be dealt with:

- the provision of a unique identification number to members;
- improved coordination between offices;
- better treasury management operations;
- improved accounting systems; and
- revamping the human resource development policies and organisational culture.

Given the political tinderbox that EPFO reform has become, however, this appears to be one reform that requires tremendous political will to implement.

For the unorganised sector, it has been shown that voluntary pension systems are not widely taken up and accessibility is a crucial issue here. Provision of financial services through the post office network would be one way to expand the reach of the sector, while with developments on the mobile banking front one can expect greater coverage in regions untouched by financial institutions so far. Here again, whether with public or private sector pension plan providers, there has been no progress on setting up low-cost solutions yet.

Given the fact that investment in physical assets like a house, land or gold rank the highest as perceived 'safe' investments and awareness of bonds, deposits and mutual funds is the lowest (ADB, 2006), it is important to market the idea of saving through financial assets in a country where levels of trust in financial systems are low. There is therefore an overwhelming need to ensure stability and efficiency in financial institutions (irrespective of ownership) to maintain the confidence of the people.

In India, where basic literacy as well as financial literacy is low, trust in financial institutions rates highest for nationalised banks, the post office and the Life Insurance Corporation of India (ibid.), which shows that in the public–private debate it will be the public sector which will win, and therefore efficiency should be bolstered in terms of the plans offered to the public, who need to be convinced that their savings are 'safe' before investing.

Most often, however, even where people have exposure to formal savings, there is a widespread lack of appreciation of the importance of planning for the future. Hence some mechanism of greater education and awareness needs to be formulated to make everyone aware of the need for pension planning. This could come about through tax incentives, marketing of pension plans, more focus in the media on the need for pensions, etc.

For the lowest-income groups, the draft Bill on social security for the unorganised sector talks of contributions of Rs1 per day from workers to fund a pension plan. While this scheme has its sceptics (Dave, 2006), universal pensions are an ideal that a society should work towards achieving. This would involve close coordination between various levels of governments in the country; given the efficiency that electronic payments and multi-purpose smart cards bring in, this aim is attainable.

It must be reiterated here that, given the need to deliver returns in the long term on investments, pension reform has to be supported by financial sector reform. This would include ensuring that the regulation of financial markets is credible and consistent; controls on banking and other financial sector participants are loosened; capital markets are allowed to extend farther and become more liquid; and that supervision of financial institutions is in line with the principles laid out in the international arena. Regulators, the central bank and the government need to recognise the interconnections in the financial sector and work towards a more open and transparent financial system, while simultaneously emphasising macroeconomic and fiscal stability in the economy.

Conclusion

Given the heterogeneity in the country in terms of income, education and therefore earning capacity, access to financial services and the nature of employment, it is clear that if pension provision is to cover the entire population, the issue will have to be tackled on various fronts, targeting different groups differently. For the poorest of the poor, this will have to take the form of a social transfer from the government but, as income levels rise, there should be a calibrated rise in the contribution levels. For all levels choices should be multiple, and investing in a public sector or private sector scheme should be consumer-driven (the banking and insurance sectors have already shown that it is possible to have efficient Public Sector Undertakings, PSUs). The choice cannot be seen as a choice between government institutions and market institutions at the current time, given the relatively low level of trust in private financial institutions. There will have to be close cooperation and more effective regulation to minimise both market as well as government failure in the sector.

The focus of pension reform in India so far has been to relieve the government of its financial burden of existing schemes that have become increasingly unviable. There are larger issues that need to be tackled, however, and the challenges before the country can be expressed as follows:

- to accelerate financial inclusion;
- to facilitate better record-keeping within the unorganised sector;
- to encourage deep and liquid financial markets;
- to increase transparency and accountability for financial institutions;
- to move towards a single regulator for all financial markets;
- to provide choice to the consumers in pension plans;
- to motivate individuals to plan for their retirement in a consistent and effective manner.

References

ADB (2006), *TA 4226-Pension Reforms for the Unorganised Sector*, Asian Development Bank.

Dave, S. (2006), *India's Pension Reform: A case study in complex institutional change*, available online at www.iief.com/ Research/Dave2006_saga.pdf.

GOI (2007), *Poverty Estimates for 2004–05*, Planning Commission press release, Press Information Bureau, March, available

online at http://planningcommission.nic.in/news/prmar07.
pdf.

NCEUS (2007), *Report on Comprehensive Legislation for Minimum
Conditions for Work and Social Security for Unorganised
Workers*, National Commission for Enterprises in the
Unorganised Sector, Ministry of Small Scale Industries,
Government of India, July.

NSSO (2004), *Morbidity, Health Care and the Condition of the
Aged*, NSS 60th Round, Report no. 507, National Sample
Survey Organisation, Government of India.

Oasis Foundation (2000), *The Project OASIS Report*, available
online at www.iief.com/oasis.htm.

ORGCC (2006), *Population Projections for India and States
2001–2026*, Office of the Registrar General and Census
Commissioner, India, available online at www.censusindia.
net/.

Srivastava, P. (2004), *Poverty Targeting in Asia: Country Experience
of India*, ADB Institute Discussion Paper no. 5, Asian
Development Bank Institute.

Thorat, U. (2007), 'Financial Inclusion – the Indian experience',
Speech by Deputy Governor, Reserve Bank of India, available
online at www.rbi.org.in.

ABOUT THE IEA

The Institute is a research and educational charity (No. CC 235 351), limited by guarantee. Its mission is to improve understanding of the fundamental institutions of a free society by analysing and expounding the role of markets in solving economic and social problems.

The IEA achieves its mission by:

- a high-quality publishing programme
- conferences, seminars, lectures and other events
- outreach to school and college students
- brokering media introductions and appearances

The IEA, which was established in 1955 by the late Sir Antony Fisher, is an educational charity, not a political organisation. It is independent of any political party or group and does not carry on activities intended to affect support for any political party or candidate in any election or referendum, or at any other time. It is financed by sales of publications, conference fees and voluntary donations.

In addition to its main series of publications the IEA also publishes a quarterly journal, *Economic Affairs*.

The IEA is aided in its work by a distinguished international Academic Advisory Council and an eminent panel of Honorary Fellows. Together with other academics, they review prospective IEA publications, their comments being passed on anonymously to authors. All IEA papers are therefore subject to the same rigorous independent refereeing process as used by leading academic journals.

IEA publications enjoy widespread classroom use and course adoptions in schools and universities. They are also sold throughout the world and often translated/reprinted.

Since 1974 the IEA has helped to create a worldwide network of 100 similar institutions in over 70 countries. They are all independent but share the IEA's mission.

Views expressed in the IEA's publications are those of the authors, not those of the Institute (which has no corporate view), its Managing Trustees, Academic Advisory Council members or senior staff.

Members of the Institute's Academic Advisory Council, Honorary Fellows, Trustees and Staff are listed on the following page.

The Institute gratefully acknowledges financial support for its publications programme and other work from a generous benefaction by the late Alec and Beryl Warren.

The Institute of Economic Affairs
2 Lord North Street, Westminster, London SW1P 3LB
Tel: 020 7799 8900
Fax: 020 7799 2137
Email: iea@iea.org.uk
Internet: iea.org.uk

311

Other papers recently published by the IEA include:

A Market in Airport Slots
Keith Boyfield (editor), David Starkie, Tom Bass & Barry Humphreys
Readings 56; ISBN 0 255 36505 5; £10.00

Money, Inflation and the Constitutional Position of the Central Bank
Milton Friedman & Charles A. E. Goodhart
Readings 57; ISBN 0 255 36538 1; £10.00

railway.com
Parallels between the Early British Railways and the ICT Revolution
Robert C. B. Miller
Research Monograph 57; ISBN 0 255 36534 9; £12.50

The Regulation of Financial Markets
Edited by Philip Booth & David Currie
Readings 58; ISBN 0 255 36551 9; £12.50

Climate Alarmism Reconsidered
Robert L. Bradley Jr
Hobart Paper 146; ISBN 0 255 36541 1; £12.50

Government Failure: E. G. West on Education
Edited by James Tooley & James Stanfield
Occasional Paper 130; ISBN 0 255 36552 7; £12.50

Corporate Governance: Accountability in the Marketplace
Elaine Sternberg
Second edition
Hobart Paper 147; ISBN 0 255 36542 x; £12.50

The Land Use Planning System
Evaluating Options for Reform
John Corkindale
Hobart Paper 148; ISBN 0 255 36550 0; £10.00

Economy and Virtue
Essays on the Theme of Markets and Morality
Edited by Dennis O'Keeffe
Readings 59; ISBN 0 255 36504 7; £12.50

Free Markets Under Siege
Cartels, Politics and Social Welfare
Richard A. Epstein
Occasional Paper 132; ISBN 0 255 36553 5; £10.00

Unshackling Accountants
D. R. Myddelton
Hobart Paper 149; ISBN 0 255 36559 4; £12.50

The Euro as Politics
Pedro Schwartz
Research Monograph 58; ISBN 0 255 36535 7; £12.50

Pricing Our Roads
Vision and Reality
Stephen Glaister & Daniel J. Graham
Research Monograph 59; ISBN 0 255 36562 4; £10.00

The Role of Business in the Modern World
Progress, Pressures, and Prospects for the Market Economy
David Henderson
Hobart Paper 150; ISBN 0 255 36548 9; £12.50

Public Service Broadcasting Without the BBC?
Alan Peacock
Occasional Paper 133; ISBN 0 255 36565 9; £10.00

The ECB and the Euro: the First Five Years
Otmar Issing
Occasional Paper 134; ISBN 0 255 36555 1; £10.00

Towards a Liberal Utopia?
Edited by Philip Booth
Hobart Paperback 32; ISBN 0 255 36563 2; £15.00

The Way Out of the Pensions Quagmire
Philip Booth & Deborah Cooper
Research Monograph 60; ISBN 0 255 36517 9; £12.50

Black Wednesday
A Re-examination of Britain's Experience in the Exchange Rate Mechanism
Alan Budd
Occasional Paper 135; ISBN 0 255 36566 7; £7.50

Crime: Economic Incentives and Social Networks
Paul Ormerod
Hobart Paper 151; ISBN 0 255 36554 3; £10.00

The Road to Serfdom *with* **The Intellectuals and Socialism**
Friedrich A. Hayek
Occasional Paper 136; ISBN 0 255 36576 4; £10.00

Money and Asset Prices in Boom and Bust
Tim Congdon
Hobart Paper 152; ISBN 0 255 36570 5; £10.00

The Dangers of Bus Re-regulation
and Other Perspectives on Markets in Transport
John Hibbs et al.
Occasional Paper 137; ISBN 0 255 36572 1; £10.00

The New Rural Economy
Change, Dynamism and Government Policy
Berkeley Hill et al.
Occasional Paper 138; ISBN 0 255 36546 2; £15.00

The Benefits of Tax Competition
Richard Teather
Hobart Paper 153; ISBN 0 255 36569 1; £12.50

Wheels of Fortune
Self-funding Infrastructure and the Free Market Case for a Land Tax
Fred Harrison
Hobart Paper 154; ISBN 0 255 36589 6; £12.50

Were 364 Economists All Wrong?
Edited by Philip Booth
Readings 60; ISBN 978 0 255 36588 8; £10.00

Europe After the 'No' Votes
Mapping a New Economic Path
Patrick A. Messerlin
Occasional Paper 139; ISBN 978 0 255 36580 2; £10.00

The Railways, the Market and the Government
John Hibbs et al.
Readings 61; ISBN 978 0 255 36567 3; £12.50

Corruption: The World's Big C
Cases, Causes, Consequences, Cures
Ian Senior
Research Monograph 61; ISBN 978 0 255 36571 0; £12.50

Choice and the End of Social Housing
Peter King
Hobart Paper 155; ISBN 978 0 255 36568 0; £10.00

Sir Humphrey's Legacy
Facing Up to the Cost of Public Sector Pensions
Neil Record
Hobart Paper 156; ISBN 978 0 255 36578 9; £10.00

The Economics of Law
Cento Veljanovski
Second edition
Hobart Paper 157; ISBN 978 0 255 36561 1; £12.50

Living with Leviathan
Public Spending, Taxes and Economic Performance
David B. Smith
Hobart Paper 158; ISBN 978 0 255 36579 6; £12.50

The Vote Motive
Gordon Tullock
New edition
Hobart Paperback 33; ISBN 978 0 255 36577 2; £10.00

Waging the War of Ideas
John Blundell
Third edition
Occasional Paper 131; ISBN 978 0 255 36606 9; £12.50

The War Between the State and the Family
How Government Divides and Impoverishes
Patricia Morgan
Hobart Paper 159; ISBN 978 0 255 36596 3; £10.00

Capitalism – A Condensed Version
Arthur Seldon
Occasional Paper 140; ISBN 978 0 255 36598 7; £7.50

Catholic Social Teaching and the Market Economy
Edited by Philip Booth
Hobart Paperback 34; ISBN 978 0 255 36581 9; £15.00

Adam Smith – A Primer
Eamonn Butler
Occasional Paper 141; ISBN 978 0 255 36608 3; £7.50

Happiness, Economics and Public Policy
Helen Johns & Paul Ormerod
Research Monograph 62; ISBN 978 0 255 36600 7; £10.00

They Meant Well
Government Project Disasters
D. R. Myddelton
Hobart Paper 160; ISBN 978 0 255 36601 4; £12.50

Rescuing Social Capital from Social Democracy
John Meadowcroft & Mark Pennington
Hobart Paper 161; ISBN 978 0 255 36592 5; £10.00

Paths to Property
Approaches to Institutional Change in International Development
Karol Boudreaux & Paul Dragos Aligica
Hobart Paper 162; ISBN 978 0 255 36582 6; £10.00

Prohibitions
Edited by John Meadowcroft
Hobart Paperback 35; ISBN 978 0 255 36585 7; £15.00

Trade Policy, New Century
The WTO, FTAs and Asia Rising
Razeen Sally
Hobart Paper 163; ISBN 978 0 255 36544 4; £12.50

Sixty Years On – Who Cares for the NHS?
Helen Evans
Research Monograph 63; ISBN 978 0 255 36611 3; £10.00

Taming Leviathan
Waging the War of Ideas Around the World
Edited by Colleen Dyble
Occasional Paper 142; ISBN 978 0 255 36607 6; £12.50

The Legal Foundations of Free Markets
Edited by Stephen F. Copp
Hobart Paperback 36; ISBN 978 0 255 36591 8; £15.00

Climate Change Policy: Challenging the Activists
Edited by Colin Robinson
Readings 62; ISBN 978 0 255 36595 6; £10.00

Should We Mind the Gap?
Gender Pay Differentials and Public Policy
J. R. Shackleton
Hobart Paper 164; ISBN 978 0 255 36604 5; £10.00

Other IEA publications
Comprehensive information on other publications and the wider work of the IEA can be found at www.iea.org.uk. To order any publication please see below.

Personal customers
Orders from personal customers should be directed to the IEA:
Bob Layson
IEA
2 Lord North Street
FREEPOST LON10168
London SW1P 3YZ
Tel: 020 7799 8909. Fax: 020 7799 2137
Email: blayson@iea.org.uk

Trade customers
All orders from the book trade should be directed to the IEA's distributor:
Gazelle Book Services Ltd (IEA Orders)
FREEPOST RLYS-EAHU-YSCZ
White Cross Mills
Hightown
Lancaster LA1 4XS
Tel: 01524 68765, Fax: 01524 53232
Email: sales@gazellebooks.co.uk

IEA subscriptions
The IEA also offers a subscription service to its publications. For a single annual payment (currently £42.00 in the UK), subscribers receive every monograph the IEA publishes. For more information please contact:
Adam Myers
Subscriptions
IEA
2 Lord North Street
FREEPOST LON10168
London SW1P 3YZ
Tel: 020 7799 8920, Fax: 020 7799 2137
Email: amyers@iea.org.uk